GUIDELINES FOR
CONSTRUCTION
AND EQUIPMENT OF

1992-93

HOSPITAL
AND
MEDICAL
FACILITIES

■ The American Institute of Architects Committee
on Architecture for Health with assistance from
the U.S. Department of Health and Human Services

The American Institute of Architects Press
WASHINGTON, D.C.

The American Institute of Architects Press
1735 New York Avenue, N.W.
Washington, D.C. 20006

Library of Congress Cataloging-in-Publication Data
Guidelines for construction and equipment of hospitals and
  medical facilities/The American Institute of Architects
  Committee on Architecture for Health, with assistance
  from the U.S. Dept. of Health and Human Services—
  1992–93 ed.
     p.   cm.
  ISBN 1-55835-086-1
  1. Hospitals—United States—Design and construction.
2. Clinics—United States—Design and construction.
I. American Institute of Architects. Committee on
Architecture for Health. II. United States. Bureau of
Maternal and Child Health and Resources Development.
RA967.G83 1993
725'.51'0973—dc20   92-42212
                                               CIP

Cover design by Whitney-Edwards, Easton, Maryland
Layout and type by Studio 405, Washington, D.C.

CONTENTS

Tables

PREFACE

This is the latest in a 45-year series of guidelines to aid in the design and construction of hospital and medical facilities.

The original *General Standards* appeared in the *Federal Register* on February 14, 1947, as part of the implementing regulations for the Hill-Burton program. The standards were revised from time to time as needed. In 1973, the document was retitled *Minimum Requirements of Construction and Equipment for Hospital and Medical Facilities* to emphasize that the requirements were generally minimum, rather than recommendations of ideal, standards.

Sections 603(b) and 1620(2) of the Public Health Service Act require the secretary of the Department of Health and Human Services (HHS) to prescribe by regulation general standards of construction, renovation, and equipment for projects assisted under Title VI and Title XVI, respectively, of the act. Since Title VI and Title XVI grant and loan authorities have expired, there is no need to retain the standards in regulation.

In 1984, HHS removed from regulation the requirements relating to minimum standards of construction, renovation, and equipment of hospitals and other medical facilities, as cited in the *Minimum Requirements*, DHEW Publication No. (HRA) 81-14500. To reflect the nonregulatory status, the title was changed to *Guidelines for Construction and Equipment of Hospital and Medical Facilities*.

It is emphasized that projects with respect to which applications were approved or grants awarded under Titles VI and XVI, but for which full project reimbursement has not yet been made, may be subject to continuing compliance with the *Guidelines* as incorporated by reference in the Code of Federal Regulations, Title 42, Parts 53 and 124, at the time of the initial approval.

The *Guidelines* will be used by HHS to assess Department of Housing and Urban Development Section 242 applications for hospital mortgage insurance and the Indian Health Service construction projects. The *Guidelines* may also be used by other entities, such as state licensure agencies. For this reason, regulatory language was retained. The 1992–93 edition of the *Guidelines* follows these principles. Explanatory and guide material is included in appendices A and B, neither of which is mandatory.

The Health Care Financing Administration, within the Department of Health and Human Services, is supporting the efforts of the 1992–93 *Guidelines* both financially and with support staff. HCFA has the responsibility for the reimbursement and operation of the Medicare and Medicaid Programs. Hospital construction and costs are directly related to the charge of HCFA's mission. Although HCFA is not adopting the *Guidelines* as regulations, the agency does concur with the construction recommendations.

This edition of the *Guidelines* reflects the work of advisory groups from private, state, and federal sectors, representing expertise in design, operation, and construction of health facilities. Advisory group members reviewed the 1987 edition of the *Guidelines* line by line, revising details as necessary to accommodate current health care procedures and to provide a desirable environment for patient care at a reasonable facility cost.

As in the past, the *Guidelines* standards are performance oriented for desired results. Prescriptive measurements, where given, have been carefully considered relative to generally recognized standards and do not require detail specification. For example, experience has shown that it would be extremely difficult to design a patient bedroom smaller than the size suggested and have space for functions and procedures that are normally expected.

Authorities adopting the *Guidelines* standards should encourage design innovations and grant exceptions where the intent of the standards is met. These standards assume that appropriate architectural and engineering practice and compliance with applicable codes will be observed as part of normal professional service and require no separate detailed instructions.

In some facility areas or sections, it may be desirable to exceed the *Guidelines* standards for optimum function. For example, door widths for inpatient hospital rooms are noted as 3 feet 8 inches, which satisfies most applicable codes, to permit passage of patient beds. However, wider widths of 3 feet 10 inches or even 4 feet may be desirable to reduce damage to doors and frames where frequent movement of beds and large equipment may occur. The decision to exceed the standards should be made by the individuals involved.

As in previous editions, details of plan preparation, specifications, engineering procedures, etc., are omitted. These may appear in other technical manuals. Instances where details are mentioned are for emphasis only.

This publication supersedes DHHS Publication No. (HRS-M-HF) 84-1, DHEW Publication No. (HRA) 79-14500, DHEW Publication No. (HRA) 76-4000, and the 1987 edition of the *Guidelines*.

Inquiries or questions on the *Guidelines* may be addressed to the following groups:

American Institute of Architects
Committee on Architecture for Health
1735 New York Avenue, N.W.
Washington, D.C. 20006

Health Resources and Services Administration
Bureau of Maternal and Child Health and Resources Development
Division of Assistance and Recovery
5600 Fishers Lane, Room 11A-19
Rockville, Maryland 20857

Office of Engineering Services
PHS Region II
26 Federal Plaza
New York, New York 10267

MAJOR ADDITIONS AND REVISIONS

The general format and technical content follow the previous document, *Guidelines for Construction and Equipment of Hospital and Medical Facilities*, 1987 edition. An Appendix A was added to separate minimum standards from explanatory or educational material, so that this document may be adopted as requirements by authorities having jurisdiction or used as a basic guide for other standards. An asterisk (*) before a paragraph number indicates that explanatory or educational material related to this paragraph is found in Appendix A. Changes from the 1987 *Guidelines* are marked in this edition with beginning (▼) and ending (▲) arrows.

Many changes, too numerous to mention, were made to correct errors, clarify intent, and generally update the standards. Listed below, however, are major additions and revisions made in conformance with current, minimum needs and state-of-the-art medical and design procedures:

1. There are five entirely new sections: Section 7.3.E, Newborn Intensive Care Units; Section 9.7, Freestanding Birth Center; Section 9.8, Freestanding Outpatient Diagnostic and Treatment Facility; Section 11, Psychiatric Hospital; and Section 12, Mobile, Transportable, and Relocatable Units. These sections establish minimum standards for the designated type of facility. Additional guide material may be found in Appendix A.

2. Section 1.2. The title "Modernization" was changed to "Renovation." The section states that all new work shall comply, insofar as practicable, with these Guidelines and with appropriate parts of the Life Safety Code, NFPA 101, covering Health Care Occupancies.

3. Section 1.3, Design Standards for the Disabled, was changed to state that all public, private, and public service hospitals must comply with the Americans with Disabilities Act (ADA) and that United States government facilities must comply with the Uniform Federal Accessibility Standards (UFAS).

4. Section 7.2.A, Patient Rooms, was changed to permit a maximum of two patients per room and to require a minimum of 100 square feet per bed in multibed rooms and 120 square feet in single rooms in all new construction. Renovation projects may continue to use four-patient bedrooms, if they are existing, and to use 80 square feet per bed in multibed rooms and 100 square feet in singles.

5. Sections 7.2.C and 7.2.D have replaced the old requirements for Isolation Rooms with Infectious Isolation Rooms and Protective Isolation Rooms.

6. Section 7.3, Intensive Care, was changed to Critical Care, and the required area increased to 150 sq. ft. per bed in new construction. Renovation projects may use the old requirement of 120 sq. ft. in single rooms and 100 sq. ft. per bed in multibed critical care units.

7. Section 7.5, Pediatric and Adolescent Unit, maximum occupancy was reduced to four patients per room and the minimum size increased to 100 sq. ft. per bed in multibed rooms and 120 sq. ft. in single rooms in new construction. In renovation projects, the old requirements of 80 sq. ft. per bed in multibed rooms and 100 sq. ft. in single rooms are approvable.

8. Section 7.7.A, Surgery, increased the minimum areas of surgical procedure rooms in new construction as follows:

   • General operating rooms from 360 sq. ft. to 400 sq. ft.

   • Orthopedic operating rooms from 360 sq. ft. to 600 sq. ft.

   • Cardiovascular and neurological operating rooms from 400 sq. ft. to 600 sq. ft.

   • Surgical cystoscopy from 250 sq. ft. to 350 sq. ft.

   • Renovation projects may continue to use the old minimum area requirements.

9. Section 7.7.B, Recovery Room, was changed to Post-Anesthetic Care Unit, and a new minimum area requirement of 80 sq. ft. per bed was added.

10. Section 7.8, Obstetrical Facilities. Postpartum bedrooms have been moved to this section. The maximum number of patients per room and minimum area per bed requirements for all patient rooms in new construction apply as do the renovation exceptions. The minimum area per labor bed was increased from 100 sq. ft. per bed to 120 sq. ft. per bed. Renovation projects may use the old requirement.

    The minimum area for LDR and LDRP facilities was increased from 200 sq. ft. to 250 sq. ft. in new construction. Renovation projects may continue to use 200 sq. ft.

Major Additions and Revisions

11. Section 7.9.8, Definitive Emergency Care. The minimum size of the trauma/cardiac rooms was increased from 240 sq. ft. to 250 sq. ft. in new construction. In renovation projects, the old figure is approvable. Two new added requirements are for at least one infectious isolation room and one holding/seclusion room in each emergency department.

12. Table 2 (previously table 3). The format was changed to have categories grouped under headings, but the table is otherwise essentially unchanged. Table 5 has been revamped to eliminate the need for a key and is cross-referenced to the appropriate section containing basic requirements for the room or service.

13. Section 8 has been retitled Nursing Facilities and is now a complete section on its own, including Table 6, ventilation; Table 7, filter efficiencies; Table 8, hot water use; and Table 10, illuminance.

ACKNOWLEDGMENTS

The Committee on Architecture for Health (CAH) of the American Institute of Architects (AIA) was privileged to convene and work with an interdisciplinary committee to revise the *Guidelines for Construction and Equipment of Hospital and Medical Facilities*. This is the second revision cycle for which the CAH/AIA has been honored to serve in this capacity. They played a major role in the preparation of this edition.

These revised *Guidelines* are the result of many hours of concentrated work by dedicated professionals concerned with the health care industry from private practice, professional organizations, and state and federal agencies. More than 2,000 proposals for change and comments on proposed changes were received and processed by the CAH at three meetings held in Washington D.C., Chicago, and San Diego. Approximately 50 members attended each meeting and gave serious and full consideration to all written comments and proposals. The AIA wishes to express its sincere gratitude to all who sent comments and to those organizations whose representatives served on the Guidelines Revision Committee.

Glenn A. Aker
Healthcare Environment Design

David Altman
Texas Department of Health

Michael Arnold, Architect, AIA
Medifac Architects

Autumn Blakeley, Architect, AIA
Quality Health Facilities, Inc.

Lee Boland, P.E.
Wisconsin Division of Health

Mary Jo Breslin, R.N.
Georgetown University Medical Center

J. Armand Burgun, Architect, FAIA
Rogers Burgun Shahine Deschler

Raymond Buttaro
Applied Management Systems

Jack Chamblee
Healthsouth Rehabilitation Corporation

Martin H. Cohen, Architect, FAIA
Forum for Health Care Planning

Michael Cohn
National Institute of Building Sciences

Walter Collins
Parsons Birnckerhoff Facilities Services

Barry Davis, P.E.
Centers for Disease Control

Michelle Donovan, R.N.
American Nurses Association

Douglas S. Erickson, FASHE
American Hospital Association

Michael Ferber
Hospital Association of Pennsylvania

Marjorie Geist, R.N.
American College of Emergency Physicians

Rita A. Gore
New Jersey Department of Health

Kerry Gragg, P.E.
Indian Health Service

Edwin S. Green, Architect, AIA
Humana, Inc.

Ken Gurtowski
Calumet Coach, Inc.

John M. Hamilton, M.D.
American Psychiatric Association

Cynthia Hayward, Architect, AIA
CHI Systems, Inc.

Daniel L. Hightower
Public Health Service

William T. Holmes
Rutherford and Chekene

Dwight H. Jones, P.E.
W.L. Thompson Consulting Engineers, Inc.

Ode R. Keil, P.E.
Joint Commission on Accreditation of Healthcare Organizations

James Lefter
Newmark Civil Engineering Laboratory
University of Illinois

Theodore R. Lentz, Architect, AIA
Horty Elving

Daniel Lerman
Society for Ambulatory Care Professionals

Nancy J. Lescavage, NC, USN
Department of Defense

Stephan G. Lynn, M.D., FACEP
American College of Emergency Physicians

John D. MacLeod
OSHPD, California

Ted Matson
Ambulatory Care Advisory Group

Robert A. Michaels, Ph.D., C.E.P.
RAM TRAC Corporation

Audrey Morgan, Architect, AIA
Audrey Morgan, AIA Architects

Hugh Nash, P.E.
Smith Seckman Reid, Inc.

Frederick C. Neale, Architect, AIA
Neale & Company

Paul Ninomura, P.E.
Department of Health and Human Services

Yosh Onoyama
California Office of Statewide Health Planning

Douglas Pendergras
American Health Care Association

Emilio M. Pucillo, Architect
Public Health Service
Office of Engineering Services

David A. Rhodes, Architect, AIA
Jones, Mah, Gaskill, Rhodes, Inc.

Cheryl Riskin
The Jewish Home for the Aged

Richard C. Rosenvold, Architect, AIA
Florida Department of Health and Rehabilitation Services

Vernon M. Rozas, Architect, AIA
Farmers Home Administration

Sylvester A. Sampson
Department of Health and Human Services

Surinder K. Sharma, P.E.
Department of Defense

Lloyd H. Siegel, Architect, FAIA
Department of Veterans Affairs

Grady Smith, Architect, AIA

Judith A. Smith
Ross Planning Associates

Joseph G. Sprague, Architect, AIA
HKS Architects, Inc.

Joseph J. Strauss, Architect, AIA
Lammers & Gershon Associates, Inc.

John P. Swope, M.D.
George Washington University

Charles Talmage
T.R. Arnold & Associates, Inc.

Conrad M. Taylor, Architect
Association of State and Territorial Health Officials

Drexel Toland
Drexel Toland & Associates

George Tsigounis
Department of Health and Human Services

Annette L. Valenta
Health Facilities Institute

Barbara Vaughey, R.N.
Birthing Center, Bethesda, Md.

Marjorie E. Vincent, R.N., MBA
The Garvin Group

Voya Vitorovich
Kettering Medical Center

Special thanks are due to the Health Care Finance Administration, Department of Health and Human Services and the American Hospital Association, which provided major funding for the project, and to Todd S. Phillips, AIA, of the American Institute of Architects staff. His efforts and attention to detail ensured that this edition proceeded on schedule.

J. Armand Burgun, FAIA
Chairman
Guidelines Revision Committee

1. INTRODUCTION

1.1 General

1.1.A.

This document contains information intended as model standards for constructing and equipping new medical facility projects. For brevity and convenience these standards are presented in "code language." Use of words such as *shall* is mandatory only where applied by an adopting authority having jurisdiction. Insofar as practical, these standards relate to desired performance or results or both. Details of construction and engineering are assumed to be part of good design practice and ▼ local building regulations. Design and construction shall conform to the requirements of these Guidelines. Requirements set forth in these Guidelines shall be considered as minimum. For aspects of design and construction not included in these Guidelines, local governing building codes shall apply. Where there is no local governing building code, the prevailing model code used within the geographic area is hereby specified for all requirements not otherwise specified in these Guidelines. (See Section 1.4 for wind and seismic local requirements.)

Where ASCE 7-92 is referenced, similar provisions in the model building code are considered substantially ▲ equivalent.

1.1.B.

This document covers health facilities common to communities in this country. Facilities with unique services will require special consideration. However, sections herein may be applicable for parts of any facility and may be used where appropriate.

▼ 1.1.C.

The model standards are not intended to restrict innovations and improvements in design or construction techniques. Accordingly, authorities adopting these standards as codes may approve plans and specifications which contain deviations if it is determined that the respective intent or objective has been met. Final implementation may be subject to requirements of the authority having jurisdiction.

1.1.D.

Some projects may be subject to the regulations of several different programs, including those of state, local, and federal authorities. While every effort has been made for coordination, individual project requirements should be verified, as appropriate. Should requirements be conflicting or contradictory, the authority having primary ▲ mary responsibility for resolution should be consulted.

1.1.E.

The Health Care Financing Administration, which is responsible for Medicare and Medicaid reimbursement, has adopted the National Fire Protection Association 101 Life Safety Code (NFPA 101). Facilities participating in Medicare and Medicaid programs shall comply with that code.

1.1.F.

The health-care provider shall supply for each project a functional program for the facility that describes the purpose of the project, the projected demand or utilization, staffing patterns, departmental relationships, space requirements, and other basic information relating to fulfillment of the institution's objectives. This program may include a description of each function or service; the operational space required for each function; the quantity of staff or other occupants of the various spaces; the numbers, types, and areas (in net square feet) of all spaces; the special design features; the systems of operation; and the interrelationships of various functions and spaces. The functional program should include a description of those services necessary for the complete operation of the facility. Those services available elsewhere in the institution or community need not be duplicated in the facility. The functional program should also address the potential future expansion of essential services which may be needed to accommodate increased demand. The approved functional program shall be made available for use in the development of project design and construction documents.

1.2 Renovation

1.2.A.

Where renovation or replacement work is done within an existing facility, all new work or additions, or both, shall comply, insofar as practical, with applicable sections of these Guidelines and with appropriate parts of NFPA 101, covering New Health Care Occupancies. Where major structural elements make total compliance impractical or impossible, exceptions should be considered. ▼ ered. This does not guarantee that an exception will be granted, but does attempt to minimize restrictions on those improvements where total compliance would not substantially improve safety, but would create an unreasonable hardship. These standards should not be construed as prohibiting a single phase of improvement.

(For example, a facility may plan to replace a flammable ceiling with noncombustible material but lacks
▲ funds to do other corrective work.) However, they are not intended as an encouragement to ignore deficiencies when resources are available to correct life-threatening problems. (See Section 1.4.A.)

1.2.B.

When construction is complete, the facility shall satisfy functional requirements for the appropriate classification (general hospital, skilled nursing facility, etc.) in an environment that will provide acceptable care and safety to all occupants.

1.2.C.

In renovation projects and those making additions to existing facilities, only that portion of the total facility affected by the project shall comply with applicable sections of the Guidelines and with appropriate parts of NFPA 101 covering New Health Care Occupancies.

1.2.D.

Those existing portions of the facility which are not included in the renovation but which are essential to the functioning of the complete facility, as well as existing building areas that receive less than substantial amounts of new work shall, at a minimum, comply with that section of NFPA 101 for Existing Health Care Occupancies.

1.2.E.

Conversion to other appropriate use or replacement should be considered when cost prohibits compliance with acceptable standards.

1.2.F.

When a building is converted from one occupancy to another, it shall comply with the new occupancy requirements. For purpose of life safety, a conversion from a hospital to a nursing home or vice versa is not considered a change in occupancy.

1.2.G.

When parts of an existing facility essential to continued overall facility operation cannot comply with particular standards, those standards may be temporarily or permanently waived if patient care and safety are not jeopardized.

1.2.H.

Renovations, including new additions, shall not diminish the safety level that existed prior to the start of the work; however, safety in excess of that required for new facilities is not required to be retained.

1.2.I.

Nothing in these Guidelines shall be construed as restrictive to a facility that chooses to do work or alterations as part of a phased long-range safety improvement plan. It is emphasized that all hazards to life and safety and all areas of noncompliance with applicable codes and regulations, should be corrected as soon as possible in accordance with a plan of correction.

1.3 Design Standards for the Disabled

▼ In July of 1990, President Bush signed into law the Americans with Disabilities Act (ADA). This new law extends comprehensive civil rights protection to individuals with disabilities. Under Titles II and III of the ADA, public, private, and public service hospitals and other health care facilities will need to comply with the *Accessibility Guidelines for Buildings and Facilities* (ADAAG) for alterations and new construction. United States government facilities are exempt from the ADA as they must comply with the *Uniform Federal Accessibility Standards* (UFAS), which was effective August 7, 1984.

Also available for use in providing quality design for the disabled is the American National Standards Institute (ANSI) A117.1 *American National Standard for Accessible and Usable Buildings and Facilities.*

State and local standards for accessibility and usability may be more stringent than ADA, UFAS, or ANSI A117.1. Designers and owners, therefore, must assume responsibility for verification of all applicable requirements.

*1.4 Provisions for Disasters

In locations where there is a history of hurricanes, tornadoes, flooding, earthquakes, or other regional disasters, planning and design shall consider the need to protect the life safety of all health care facility occupants and the potential need for continuing services following such a disaster.

1.4.A. Wind and Earthquake Resistant Design for New Buildings

Facilities shall be designed to meet the requirements of the building codes specified in Section 1.1.A., provided these requirements are substantially equivalent to ASCE 7-92. Design shall meet the requirements of ASCE 7-92 Section 9.1.4.2, "Seismic Hazards Exposure Groups."

The following model codes and provisions are essentially equivalent to the ASCE 7-92 requirements:

1988 NEHRP Provisions
1991 ICBO Uniform Building Code
1992 Supplement to the BOCA National
   Building Code
1992 Amendments to the SBCC Standard
   Building Code

1.4.A1. For those facilities that must remain operational after a disaster, special design is needed to protect essential building services such as power, medical gas systems, and, in certain areas, air conditioning. In addition, consideration must be given to the likelihood of temporary loss of externally supplied power, gas, water, and communications.

1.4.A2. The owner shall provide special inspection during construction of seismic systems described in Section A.9.1.6.2 and testing in Section A.9.1.6.3 of ASCE 7-92.

1.4.A3. Roof coverings shall be securely fastened or ballasted to the supporting roof construction and shall provide weather protection for the building at the roof. Roof covering shall be applied on clean and dry decks in accordance with the manufacturer's instructions, these Guidelines, and related references. In addition to the wind force design and construction requirements specified, particular attention shall be given to roofing, glazing, and flashing details to minimize uplift and other damage that might allow entry of water that could seriously impair functioning of the building.

1.4.B.
Flood Protection, Executive Order No. 11296, was issued to minimize financial loss from flood damage to facilities constructed with federal assistance. In accordance with that order, possible flood effects shall be considered when selecting and developing the site. Insofar as possible, new facilities shall *not* be located on designated flood plains. Where this is unavoidable, consult the Corps of Engineers regional office for the latest applicable regulations pertaining to flood insur-
▲ ance and protection measures that may be required.

1.4.C.
Should normal operations be disrupted, the facility shall provide adequate storage capacity for, or a functional program contingency plan to obtain, the following supplies: food, sterile supplies, pharmacy supplies, linen, and water for sanitation. Such storage capacity or plans shall be sufficient for at least four continuous days of operation.

1.5 Codes and Standards

1.5.A.
Every health facility shall provide and maintain a safe environment for patients, personnel, and the public.

1.5.B.
References made in these Guidelines to appropriate model codes and standards do not, generally, duplicate wording of the referenced codes.

NFPA's standards, especially the NFPA 101, are the basic codes of reference; but other codes and/or standards may be included as part of these standards. In the absence of state or local requirements, the project shall also comply with approved nationally recognized building codes except as modified in the latest edition of the NFPA 101, and/or herein.

▼ Design standards for insuring accessibility for the handicapped may be based upon either ADA or UFAS, in accordance with the local authority having jurisdiction.
▲ Federally assisted construction shall comply with UFAS.

Referenced code material is contained in the issue current at the time of this publication. The latest revision of code material is usually a clarification of intent and/or general improvement in safety concepts and may be used as an explanatory document for earlier code editions. Questions of applicability should be addressed as the need occurs.

1.5.C. Equivalency
Insofar as practical, these model standards have been established to obtain a desired performance result. Prescriptive limitations, when given, such as exact minimum dimensions or quantities, describe a condition that is commonly recognized as a practical standard for normal operation. For example, reference to a room area is for patient, equipment, and staff activities; this avoids the need for complex descriptions of procedures for appropriate functional planning.

In all cases where specific limits are described, equivalent solutions will be acceptable if the authority having jurisdiction approves them as meeting the intent of these standards. *Nothing in this document shall be construed as restricting innovations that provide an equivalent level of performance with these standards in a manner other than that which is prescribed by this document, provided that no other safety element or system is compromised in order to establish equivalency.*

▼ National Fire Protection Association (NFPA) document 101M is a technical standard for evaluating equivalency to certain Life Safety Code 101 requirements. The Fire Safety Evaluation System (FSES) has become widely recognized as a method for establishing a safety level equivalent to the Life Safety Code. It may be useful for evaluating *existing* facilities that will be affected by renovation. For purposes of these Guidelines, the FSES
▲ is not intended to be used for *new* construction.

1.5.D. English/Metric Measurements
Metric standards of measurement are the norm for most international commerce and are being used increasingly in health facilities in the United States. Where measurements are a part of this document, English units are given as the basic standards with metric units in parenthesis.

1.5.E. List of Referenced Codes and Standards

Codes and standards which have been referenced in whole or in part in the various sections of this document are listed below. Names and addresses of originators are also included for information. The issues available at the time of publication are used. Later issues will normally be acceptable where requirements for function and safety are not reduced; however, editions of different dates may have portions renumbered or retitled. Care must be taken to insure that appropriate sections are used.

▼ American National Standards Institute. Standard A17.1 (ANSI A17.1), *American National Standard Safety Code for Elevators, Dumbwaiters, Escalators, and Moving Stairs.*

American Society of Civil Engineers. ASCE 9-72, formerly ANSI A58.1, *Minimum Design Loads for* ▲ *Buildings and Other Structures.*

American Society of Heating, Refrigerating, and Air-Conditioning Engineers (ASHRAE). *Handbook of Fundamentals.*

American Society of Heating, Refrigerating, and Air-Conditioning Engineers. Standard 52-76 (ASHRAE 52-76), *Method of Testing Air Cleaning Devices Used in General Ventilation for Removing Particulate Matter.*

► Americans with Disabilities Act (ADA)

Building Officials and Codes Administrators International, Inc. *The BOCA Basic Building Code.*

Building Officials and Codes Administrators International, Inc. *The BOCA Basic Plumbing Code.*

Code of Federal Regulations. Title 10, parts 20 and 35, *Handling of Nuclear Materials.*

Code of Federal Regulations. Title 29, part 1910, *Employee Safety and Health.*

▼ College of American Pathologists. *Medical Laboratory* ▲ *Design Manual.*

Compressed Gas Association (CGA). *Standards for Medical-Surgical Vacuum Systems in Hospitals.*

DOP Penetration Test Method. MIL STD no. 282, *Filter Units, Protective Clothing, Gas-Masking Components and Related Products: Performance Test Methods.*

General Services Administration, Department of Defense, Department of Housing and Urban Development, U.S. Postal Service. *Uniform Federal Accessibility Standard* (UFAS).

Health Education and Welfare. HEW publication no. (FDA)78-2081 (available through GPO), *Food Service Sanitation Manual.*

Hydronics Institute. *Boiler Ratings: I-B-R, Cast Iron, and SBI Steel Boilers.*

Illuminating Engineering Society of North America. IESNA publication CP29, *Lighting for Health Facilities.*

International Conference of Building Officials (ICBO). *Uniform Building Code.*

National Association of Plumbing-Heating-Cooling Contractors (PHCC). *National Standard Plumbing Code.*

▼ National Bureau of Standards Interagency Report. NBSIR 81-2195, *Draft Seismic Standards for Federal Buildings Prepared by Interagency Committee on Seismic Safety in Construction* (available from NTIS as ▲ no. PB81-163842).

National Council on Radiation Protection (NCRP). *Medical X-ray and Gamma Ray Protection for Energies up to 10 MeV Equipment Design and Use.*

▼ National Council on Radiation Protection (NCRP). *Medical X-ray and Gamma Ray Protection for Energies up to 10 MeV Structural Shielding Design and* ▲ *Evaluation.*

National Council on Radiation Protection (NCRP). *Radiation Protection Design Guidelines for 0.1pi29100, MeV Particle Accelerator Facilities.*

National Fire Protection Association. NFPA 20. *Centrifugal Fire Pumps.*

NFPA 70. *National Electrical Code.*

NFPA 72. *Standard for the Installation, Maintenance, and Use of Protective Signaling Systems.*

NFPA 72E. *Standard for Automatic Fire Detectors.*

NFPA 80. *Standard for Fire Doors and Windows.*

NFPA 82. *Standard on Incinerators, Waste and Linen Handling Systems and Equipment.*

NFPA 90A. *Standard for the Installation of Air Conditioning and Ventilating Systems.*

NFPA 96. *Standard for the Installation of Equipment for the Removal of Smoke and Grease-Laden Vapors from Commercial Cooking Equipment.*

► NFPA 99. *Standard for Health Care Facilities.*

NFPA 101. *Life Safety Code.*

NFPA 110. *Emergency and Standby Power Systems.*

NFPA 253. *Standard Method of Test for Critical Radiant Flux of Floor Covering Systems Using a Radiant Heat Energy Source.*

NFPA 255. *Standard Method of Test of Surface Burning Characteristics of Building Materials.*

NFPA 258. *Standard Research Test Method for Determining the Smoke Generation of Solid Materials.*

NFPA 701. *Standard Method of Fire Tests for Flame-Resistant Textiles and Films.*

NFPA 801. *Recommended Fire Protection Practice for Facilities Handling Radioactive Materials.*

Southern Building Code Congress International, Inc. *Standard Building Code.*

Underwriter's Laboratories, Inc. Publication no.181.

▼ U.S. EPA. *Methodology for Assessing Health Risks Associated with Indirect Exposure to Combustor Emissions—International.* EPA/600/6-90/003.

U.S. EPA. *The Risk Assessment Guidelines of 1986.*
▲ EPA/600/8-87/045.

1.5.F. Availability of Codes and Standards
The codes and standards that are government publications can be ordered from the Superintendent of Documents, U.S. Government Printing Office (GPO), Washington, D.C. 20402.

Copies of nongovernment publications can be obtained at the addresses listed below.

Air Conditioning and Refrigeration Institute
1501 Wilson Boulevard
Arlington, Va. 22209

American National Standards Institute
1430 Broadway
New York, N.Y. 10018

American Society of Civil Engineers
345 East 47th Street
New York, N.Y. 10017

American Society of Heating, Refrigerating, and
Air-Conditioning Engineers
1741 Tullie Circle, NE
Atlanta, Ga. 30329

American Society for Testing and Materials (ASTM)
1916 Race Street
Philadelphia, Pa. 19103

Architectural and Transportation Barriers Compliance
Board (ATBCB)
Office of Technical Services
330 C Street, SW
Washington, D.C. 20202

Building Officials and Code Administrators, Inc.
4051 West Flossmoor Road
Country Club Hills, Ill. 60477

Compressed Gas Association
1235 Jefferson Davis Highway
Arlington, Va. 22202

Hydronics Institute
35 Russo Place
Berkeley Heights, N.J. 07922

Illuminating Engineering Society of North America
(IESNA)
IES Publication Sales
345 East 47th Street
New York, N.Y. 10017

International Conference of Building Officials
5360 South Workman Mill Road
Whittier, Calif. 90601

National Association of Plumbing-Heating-Cooling
Contractors
Box 6808
180 South Washington Street
Falls Church, Va. 22046

National Council on Radiation Protection and
Measurement
7910 Woodmont Avenue, Suite 1016
Bethesda, Md. 20814

National Fire Protection Association
1 Batterymarch Park
P.O. Box 9101
Quincy, Mass. 02269-9101

National Technical Information System (NTIS)
5285 Port Royal Road
Springfield, Va. 22161

Naval Publications and Form Center
5801 Tabor Avenue
Philadelphia, Pa. 19120
(for DOP Penetration Test Method)

Southern Building Code Congress International, Inc.
900 Montclair Road
Birmingham, Ala. 35213

Underwriters Laboratories, Inc.
333 Pfingsten Road
Northbrook, Ill. 60062

▼ U.S. Department of Justice
▲ Americans with Disabilities Act

Introduction

2. ENERGY CONSERVATION

3. SITE

2.1 General

The importance of energy conservation shall be considered in all phases of facility development or renovation. Proper planning and selection of mechanical and electrical systems, as well as efficient utilization of space and climatic characteristics, can significantly reduce overall energy consumption. The quality of the health facility environment must, however, be supportive of the occupants and functions served. Design for energy conservation shall not adversely affect patient health, safety, or accepted personal comfort levels. New and innovative systems which accommodate these considerations while preserving cost effectiveness are encouraged. A discussion of energy conservation considerations is included as Appendix B.

3.1 Location

3.1.A. Access
The site of any medical facility shall be convenient both to the community and to service vehicles, including fire protection apparatus, etc.

3.1.B. Availability of Transportation
Facilities should be located so that they are convenient to public transportation where available.

3.1.C. Security
Health facilities shall have security measures for patients, personnel, and the public consistent with the conditions and risks inherent in the location of the facility. These measures shall include a program designed to protect human and capital resources.

3.1.D. Availability of Utilities
Facilities shall be located to provide reliable utilities (water, gas, sewer, electricity). The water supply shall have the capacity to provide normal usage plus fire-fighting requirements. The electricity shall be of stable voltage and frequency.

3.2 Facility Site Design

3.2.A. Roads
▼ Paved roads shall be provided within the property for access to all entrances and to loading and unloading docks (for delivery trucks). Hospitals with an organized emergency service shall have the emergency access well marked to facilitate entry from the public roads or streets serving the site. Other vehicular or pedestrian traffic should not conflict with access to the emergency station. In addition, access to emergency services shall be located to incur minimal damage from floods and other natural disasters. Paved walkways shall be provid-
▲ ed for pedestrian traffic.

3.2.B. Parking
Parking shall be made available for patients, personnel, and the public, as described in the individual sections for specific facility types.

3.3 Environmental Pollution Control

▼ **3.3.A. Environmental Pollution**
The design, construction, renovation, expansion, equipment, and operation of hospitals and medical facilities are all subject to provisions of several federal environmental pollution control laws and associated agency regulations. Moreover, many states have enacted substantially equivalent or more stringent statutes and regulations, thereby implementing national priorities under local jurisdiction while additionally incorporating local priorities (e.g., air quality related to incinerators and gas sterilizers; underground storage tanks; hazardous materials and wastes storage, handling, and disposal; storm water control; medical waste storage and disposal; and asbestos in building materials).

The principal federal environmental statutes under which hospitals and medical facilities may be regulated include, most notably, the following:

- National Environmental Policy Act (NEPA)

- Resource Conservation and Recovery Act (RCRA)

- Superfund Amendments and Reauthorization Act (SARA)

- Clean Air Act (CAA)

- Safe Drinking Water Act (SDWA)

- Occupational Safety and Health Act (OSHA)

- Medical Waste Tracking Act (MWTA).

Consult the appropriate U.S. Department of Health and Human Services (HHS) and U.S. Environmental Protection Agency (EPA) regional offices and any other federal, state, or local authorities having jurisdiction for the latest applicable state and local regulations pertaining to environmental pollution that may affect the design, construction, or operation of the facility, including the management of industrial chemicals, pharmaceuticals, radionuclides, and wastes thereof, as well as trash, noise, and traffic (including air traffic).

Hospital and medical facilities regulated under federal, state, and local environmental pollution laws may be required to support permit applications with appropriate documentation of proposed impacts and mitigations. Such documentation is typically reported in an Environmental Impact Statement (EIS) with respect to potential impacts on the environment and in a Health Risk Assessment (HRA) with respect to potential impacts upon public health. The HRA may constitute a part or appendix of the EIS. The scope of the EIS and HRA is typically determined via consultation with appropriate regulatory agency personnel and, if required, via a "scoping" meeting at which members of the interested public are invited to express their particular concerns.

Once the EIS and/or HRA scope is established, a *Protocol* document shall be prepared for agency approval. The *Protocol* shall describe the scope and procedures to be used to conduct the assessment(s). The EIS and/or HRA shall then be prepared in accordance with a final *Protocol* approved by the appropriate agency or agencies. Approval is most likely to be obtained in a timely manner and with minimum revisions if standard methods are initially proposed for use in the EIS and/or HRA. Standard methods suitable for specific assessment tasks are set forth in particular EPA documents.

3.3.B. Equipment
Equipment should minimize the release of chlorofluorocarbons (CFCs) and any potentially toxic substances that may be used in their place. For example, the design of air conditioning systems should specify CFC alternatives and recovery systems as may be practicable. ▲

4. EQUIPMENT

4.1 General

▼ **4.1.A.**
An equipment list showing all items of equipment necessary to operate the facility shall be included in the contract documents. This list will assist in the overall coordination of the acquisition, installation, and relocation of equipment. The equipment list should include the classifications identified in Section 4.2 below and whether the items are new, existing to be relocated, owner provided, or not-in-contract.

4.1.B.
The drawings shall indicate provisions for the installation of equipment that requires dedicated building services, or special structures, or that illustrate a major function of the space. Adjustments shall be made to the construction documents when final selections are made.

4.1.C.
Space for accessing and servicing fixed and building service equipment shall be provided.

4.1.D.
Some equipment may not be included in the construction contract but may require coordination during construction. Such equipment shall be shown in the construction documents as owner-provided or not-in-contract for purposes of coordination.

4.2 Classification

Equipment will vary to suit individual construction projects and therefore will require careful planning. Equipment to be used in projects shall be classified as building service equipment, fixed equipment, or movable equipment.

4.2.A. Building Service Equipment
Building service equipment shall include such items as heating, air conditioning, ventilation, humidification, filtration, chillers, electrical power distribution, emergency power generation, energy management systems, conveying systems, and other equipment with a primary function of building service.

4.2.B. Fixed Equipment (Medical and Nonmedical)

4.2.B1. Fixed equipment includes items that are permanently affixed to the building or permanently connected to a service distribution system that is designed and installed for the specific use of the equipment. Fixed equipment may require special structural designs, electromechanical requirements, or other considerations.

    a. Fixed medical equipment includes, but is not limited to, such items as fume hoods, sterilizers, communication systems, built-in casework, imaging equipment, radiotherapy equipment, lithotripters, hydrotherapy tanks, audiometry testing chambers, and lights.

    b. Fixed nonmedical equipment includes, but is not limited to, items such as walk-in refrigerators, kitchen cooking equipment, serving lines, conveyors, mainframe computers, laundry, and similar equipment.

4.2.C. Movable Equipment (Medical and Nonmedical)

*__4.2.C1.__ Movable equipment includes items that require floor space or electrical connections but are portable, such as wheeled items, portable items, office-type furnishings, and monitoring equipment.

    a. Movable medical equipment includes, but is not limited to, portable X-ray, electroencephalogram (EEG), electrocardiogram (EKG), treadmill and exercise equipment, pulmonary function equipment, operating tables, laboratory centrifuges, examination and treatment tables, and similar equipment.

    b. Movable nonmedical equipment includes, but is not limited to, personal computer stations, patient room furnishings, food service trucks, and other portable equipment.

*4.3 Major Technical Equipment

Major technical equipment is specialized equipment (medical or nonmedical) that is customarily installed by the manufacturer or vendor. Since major technical equipment may require special structural designs, electromechanical requirements, or other considerations, close coordination between owner, building designer, installer, construction contractors, and others is required.

4.4 Equipment Shown on Drawings

Equipment which is not included in the construction contract but which requires mechanical or electrical service connections or construction modifications shall, insofar as practical, be identified on the design development documents to provide coordination with the architectural, mechanical, and electrical phases of construction.

4.5 Electronic Equipment

Special consideration shall be given to protecting computerized equipment such as multiphasic laboratory testing units, as well as computers, from power surges and spikes that might damage the equipment or programs. Consideration shall also be given to the addition of a constant power source where loss of data input
▲ might compromise patient care.

5. CONSTRUCTION

5.1 Construction Phasing

Projects involving alterations and/or additions to existing buildings should be programmed and phased to minimize disruptions of retained, existing functions. Access, exits, and fire protection shall be so maintained that the occupants' safety will not be jeopardized during construction.

5.2 Nonconforming Conditions

▼ It is not always financially feasible to renovate the entire existing structure in accordance with these Guidelines. In such cases, authorities having jurisdiction may grant approval to renovate portions of the structure if facility operation and patient safety in the renovated areas are not jeopardized by the existing features of sections retained without complete corrective
▲ measures.

6. RECORD DRAWINGS AND MANUALS

6.1 Drawings

Upon occupancy of the building or portion thereof, the owner shall be provided with a complete set of legible drawings showing construction, fixed equipment, and mechanical and electrical systems, as installed or built. Drawings shall include a fire protection plan for each floor reflecting NFPA 101 requirements.

6.2 Equipment Manuals

Upon completion of the contract, the owner shall be furnished with a complete set of manufacturers' operating, maintenance, and preventive maintenance instructions; parts lists; and procurement information with numbers and a description for each piece of equipment. Operating staff shall also be provided with instructions on how to properly operate systems and equipment. Required information shall include energy ratings as needed for future conservation calculations.

6.3 Design Data

The owners shall be provided with complete design data for the facility. This shall include structural design loadings; summary of heat loss assumption and calculations; estimated water consumption; and electric power requirements of installed equipment. All such data shall be supplied to facilitate future alterations, additions, and changes, including, but not limited to, energy audits and retrofit for energy conservation (see Appendix B).

7. GENERAL HOSPITAL

7.1 General Considerations

7.1.A. Functions
There shall be for each project a functional program for the facility in accordance with Section 1.1.F.

7.1.B. Standards
The general hospital shall meet all the standards described herein. Deviations shall be described and justified in the functional program for specific approval by the authorities having jurisdiction.

▼ 7.1.C. Sizes
Department size and clear floor areas will depend upon program requirements and organization of services within the hospital. Some functions may be combined or shared providing the layout does not compromise safety standards and medical and nursing practices.

7.1.D. Parking
Each new facility, major addition, or major change in function shall have parking space to satisfy the needs of patients, personnel, and public. *A formal parking study is desirable.* In the absence of such a study, provide one space for each bed plus one space for each employee normally present on any single weekday shift. This ratio may be reduced in an area convenient to public transportation or public parking facilities, or where carpool or other arrangements to reduce traffic have been developed. Additional parking may be required to accommodate outpatient and other services. Separate and additional space shall be provided for service delivery vehicles and vehicles utilized for emergency patients.

7.1.E. Swing Beds
When the concept of swing beds is part of the functional program, care shall be taken to include requirements for all intended categories. Facility design for swing beds often requires additional corridor doors and provisions for switching nurse call operations from one nurse
▲ station to another depending on use.

7.2 Nursing Unit (Medical and Surgical)

See other sections of this document for special-care area units such as recovery rooms, critical care units, pediatric units, rehabilitation units, and skilled nursing care or other specialty units.

Each nursing unit shall include the following (see Section 1.2 for waiver of standards where existing conditions make absolute compliance impractical):

▼ **7.2.A. Patient Rooms**
Each patient room shall meet the following standards:

7.2.A1. Maximum room capacity shall be two patients.

Note: In new construction, the maximum room capacity shall be two patients. Where renovation work is undertaken and the present capacity is four patients, maximum room capacity may be four patients.

7.2.A2. In new construction, patient rooms shall have a minimum of 100 square feet (9.29 square meters) of clear floor area per bed in multiple-bed rooms and 120 square feet (10.8 square meters) of clear floor area for single-bed rooms, exclusive of toilet rooms, closets, lockers, wardrobes, alcoves, or vestibules. The dimensions and arrangement of rooms should be such that there is a minimum of 3 feet (0.91 meter) between the sides and foot of the bed and any wall or any other fixed obstruction. In multiple-bed rooms, a clearance of 4 feet (1.22 meters) shall be available at the foot of each bed to permit the passage of equipment and beds. Minor encroachments, including columns and lavatories, that do not interfere with functions may be ignored when determining space requirements for patient rooms. Where renovation work is undertaken, patient rooms shall have a minimum of 80 square feet (7.43 square meters) of clear floor area per bed in multiple-bed areas and 100 square feet (9.29 square meters) of clear floor area in single-bed rooms.

Note: These areas are recognized as minimums and do not prohibit the use of larger rooms where required for needs and functions. The degree of acuteness of care being provided should be the
▲ *determining factor.*

7.2.A3. Each patient room shall have a window in accordance with Section 7.28.A10.

Note: Windows are important for the psychological well-being of many patients, as well as for meeting fire safety code requirements. They are also essential for continued use of the area in the event of mechanical ventilation system failure.

7.2.A4. Nurse calling systems for two-way voice communication shall be provided in accordance with Section 7.32.G.

7.2.A5. In new construction, handwashing facilities shall be provided in each patient room. In renovation projects, the handwashing fixture may be omitted from the bedroom where a water closet and handwashing fixture are provided in a toilet room designed to serve one single-bed room or one two-bed room. This exception does not apply to postpartum rooms. (See Section 7.8.B2.)

7.2.A6. Each patient shall have access to a toilet room without having to enter the general corridor area. One toilet room shall serve no more than four beds and no more than two patient rooms. The toilet room shall contain a water closet and a handwashing fixture and the door should swing outward or be double acting. The handwashing fixture may be omitted from a toilet room if each patient room served by that toilet contains a handwashing fixture.

7.2.A7. Each patient shall have within his or her room a separate wardrobe, locker, or closet suitable for hanging full-length garments and for storing personal effects.

7.2.A8. In multiple-bed rooms, visual privacy from casual observation by other patients and visitors shall be provided for each patient. The design for privacy shall not restrict patient access to the entrance, lavatory, or toilet.

▼ **7.2.A9.** See Sections 7.31 and 7.32 for ventilation,
▲ oxygen, vacuum, air, and electrical standards.

7.2.B. Service Areas
Provision for the services listed below shall be in or readily available to each nursing unit. The size and location of each service area will depend upon the numbers and types of beds served. Identifiable spaces are required for each of the indicated functions. Each service area may be arranged and located to serve more than one nursing unit but, unless noted otherwise, at least one such service area shall be provided on each nursing floor. Where the words *room* or *office* are used, a separate, enclosed space for the one named function is intended; otherwise, the described area may be a specific space in another room or common area.

▼ **7.2.B1.** Administrative center or nurse station. This area shall have space for counters and storage and shall have convenient access to handwashing facilities. It may be combined with or include centers for reception and communication. Preferably, the station should permit visual observation of all traffic into
▲ the unit.

7.2.B2. Dictation area. This area should be adjacent to but separate from the nurse station.

7.2.B3. Nurse or supervisor office.

7.2.B4. Handwashing fixtures, conveniently accessible to the nurse station, medication station, and nourishment center. One handwashing fixture may serve several areas if convenient to each.

7.2.B5. Charting facilities.

▼ **7.2.B6.** Toilet room(s) conveniently located for staff
▲ use (may be unisex).

7.2.B7. Staff lounge facilities shall be provided. These facilities may be on another floor.

7.2.B8. Securable closets or cabinet compartments for the personal articles of nursing personnel, located in or near the nurse station. At a minimum, these shall be large enough for purses and billfolds. Coats may be stored in closets or cabinets on each floor or in a central staff locker area.

7.2.B9. Multipurpose room(s) for staff, patients, patients' families for patient conferences, reports, education, training sessions, and consultation. These rooms must be accessible to each nursing unit. They may be on other floors if convenient for regular use. One such room may serve several nursing units and/or departments.

▼ **7.2.B10.** Examination/treatment room(s). Such rooms may be omitted if all patient rooms in the nursing unit are single-bed rooms. Centrally located examination and treatment room(s) may serve more than one nursing unit on the same floor. Such rooms shall have a minimum floor area of 120 square feet (10.8 square meters). The room shall contain a handwashing fixture; storage facilities; and a desk, counter, or shelf space for writing.

7.2.B11. Clean workroom or clean supply room. If the room is used for preparing patient care items, it shall contain a work counter, a handwashing fixture, and storage facilities for clean and sterile supplies. If the room is used only for storage and holding as part of a system for distribution of clean and sterile materials, the work counter and handwashing fixture may be omitted. Soiled and clean workrooms or holding rooms shall be separated and have no direct connection.

7.2.B12. Soiled workroom or soiled holding room. This room shall be separate from the clean workroom and shall have separate access doors. The soiled workroom shall contain a clinical sink (or equivalent flushing-rim fixture). The room shall con-

tain a lavatory (or handwashing fixture). The above fixtures shall both have a hot and cold mixing faucet. The room shall have a work counter and space for separate covered containers for soiled linen and waste. Rooms used only for temporary holding of soiled material may omit the clinical sink and work counter. If the flushing-rim clinical sink is eliminated, facilities for cleaning bedpans shall be provided
▲ elsewhere.

7.2.B13. Medication station. Provision shall be made for 24-hour distribution of medications. This may be done from a medicine preparation room or unit, from a self-contained medicine dispensing unit, or by another approved system.

▼ a. Medicine preparation room. This room shall be under visual control of the nursing staff. It shall contain a work counter, a sink adequate for handwashing, refrigerator, and locked storage for controlled drugs, and shall have a minimum area of 50 square feet (4.65 square meters). When a medicine preparation room is to be used to store one or more self-contained medicine dispensing units, the room shall be designed with adequate space to prepare medicines with the self-contained medicine dispensing unit(s) present.

b. Self-contained medicine dispensing unit. A self-contained medicine dispensing unit may be located at the nurse station, in the clean workroom, or in an alcove, provided the unit has adequate security for controlled drugs and adequate lighting to easily identify drugs. Convenient access to handwashing facilities shall be provided. (Standard cup-sinks provided in many self-contained units are not adequate for handwashing.)

7.2.B14. Clean linen storage. Each nursing unit shall contain a designated area for clean linen storage. This may be within the clean workroom, a separate closet, or an approved distribution system on each floor. If a closed cart system is used, storage may be in an alcove. It must be out of the path of normal traffic and under staff control.

7.2.B15. Nourishment station. There shall be a nourishment station with sink, work counter, refrigerator, storage cabinets, and equipment for hot and cold nourishments between scheduled meals. The nourishment station shall include space for trays and dishes used for nonscheduled meal service. Provisions and space shall be included for separate temporary storage of unused and soiled dietary trays not picked up at meal time. Handwashing facilities shall be in or immediately accessible from the nour-
▲ ishment station.

7.2.B16. Ice machine. Each nursing unit shall have equipment to provide ice for treatments and nourishment. Ice-making equipment may be in the clean work room/holding room or at the nourishment station. Ice intended for human consumption shall be from self-dispensing ice makers.

▼ **7.2.B17.** Equipment storage room or alcove. Appropriate room(s) or alcove(s) shall be provided for storage of equipment necessary for patient care and as required by the functional program. This room may serve more than one unit on the same floor. Its location shall not interfere with the flow of
▲ traffic.

7.2.B18. Storage space for stretchers and wheelchairs shall be provided in a strategic location, without restricting normal traffic.

▼ **7.2.B19.** Showers and bathtubs. When individual bathing facilities are not provided in patient rooms, there shall be at least one shower and/or bathtub for each 12 beds without such facilities. Each bathtub or shower shall be in an individual room or enclosure that provides privacy for bathing, drying, and dressing. Special bathing facilities, including space for attendant, shall be provided for patients on stretchers, carts, and wheelchairs at the ratio of one per 100 beds or a fraction thereof. This may be on a separate floor if convenient for use.

7.2.B20. Patient toilet room(s), in addition to those serving bed areas, shall be conveniently located to multipurpose room(s) and to each central bathing facility. Patient toilet rooms serving multipurpose
▲ rooms may also be designated for public use.

7.2.B21. Emergency equipment storage. Space shall be provided for emergency equipment that is under direct control of the nursing staff, such as a cardiopulmonary resuscitation (CPR) cart. This space shall be located in an area appropriate to the functional program, but out of normal traffic.

7.2.B22. Housekeeping room. One housekeeping room shall be provided for each nursing unit or nursing floor. It shall be directly accessible from the unit or floor and may serve more than one nursing unit on a floor. At least one housekeeping room per floor shall contain a service sink or floor receptor and provisions for storage of supplies and housekeeping equipment.

▼ *Note: This housekeeping room may not be used for other departments and nursing units that require*
▲ *separate housekeeping rooms.*

7.2.C. Infectious Isolation Room(s)

Note: Details and numerical ratios of this section apply to those areas of the facility covered by new design, including replacement and/or major renovation. Existing nursing units and beds not affected by project work that have approved isolation procedures may be acceptable without changes or additions. Existing beds that are retained without change and psychiatric beds need not be counted in the ratios required below.

▼ At least one isolation room, designed to minimize infection hazards to or from the patient, shall be provided for each 30 acute-care beds or a fraction thereof (except as noted above). The number and type of isolation beds required may need to be increased where large numbers of patients likely to transmit diseases that are communicable via the airborne route (e.g., tuberculosis or multiple-resistant staph diseases) are treated. These may be located within individual nursing units and used for normal acute care when not required for isolation cases, or they may be grouped as a separate isolation unit. Each isolation room shall contain only one bed and shall comply with the acute-care patient room sec-
▲ tion of this document as well as the following:

7.2.C1. Room entry shall be through a work area that provides for facilities that are separate from patient areas for handwashing, gowning, and storage of clean and soiled materials. The work area entry may be a separate enclosed anteroom. The vestibule workspace open to the room may be used for other functions when not needed for isolation. However, where the program function requires strict isolation, at least one isolation room may need to be designed for entry only through an enclosed anteroom.

7.2.C2. Separate enclosed anteroom(s) for isolation rooms are not required as a minimum but, if used, viewing panel(s) shall be provided for observation of each patient by staff from the anteroom.

7.2.C3. One separate anteroom may serve several isolation rooms.

7.2.C4. Toilet, bathtub (or shower), and handwashing facilities are required for each isolation room. These shall be arranged to permit access from the bed area without the need to enter or pass through the work area of the vestibule or anteroom.

▼ **7.2.D. Protective Isolation Room(s)**
In facilities where procedures such as those for organ transplants, burn therapy, and immunosuppressive treatments are performed, special design provisions, including special ventilation, will be necessary to meet the needs of the functional program. (See Table 2 in Section 7.31 for specific ventilation requirements.)

7.2.E. Security Room(s)

The hospital shall provide one or more single bedrooms for patients needing close supervision for medical and/or psychiatric care. This may be part of the psychiatric unit described in Section 7.6. If the single bedroom(s) is part of the acute-care nursing unit, the provisions of Section 7.6.A shall apply, with the following exceptions: each room shall be for single occupancy; each shall be located to permit staff observation of the entrance, preferably adjacent to the nurse station; and each shall be designed to minimize the potential for escape, hiding, injury, or suicide. If vision panels are used for observation of patients, the arrangement shall insure patient privacy and prevent casual observation by visitors and other
▲ patients.

7.3 Critical Care Units

The critical care units require special space and equipment considerations for effective staff functions. In addition, space arrangement shall include provisions for immediate access of emergency equipment from other departments.

Not every hospital will provide all types of critical care. Some hospitals may have a small combined unit; others may have separate, sophisticated units for highly specialized treatments. Critical care units shall comply in size, number, and type with these standards and with the functional program. The following standards are intended for the more common types of critical care services and shall be appropriate to needs defined in functional programs. Where specialized services are required, additions and/or modifications shall be made as necessary for efficient, safe, and effective patient care.

7.3.A. Critical Care (General)
▼ The following shall apply to all types of critical care units unless otherwise noted. Each unit shall comply
▲ with the following provisions:

7.3.A1. The location shall offer convenient access from the emergency, respiratory therapy, laboratory, radiology, surgery, and other essential departments and services as defined by the functional program. It shall be located so that the medical emergency resuscitation teams may be able to respond promptly to emergency calls within minimum travel time.

▼ **7.3.A2.** The location shall be arranged to eliminate the need for through traffic. Transportation of patients to and from the critical care unit should ideally be separated from public corridors and visitor waiting areas. Where elevator transport is required for critically ill patients, the size of the cab and mechanisms and controls should be carefully planned to meet the specialized needs.

7.3.A3. In new construction, each patient space (whether separate rooms, cubicles, or multiple bed space) shall have a minimum of 150 square feet (13.94 square meters) of clear floor area with a minimum headwall width of 12 feet (3.66 meters) per bed, exclusive of anterooms, vestibules, toilet rooms, closets, lockers, wardrobes, and/or alcoves.

In renovation of existing intensive care units, separate rooms or cubicles for single patient use shall be at least 120 square feet (11.15 square meters) and multiple bed space shall contain at least 100 square feet (9.29 square meters) per bed.

A staff emergency assistance system shall be provided on the most accessible side of the bed. The system shall annunciate at the nurse station with backup from another staffed area from which assistance can be summoned.

Provision should be made for rapid and easily accessible information exchange and communication within the unit and the hospital.

The unit shall provide the ability to continuously monitor the physiological parameters appropriate for the types of patients the unit is expected to care for.

7.3.A4. When private rooms or cubicles are provided, view panels to the corridor shall be required and shall have drapes or curtains which may be closed. Where only one door is provided to a bed space, it shall be at least 4 feet (1.22 meters) wide and arranged to minimize interference with movement of beds and large equipment. Sliding doors shall not have floor tracks and shall have hardware that minimizes jamming possibilities. Where sliding doors are used for access to cubicles within a suite, a 3-foot-wide swinging door may also be provided for personnel communication.

7.3.A5. Each patient bed area should have space at each bedside for visitors, and provisions for visual privacy from casual observation by other patients and visitors. For both adult and pediatric units, there must be a minimum of 8 feet (2.44 meters) between beds.

7.3.A6. Each patient bed shall have visual access, other than skylights, to the outside environment with not less than one outside window in each patient bed area. In renovation projects, clerestory windows with windowsills above the heights of adjacent ceilings may be used, provided they afford patients a view of the exterior and are equipped with appropriate forms of glare and sun control. Distance from the patient bed to the outside window shall not exceed 50 feet (15.24 meters). When partitioned cubicles are used, patients' view to outside windows may be through no more than two separate clear vision panels.

7.3.A7. Nurse calling systems for two-way voice communication shall be provided in accordance with Section 7.32.G. The call system for the unit shall include provisions for an emergency code resuscitation alarm to summon assistance from outside the critical care unit.

7.3.A8. Handwashing fixtures shall be convenient to nurse stations and patient bed areas. There shall be at least one handwashing fixture for every three beds in open plan areas, and one in each patient room. The handwashing fixture should be located near the entrance to the patient cubicle or room, should be sized to minimize splashing water onto the floor, and should be equipped with elbow-, knee-, or foot-operated controls.

*7.3.A9. Administrative center or nurse station. This area shall have space for counters and storage. It may be combined with or include centers for reception and communication.

Patients should be visually observed at all times. This can be achieved in a variety of ways.

If a central station is chosen, it will be geographically located to allow for complete visual control of all patient beds in the critical care unit. It will be designed to maximize efficiency in traffic patterns. There will be visual contact between the nurse and the patient at all times. Patients should be oriented so that they can see the nurse but cannot see the other patients. There should be an ability to communicate with the clerical staff without having to enter the central station.

If a central station is not chosen, the unit should be designed to provide visual contact between patient beds so that there can be constant visual contact between the nurse and patient.

7.3.A10. Each unit shall contain equipment for continuous monitoring, with visual displays for each patient at the bedside and at the nurse station. Monitors shall be located to permit easy viewing and access but not interfere with access to the patient.

7.3.A11. Emergency equipment storage. Space that is easily accessible to the staff shall be provided for emergency equipment such as a CPR cart.

7.3.A12. Medication station. Provision shall be made for 24-hour storage and distribution of emergency drugs and routine medications. This may be done from a medicine preparation room or unit, from a self-contained medicine dispensing unit, or by another system. If used, a medicine preparation room or unit shall be under visual control of nursing staff. It shall contain a work counter, cabinets

for storage of supplies, sink with hot and cold water supply, refrigerator for pharmaceuticals, and doubled locked storage for controlled substances, and shall have a minimum area of 50 square feet (4.65 square meters). To minimize distraction of those preparing medications, the area should be enclosed. A glass wall or walls may be advisable to permit visualization of patients and unit activities. A self-contained medicine dispensing unit may be located at the nurses station, in the clean workroom, in an alcove, or in another area directly under visual control of nursing or pharmacy staff. Convenient access to handwashing facilities shall be provided. (Standard cup-sinks provided in many self-contained units are not adequate for handwashing.)

7.3.A13. The electrical, medical gas, heating, and air conditioning shall support the needs of the patients and critical care team members under normal and emergency situations. See Sections 7.31 and 7.32 for specific requirements.

7.3.A14. Isolation rooms with separate washing and gowning facilities will be provided within the critical care unit. Isolation rooms shall contain a minimum of 150 square feet (13.94 square meters) plus space for an anteroom. An anteroom shall be provided and shall consist of at least 20 square feet (1.86 square meters) to accommodate washing, gowning, and storage. If the functional program requires, both normal and protective isolation shall be provided. If a toilet is provided, it must be connected only to this room. If a toilet is not provided, a means must be provided within the room or anteroom for the disposal of the patient's body waste.

7.3.A15. The following additional service spaces shall be immediately available within each critical care suite. These may be shared by more than one critical care unit provided that direct access is available from each.

a. Securable closets or cabinet compartments for the personal effects of nursing personnel, located in or near the nurse station. At a minimum, these shall be large enough for purses and billfolds. Coats may be stored in closets or cabinets on each floor or in a central staff locker area.

b. Clean workroom or clean supply room. If the room is used for preparing patient care items, it shall contain a work counter, a handwashing fixture, and storage facilities for clean and sterile supplies. If the room is used only for storage and holding as part of a system for distribution of clean and sterile supply materials, the work counter and handwashing fixture may be omitted. Soiled and clean workrooms or holding rooms shall be separated and have no direct connection.

c. Clean linen storage. There shall be a designated area for clean linen storage. This may be within the clean workroom, a separate closet, or an approved distribution system on each floor. If a closed cart system is used, storage may be in an alcove. It must be out of the path of normal traffic and under staff control.

d. Soiled workroom or soiled holding room. This room shall be separate from the clean workroom and shall have separate access doors. The soiled workroom shall contain a clinical sink (or equivalent flushing-rim fixture). The room shall contain a lavatory (or handwashing fixture). The above fixtures shall both have a hot and cold mixing faucet. The room shall have a work counter and space for separate covered containers for soiled linen and waste. Rooms used only for temporary holding of soiled material may omit the clinical sink and work counter. If the flushing-rim clinical sink is eliminated, facilities for cleaning bedpans shall be provided elsewhere.

e. Nourishment station. There shall be a nourishment station with sink, work counter, refrigerator, storage cabinets, and equipment for hot and cold nourishments between scheduled meals. The nourishment station shall include space for trays and dishes used for nonscheduled meal service. Provisions and space shall be included for separate temporary storage of unused and soiled dietary trays not picked up at meal time. Handwashing facilities shall be in or immediately accessible from the nourishment station.

f. Ice machine. There shall be available equipment to provide ice for treatments and nourishment. Ice-making equipment may be in the clean work room or at the nourishment station. Ice intended for human consumption shall be from self-dispensing ice makers.

*g. Equipment storage room or alcove. Appropriate room(s) or alcove(s) shall be provided for storage of large items of equipment necessary for patient care and as required by the functional program. Its location shall not interfere with the flow of traffic.

h. An X-ray viewing facility shall be in the unit.

*i. Twenty-four hour laboratory, radiology, and pharmacy services shall be available. These services may be provided from the central departments or from satellite facilities as required by the functional program.

7.3.A16. The following shall be provided and may be located outside the unit if conveniently accessible.

a. A visitors' waiting room will be provided with convenient access to telephones and toilets. One waiting room may serve several critical care units.

b. Adequate office space immediately adjacent to the critical care unit will be available for critical care medical and nursing management/administrative personnel. The offices should be large enough to permit consulting with members of the critical care team and visitors. The offices will be linked with the unit by telephone or an intercommunications system.

c. Staff lounge(s) and toilet(s) located so that staff may be recalled quickly to the patient area in emergencies. The lounge shall have telephone or intercom and emergency code alarm connections to the critical care unit it serves. If not provided elsewhere, provision for the storage of coats, etc., shall be made in this area. Consideration should be given to providing adequate furnishings, equipment, and space for comfortable seating and the preparation and consumption of snacks and beverages. One lounge may serve adjacent critical care areas.

*d. See Appendix A. (Other critical care considerations.)

e. A special procedures room shall be provided if ▲ required by the functional program.

f. Sleeping and personal care accommodations for staff on 24-hour, on-call work schedules.

▼ g. Multipurpose room(s) for staff, patients, and patients' families for patient conferences, reports, education, training sessions, and consultation. These rooms must be accessible to each nursing unit.

h. A housekeeping room shall be provided within or immediately adjacent to the critical care unit. It shall not be shared with other nursing units or departments. It shall contain a service sink or floor receptor and provisions for storage of supplies and housekeeping equipment.

i. Storage space for stretchers and wheelchairs shall be provided in a strategic location, without ▲ restricting normal traffic.

7.3.B. Coronary Critical Care Unit

Coronary patients have special needs. They are often fully aware of their surroundings but still need immediate and critical emergency care. In addition to the standards set forth in Section 7.3.A, the following standards apply to the coronary critical care unit:

7.3.B1. Each coronary patient shall have a separate room for acoustical and visual privacy.

7.3.B2. Each coronary patient shall have access to a toilet in the room. (Portable commodes may be used in lieu of individual toilets, but provisions must be made for their storage, servicing, and odor control.)

▼ **7.3.B3.** Each unit shall contain equipment for continuous monitoring, with visual displays for each patient at the bedside and at the nurse station. Monitors shall be located to permit easy viewing and
▲ access but not interfere with access to the patient.

7.3.C. Combined Medical/Surgical and Cardiac Critical Care

If medical, surgical, and cardiac critical care services are combined in one critical care unit, at least 50 percent of the beds must be located in private rooms or cubicles. *(**Note:** Medical/surgical patients may utilize open areas or private rooms as needed and available but, insofar as possible, cardiac patients should not be accommodated in open ward areas.)* When 50 percent of the beds are in private enclosed spaces within a combined unit, the standards set forth in Section 7.3.B2 for additional separate enclosed rooms do not apply.

7.3.D. Pediatric Critical Care

Critically ill pediatric patients have unique physical and psychological needs. Not every hospital can or should attempt to have a separate pediatric critical care unit. Many hospitals will be able to safely transfer their patients to other facilities offering appropriate services. If a facility has a specific pediatric critical care unit, the functional program must include consideration for staffing, control, and the safe transportation of critically ill pediatric patients, along with life support and environmental systems, from other areas. The pediatric critical care unit may be an open-ward plan. The total room-to-bed ratio in open-ward plans shall provide for at least one isolation room for every six ward beds and protective isolation room(s) if required by the functional program.

In addition to the standards previously listed for critical care units, each pediatric critical care unit shall include:

7.3.D1. Space at each bedside for visiting parents.

7.3.D2. Sleeping space for parents who may be required to spend long hours with the patient. This space may be separate from the patient area, but must be in communication with the critical care unit staff.

7.3.D3. Consultation/demonstration room within, or convenient to, the pediatric critical care unit for private discussions.

7.3.D4. Provisions for formula storage. These may be outside the pediatric critical care unit but must be available for use at all times.

7.3.D5. Separate storage cabinets or closets for toys and games for use by the pediatric patients.

▼ **7.3.D6.** Additional storage for cots, bed linens, and other items needed to accommodate parents overnight.

7.3.D7. Space allowances for pediatric beds and cribs equal to those required for adult beds, because of the variations in sizes and the potential for change.

7.3.D8. Examination and treatment room(s). This room may be omitted if all rooms in the unit are single-bed patient rooms. Centrally located examination and treatment room(s) may serve more than one floor and/or nursing unit. Examination and treatment rooms shall have a minimum floor area of 120 square feet (11.15 square meters). The room shall contain a handwashing fixture; storage facilities; and a desk, counter, or shelf space for writing.

7.3.E. Newborn Intensive Care Units

Each Newborn Intensive Care Unit shall include or comply with the following:

7.3.E1. A scrub/gowning area shall be provided at the entrance of each nursery but separated from the work area. The scrub/gowning area shall contain a sink and separate storage facilities for clean and soiled gowns. All sinks throughout the nursing area(s) shall be hands-free operable. One scrub/gowning area may serve more than one room.

7.3.E2. At least one door to each room in the unit must be large enough to accommodate portable X-ray equipment. A door 44 inches (111.76 centimeters) wide should accommodate most X-ray equipment. Both width and height must be considered.

7.3.E3. There should be efficient and controlled access to the unit from the Labor and Delivery area, the Emergency Room or other referral entry points.

*****7.3.E4.** (See Appendix A.)

7.3.E5. When viewing windows are provided, provision shall be made to control casual viewing of infants.

*****7.3.E6.** (See Appendix A.)

*****7.3.E7.** (See Appendix A.)

7.3.E8. In the interest of noise control, sound attenuation shall be a design factor.

*7.3.E9. Provisions shall be made for indirect lighting and high-intensity lighting in all nurseries. The level of general lighting shall be adjustable to simulate day-night patterns and to satisfy diagnostic and procedural requirements.

7.3.E10. A central area shall serve as a control station, shall have space for counters and storage, and shall have convenient access to handwashing facilities. It may be combined with or include centers for reception and communication and patient monitoring. The station should permit visual observation of all traffic entering the unit.

7.3.E11. There shall be a minimum clear space of 3 feet (0.91 meter) on each of three sides of the patient bed for work space and parental access. This minimum clearance shall exclude space for headwalls, sinks, charting areas, and other fixed equipment in the patient care area, and shall not overlap with other patient care space or aisles. There shall be an aisle for circulation adjacent to each patient care space with a minimum width of 3 feet (0.91 meter).

7.3.E12. An infectious isolation room is required in at least one level of nursery care. The isolation nursery shall be an enclosed and separate room within the nursery unit with provision for observation of the infant from adjacent nurseries or control area. This nursery shall be served by an anteroom that contains sink and separate storage facilities for clean and soiled materials and gowns. See Table 5 in Section 7.31 for oxygen, suction, and medical air systems outlet requirements.

*7.3.E13. (See Appendix A.)

7.3.E14. Blood gas lab facilities should be immediately accessible.

7.3.E15. Physician's sleeping facilities with access to a toilet and shower shall be provided. If not contained within the unit itself, the area shall have a telephone or intercom connection to the patient care area.

7.3.E16. Sleeping space may be needed for parents who may be required to spend long hours with the neonate. This space may be separate from the unit, but must be in communication with the Newborn Critical Care Unit staff.

7.3.E17. A respiratory therapy work area and storage room shall be provided.

7.3.E18. A consultation/demonstration/breast feeding or pump room shall be provided convenient to the unit. Provision shall be made, either within the room or conveniently located nearby, for sink, counter, refrigeration and freezing, storage for pump and attachments, and educational materials.

7.3.E19. Provide charting and dictation space for physicians.

7.3.E20. Medication station. Provision shall be made for 24-hour storage and distribution of emergency drugs and routine medications. This may be done from a medicine preparation room or unit, from a self-contained medicine dispensing unit, or by another system. If used, a medicine preparation room or unit shall be under visual control of nursing staff. It shall contain a work counter, sink, refrigerator, and double locked storage for controlled substances, and shall have a minimum area of 50 square feet (4.65 square meters). A self-contained medicine dispensing unit may be located at the nurse station, in the clean workroom, in an alcove, or in another area directly under visual control of nursing or pharmacy staff. Convenient access to handwashing facilities shall be provided. (Standard cup-sinks provided in many self-contained units are not adequate for handwashing.)

7.3.E21. Clean workroom or clean supply room. If the room is used for preparing patient care items, it shall contain a work counter, a handwashing sink, and storage facilities for clean and sterile supplies. If the room is used only for storage and holding as part of a system for distribution of clean and sterile supply materials, the work counter and handwashing facilities may be omitted.

7.3.E22. Soiled workroom or soiled holding room. The soiled workroom shall contain a clinical sink or equivalent flushing-rim fixture; a handwashing fixture; and space for waste receptacles and soiled linen receptacles. Rooms used only for temporary holding of soiled material may omit the handwashing fixture. However, if the flushing-rim sink is omitted, other provisions for disposal of liquid waste at each unit shall be added. Soiled and clean workrooms or holding rooms shall be separated and have no direct connection. The soiled workroom or soiled holding room shall be directly accessible to the unit and separate.

7.3.E23. Provide a lounge, locker room and staff toilet within or adjacent to the unit suite for staff use.

7.3.E24. Emergency equipment storage. Space shall be provided for emergency equipment that is under direct control of the nursing staff, such as a CPR cart. This space shall be located in an area appropriate to the functional program, but out of normal traffic.

7.3.E25. Housekeeping room. One housekeeping room shall be provided for the unit. It shall be directly accessible from the unit and be dedicated for the exclusive use of the neonatal critical care unit. It shall contain a service sink or floor receptor and provisions for storage of supplies and housekeeping equipment.

7.3.E26. Space should be provided for the following:

a. A visitors waiting room should be provided with convenient access to telephones and toilets.

b. Nurses/supervisors office or station.

c. Multipurpose room(s) for staff, patients and patients' families for patient conferences, reports, education, training sessions, and consultation. These rooms must be accessible to each nursing unit. They may be on other floors if convenient for regular use. One such room may serve several nursing units and/or departments.

*7.4 Newborn Nurseries

Hospitals having 25 or more postpartum beds shall have a separate nursery that provides continuing care for infants requiring close observation (for example, those with low birth weight). The minimum floor area per infant shall be 50 square feet (4.65 square meters), exclusive of auxiliary work areas, with provisions for at least 4 feet (1.22 meters) between and at all sides of
▲ bassinets.

Note: Normal newborn infants shall be housed in nurseries that comply with the standards below. Location shall be convenient to the postpartum nursing unit and obstetrical facilities. The nurseries shall be located and arranged to preclude the need for nonrelated pedestrian traffic. No nursery shall open directly into another nursery. See Section 7.5 for pediatric nurseries. See Section 7.3.E for critical care units for neonatal infants.

7.4.A. General
Each nursery shall contain:

7.4.A1. At least one lavatory, equipped with handwashing controls that can be operated without use of hands, for each eight infant stations.

7.4.A2. Nurse emergency calling system, for summoning assistance without leaving the patient area, shall be provided in accordance with Section 7.32.G.

7.4.A3. Glazed observation windows to permit the viewing of infants from public areas, workrooms, and adjacent nurseries.

7.4.A4. Convenient, accessible storage for linens and infant supplies at each nursery room.

▼ **7.4.A5.** See Sections 7.31 and 7.32 for ventilation, medical gas, and electrical standards. Indirect lighting or other design to minimize the UV output of
▲ flourescent fixtures shall be used.

See mechanical and electrical sections for ventilation, oxygen, suction, air, and electrical standards.

▼ **7.4.A6.** A consultation/demonstration/breast feeding or pump room shall be provided convenient to the nursery. Provision shall be made, either within the room or conveniently located nearby, for sink, counter, refrigeration and freezing, storage for pump and attachments, and educational materials. The area provided for the unit for these purposes, when conveniently located, may be shared by the newborn nursery.

▲ Enough space for parent to stay 24 hours.

7.4.B. Full-Term Nursery
Each full-term nursery room shall contain no more than 16 infant stations. The minimum floor area shall be 24 square feet (2.23 square meters) for each infant station, exclusive of auxiliary work areas. When a rooming-in program is used, the total number of bassinets provided in these units may be appropriately reduced, but the full-term nursery may not be omitted in its entirety from any facility that includes delivery services. (When facilities use a rooming-in program in which all infants are returned to the nursery at night, a reduction in nursery size may not be practical.)

▼ **7.4.B1.** Baby Holding Nurseries

Hospitals may replace traditional nurseries with baby holding nurseries in postpartum and labor-delivery-recovery-postpartum (LDRP) units. The minimum floor area per bassinet, ventilation, electrical, and medical vacuum and gases shall be the same as that required for a full-term nursery. These holding nurseries should be next to the nurse station on these units. The holding nursery shall be sized to accommodate the percentage of newborns who do not remain with their mothers during the postpartum stay.

7.4.C. Charting Facilities
Provision shall be made for physician and nurse charting and dictation. This may be in a separate room or
▲ part of the workroom.

*7.4.D. Workroom(s)
Each nursery room shall be served by a connecting workroom. The workroom shall contain scrubbing and gowning facilities at the entrance for staff and housekeeping personnel, work counter, refrigerator, storage for supplies, and handwashing fixture. One workroom may serve more than one nursery room provided that required services are convenient to each.

The workroom serving the full-term and continuing care nurseries may be omitted if equivalent work and storage areas and facilities, including those for scrubbing and gowning, are provided within that nursery. Space required for work areas located within the nursery is in addition to the area required for infant care.

Adequate provision shall be made for storage of emergency cart(s) and equipment out of traffic and for the sanitary storage and disposal of soiled waste.

7.4.E. Infant Examination and Treatment Areas
Such areas, when required by the functional program, shall contain a work counter, storage facilities, and a handwashing fixture.

7.4.F. Infant Formula Facilities

7.4.F1. Where infant formula is prepared on-site, direct access from the formula preparation room to any nursery room is prohibited. The room may be located near the nursery or at other appropriate locations in the hospital, but must include:

> a. Cleanup facilities for washing and sterilizing supplies. This area shall include a handwashing fixture, facilities for bottle washing, a work counter, and sterilization equipment.

> b. Separate room for preparing infant formula. This room shall contain warming facilities, refrigerator, work counter, formula sterilizer, storage facilities, and a handwashing fixture.

> c. Refrigerated storage and warming facilities for infant formula accessible for use by nursery personnel at all times.

7.4.F2. If a commercial infant formula is used, the separate clean-up and preparation rooms may be omitted. The storage and handling may be done in the nursery workroom or in another appropriate room in the hospital that is conveniently accessible at all hours. The preparation area shall have a work counter, a sink equipped for handwashing, and storage facilities.

▼ **7.4.G. Housekeeping/Environmental Services Room**
A housekeeping/environmental services room shall be provided for the exclusive use of the nursery unit. It shall be directly accessible from the unit and shall contain a service sink or floor receptor and provide for storage of supplies and housekeeping equipment.
▲

7.5 Pediatric and Adolescent Unit

Note: If practical, young children and adolescents shall be housed in a nursing unit separate from adults.

▼ The unit shall meet the following standards:

7.5.A. Patient Rooms
Each patient room shall meet the following standards:

> **7.5.A1.** Maximum room capacity shall be four patients.

> **7.5.A2.** The space requirements for pediatric patient beds are the same as for adult beds due to the size variation and the need to change from cribs to beds, and vice-versa. Additional provisions for hygiene, toilets, sleeping, and personal belongings shall be included where the program indicates that parents will be allowed to remain with young children. Existing crib areas with at least 60 square feet (5.57 square meters) of clear area for each crib and no more than six cribs or beds in a room may continue to be used if the use complies with the functional program. (See Sections 7.3.E for pediatric critical care units and 7.4 for newborn nurseries.)

> **7.5.A3.** In new construction, patient rooms shall have a minimum of 100 square feet (9.29 square meters) of clear floor area per bed in multiple-bed rooms and 120 square feet (11.15 square meters) of clear floor area for single-bed rooms, exclusive of toilet rooms, closets, lockers, wardrobes, alcoves, or vestibules. The dimensions and arrangement of rooms should be such that there is a minimum of 3 feet (0.91 meter) between the sides and foot of the bed and any wall, other fixed obstruction, or another bed. In multiple-bed rooms, a clearance of 4 feet (1.22 meters) shall be available at the foot of each bed to permit the passage of equipment and beds. Minor encroachments, including columns and lavatories, that do not interfere with functions may be ignored when determining space requirements for patient rooms. Where renovation work is undertaken, patient rooms shall have a minimum of 80 square feet (7.43 square meters) of clear floor area per bed in multiple-bed areas and 100 square feet
▲ (9.29 square meters) of clear floor area in single-bed rooms.

7.5.B. Nursery
To minimize the possibility of cross-infection, each nursery room serving pediatric patients shall contain no more than eight bassinets; each bassinet shall have a minimum clear floor area of 40 square feet (3.72 square meters). Each room shall contain a lavatory equipped for handwashing operable without hands, a nurses

emergency calling system, and a glazed viewing window for observing infants from public areas and workrooms. (Limitation on number of patients in a nursery room does not apply to the pediatric critical care unit.)

7.5.C. Nursery Workrooms

Each nursery shall be served by a connecting workroom. It shall contain gowning facilities at the entrance for staff and housekeeping personnel; workspace with a work counter; storage facilities; and a handwashing fixture. One workroom may serve more than one nursery.

▼ 7.5.D. Nursery Visiting and Feeding

Each pediatric nursery shall have an area for instruction and parent contact with the infant including breast and/or bottle feeding. This may be a section of the workroom with provisions for privacy and quiet.

7.5.E. Examination/Treatment Rooms

This room shall be provided for pediatric and adolescent patients and may be omitted if all rooms in the unit are single-bed patient rooms. A separate area for infant examination and treatment may be provided within the pediatric nursery workroom. Examination/treatment rooms shall have a minimum floor area of 120 square feet (11.15 square meters). The room shall contain a handwashing fixture; storage facilities; and a desk,
▲ counter, or shelf space for writing.

7.5.F. Service Areas

The service areas in the pediatric and adolescent nursing units shall conform to Section 7.2.B and shall also meet the following standards:

7.5.F1. Multipurpose or individual room(s) shall be provided for dining, education, and recreation. Insulation, isolation, and structural provisions shall minimize the transmission of impact noise through the floor, walls, or ceiling of these multipurpose room(s).

7.5.F2. Space for preparation and storage of infant formula shall be provided within the unit or other convenient location with 24-hour access. Provisions shall be made for continuation of special formula that may have been prescribed for the infant prior to admission or readmission.

7.5.F3. Patient toilet room(s), in addition to those serving bed areas, shall be conveniently located to multipurpose room(s) and to each central bathing facility.

7.5.F4. Storage closets or cabinets for toys and educational and recreational equipment shall be provided.

7.5.F5. Storage space shall be provided to permit exchange of cribs and adult beds. Provisions shall also be made for storage of equipment and supplies (including cots or recliners, extra linen, etc.) for parents who may remain with the patient overnight.

7.5.F6. At least one room for isolation shall be provided in each pediatric unit as described in Section 7.2.C.

7.5.F7. Separate clean and soiled workrooms or holding rooms shall be provided as described in Sections 7.2.B11 and 12.

7.6 Psychiatric Nursing Unit

When part of a general hospital, these units shall be designed for the care of inpatients. Nonambulatory inpatients may be treated in a medical unit until their medical condition allows for transfer to the psychiatric nursing unit. See Section 7.2.E for psychiatric care in a medical unit. Provisions shall be made in the design for adapting the area for various types of psychiatric therapies.

The environment of the unit should be characterized by a feeling of openness with emphasis on natural light and exterior views. Various functions should be accessible from common areas while not compromising desirable levels of patient privacy. Interior finishes, lighting, and furnishings should suggest a residential rather than an institutional setting. These should, however, conform with applicable fire safety codes. Security and safety devices should not be presented in a manner to attract or challenge tampering by patients.

Windows or vents in psychiatric units shall be arranged and located so that they can be opened from the inside to permit venting of combustion products and to permit any occupant direct access to fresh air in emergencies. The operation of operable windows shall be restricted to inhibit possible escape or suicide. Where windows or vents require the use of tools or keys for operation, the tools or keys shall be located on the same floor in a prominent location accessible to staff. Windows in existing buildings designed with approved, engineered smoke control systems may be of fixed construction. Where glass fragments pose a hazard to certain patients, safety glazing and/or other appropriate security features shall be used.

Details of such facilities should be as described in the approved functional program. Each nursing unit shall provide the following:

7.6.A. Patient Rooms

The standard noted in Section 7.2.A shall apply to patient rooms in psychiatric nursing units except as follows:

7.6.A1. A nurses call system is not required, but if it is included, provisions shall be made for easy removal, or for covering call button outlets.

7.6.A2. Bedpan-flushing devices may be omitted from patient room toilets in psychiatric nursing units.

7.6.A3. Handwashing facilities are not required in patient rooms.

7.6.A4. Visual privacy in multibed rooms (e.g., cubicle curtains) is not required.

7.6.B. Service Areas

The standards noted in Section 7.2.B shall apply to service areas for psychiatric nursing units with the following modifications:

▼ A secured storage area shall be provided for patients' belongings that are determined to be potentially harmful (e.g., razors, nail files, cigarette lighters); this area
▲ will be controlled by staff.

7.6.B1. Medication station shall include provisions for security against unauthorized access.

7.6.B2. Food service within the unit may be one, or a combination, of the following:

a. A nourishment station.

b. A kitchenette designed for patient use with staff control of heating and cooking devices.

c. A kitchen service within the unit including a handwashing fixture, storage space, refrigerator, and facilities for meal preparation.

7.6.B3. Storage space for stretchers and wheelchairs may be outside the psychiatric unit, provided that provisions are made for convenient access as needed for handicapped patients.

7.6.B4. In psychiatric nursing units, a bathtub or shower shall be provided for each six beds not otherwise served by bathing facilities within the patient rooms. Bathing facilities should be designed and located for patient convenience and privacy.

7.6.B5. A separate charting area shall be provided with provisions for acoustical privacy. A viewing window to permit observation of patient areas by the charting nurse or physician may be used if the arrangement is such that patient files cannot be read from outside the charting space.

7.6.B6. At least two separate social spaces, one appropriate for noisy activities and one for quiet activities, shall be provided. The combined area shall be at least 40 square feet (3.72 square meters) per patient with at least 120 square feet (11.15 square meters) for each of the two spaces. This space may be shared by dining activities.

7.6.B7. Space for group therapy shall be provided. This may be combined with the quiet space noted above when the unit accommodates not more than 12 patients, and when at least 225 square feet (20.90 square meters) of enclosed private space is available for group therapy activities.

7.6.B8. Patient laundry facilities with an automatic washer and dryer shall be provided.

The following elements shall also be provided, but may be either within the psychiatric unit or immediately accessible to it unless otherwise dictated by the program:

▼ **7.6.B9.** Room(s) for examination and treatment with a minimum area of 120 square feet (11.15 square meters). Examination and treatment room(s) for medical-surgical patients may be shared by the psychiatric unit patients. (These may be on a different
▲ floor if conveniently accessible.)

7.6.B10. Separate consultation room(s) with minimum floor space of 100 square feet (9.29 square meters) each, provided at a room-to-bed ratio of one consultation room for each 12 psychiatric beds. The room(s) shall be designed for acoustical and visual privacy and constructed to achieve a noise reduction of at least 45 decibels.

7.6.B11. Psychiatric units each containing 15 square feet (1.39 square meters) of separate space per patient for occupational therapy, with a minimum total area of at least 200 square feet (18.58 square meters), whichever is greater. Space shall include provision for handwashing, work counter(s), storage, and displays. Occupational therapy areas may serve more than one nursing unit. When psychiatric nursing unit(s) contain less than 12 beds, the occupational therapy functions may be performed within the noisy activities area, if at least an additional 10 square feet (0.93 square meter) per patient served is included.

7.6.B12. A conference and treatment planning room for use by the psychiatric unit.

7.6.C. Isolation Room(s)

The standards of Section 7.2.C for isolation rooms do not apply to a psychiatric nursing unit. Psychiatric beds are not to be included in the bed count ratio to establish the number of beds required for medical isolation.

7.6.D. Seclusion Treatment Room

▼ There shall be at least one seclusion room for up to 24 beds or a major fraction thereof. The seclusion treatment room is intended for short-term occupancy by a violent or suicidal patient. Within the psychiatric

nursing unit, this space provides for patients requiring security and protection. The room(s) shall be located for direct nursing staff supervision. Each room shall be for only one patient. It shall have an area of at least 60 square feet (5.57 square meters) and shall be constructed to prevent patient hiding, escape, injury, or suicide. Where restraint beds are required by the functional program, 80 square feet (7.43 square meters) shall be required. If a facility has more than one psychiatric nursing unit, the number of seclusion rooms shall be a function of the total number of psychiatric beds in the facility. Seclusion rooms may be grouped together. Special fixtures and hardware for electrical circuits shall be used. Minimum ceiling height shall be 9 feet (2.74 meters). Doors shall be 3 feet 8 inches (1.12 meters) wide, and shall permit staff observation of the patient while also maintaining provisions for patient privacy. Seclusion treatment rooms shall be accessed by an anteroom or vestibule which also provides direct access to a toilet room. The toilet room and anteroom
▲ shall be large enough to safely manage the patient.

Where the interior of the seclusion treatment room is padded with combustible materials, these materials shall be of a type acceptable to the local authority having jurisdiction. The room area, including floor, walls, ceilings, and all openings shall be protected with not less than one-hour-rated construction.

7.7 Surgical Suites

Note: The number of operating rooms and recovery beds and the sizes of the service areas shall be based on the expected surgical workload. The surgical suite shall be located and arranged to prevent nonrelated traffic through the suite. See Sections 7.28, 7.31, and 7.32 for details, ventilation, and electrical standards.

Additions to, and adaptations of, the following elements shall be made for the special-procedure operating rooms found in larger facilities.

The following shall be provided:

7.7.A. Surgery

▼ **7.7.A1.** General operating room(s). In new construction, each room shall have a minimum clear area of 400 square feet (37.16 square meters) exclusive of fixed or wall-mounted cabinets and built-in shelves, with a minimum of 20 feet (6.10 meters) clear dimension between fixed cabinets and built-in shelves; and a system for emergency communication with the surgical suite control station. X-ray film illuminators for handling at least four films simultaneously shall also be provided. In renovation projects, each room shall have a minimum clear area of 360 square feet (33.45 square meters), exclusive of fixed or wall-mounted

cabinets and built-in shelves, with a minimum of 18 feet (5.49 meters) clear dimension between fixed cabinets and built-in shelves. (For renovation projects, see Section 7.7.A6.)

7.7.A2. Room(s) for cardiovascular, orthopedic, neurological, and other special procedures that require additional personnel and/or large equipment. When included, this room shall have, in addition to the above, a minimum clear area of 600 square feet (55.74 square meters), with a minimum of 20 feet (6.10 meters) clear dimension exclusive of fixed or wall-mounted cabinets and built-in shelves. When open-heart surgery is performed, an additional room in the restricted area of the surgical suite, preferably adjoining this operating room, shall be designated as a pump room where extra corporeal pump(s), supplies and accessories are stored and serviced. When complex orthopedic and neurosurgical surgery is performed, additional rooms shall be in the restricted area of the surgical suite, preferably adjoining the specialty operating rooms, which shall be designated as equipment storage rooms for the large equipment used to support these procedures. Appropriate plumbing and electrical connections shall be provided in the cardiovascular, orthopedic, neurosurgical, pump, and storage rooms. In renovation projects, orthopedic surgical rooms may have a minimum clear area of 360 square feet (33.5 square meters) and a minimum dimension of 18 feet (5 meters). Rooms for cardiovascular, neurological, and other special procedures may have a minimum clear area
▲ of 400 square feet (44.39 square meters).

7.7.A3. A room for orthopedic surgery. When included, this room shall, in addition to the above, have enclosed storage space for splints and traction equipment. Storage may be outside the operating room but must be conveniently located. If a sink is used for the disposal of plaster of paris, a plaster trap shall be provided.

▼ **7.7.A4.** Room(s) for surgical cystoscopic and other endo-urologic procedures. This room shall have a minimum clear area of 350 square feet (32.52 square meters) exclusive of fixed or wall-mounted cabinets and built-in shelves with a minimum of 15 feet (4.57 meters) clear dimension between fixed cabinets and built-in shelves. X-ray viewing capability to accommodate at least four films simultaneously will be provided. In renovation projects, rooms for surgical cystoscopy may have a minimum clear area of 250
▲ square feet (23.28 square meters).

7.7.A5. Endoscopy suite requirements. (See Section 9.9.)

7.7.A6. The functional program may require additional clear space, plumbing, and mechanical facilities to accommodate special functions in one or more of these rooms. When existing functioning operating rooms are modified, and it is impractical to increase the square foot area because of walls or structural members, the operating room may continue in use when requested by the hospital.

7.7.B. Post-Anesthetic Care Units (PACUs)

▼ Each PACU shall contain a medication station; handwashing facilities; nurse station with charting facilities; clinical sink; provisions for bedpan cleaning; and storage space for stretchers, supplies, and equipment. Additionally, the design shall provide a minimum of 80 square feet for each patient bed with a space for additional equipment described in the functional program, and for clearance of at least 4 feet (1.22 meters) between patient beds and between patient bedsides and adjacent walls. Provisions shall be made for the isolation of infectious patients. Provisions for patient privacy such as cubicle curtains shall be made. In new construction, at least one door to the recovery room shall access directly from the surgical suite without crossing public hospital corridors. Separate and additional recovery space may be necessary to accommodate surgical outpatients and pediatric patients. (See Sections 7.7.C14, 7.7.C17, and 9.5.)

A staff toilet shall be located within the working area to maintain staff availability to patients.

Handwashing sinks with foot or elbow controls should be available in sufficient number, at least one for every four beds uniformly distributed to provide equal access
▲ from each patient bed.

7.7.C. Service Areas

Services, except for the enclosed soiled workroom mentioned in item 7.7.C6 and the housekeeping room in item 7.7.C19, may be shared with the obstetrical facilities if the functional program reflects this concept. Service areas, when shared with delivery rooms, shall be designed to avoid the passing of patients or staff between the operating room and the delivery room areas. The following services shall be provided:

7.7.C1. A control station located to permit visual observation of all traffic into the suite.

7.7.C2. A supervisor's office or station.

▼ **7.7.C3.** A sterilizing facility(ies) with high-speed sterilizer(s) or other sterilizing equipment for immediate or emergency use must be grouped to several operating rooms for convenient, efficient use. A work space and handwashing facility may be included. Other facilities for processing and sterilizing reusable instruments, etc., may be located in another hospital department such as central services.

7.7.C4. Medication station. Provision shall be made for storage and distribution of drugs and routine medications. This may be done from a medicine preparation room or unit, from a self-contained medicine dispensing unit, or by another system. If used, a medicine preparation room or unit shall be under visual control of nursing staff. It shall contain a work counter, sink, refrigerator, and double-locked storage for controlled substances and shall have a minimum area of 50 square feet (4.65 square meters). Convenient access to handwashing facilities shall be provided. (Standard cup-sinks provided in many self-contained units are not adequate for handwashing.)

7.7.C5. Scrub facilities. Two scrub positions shall be provided near the entrance to each operating room. Two scrub positions may serve two operating rooms if both are located adjacent to the entrance of each operating room. Scrub facilities should be arranged to minimize incidental splatter on nearby personnel, medical equipment, or supply carts. In new construction, view windows at scrub stations permitting observation of room interiors should be provided. The scrub sinks should be recessed into an alcove out of the main traffic areas.

7.7.C6. An enclosed soiled workroom (or soiled holding room that is part of a system for the collection and disposal of soiled material) for the exclusive use of the surgical suite shall be provided. It shall be located in the restricted area. The soiled workroom shall contain a flushing-rim clinical sink or equivalent flushing-rim fixture, a handwashing fixture, a work counter, and space for waste receptacles and soiled linen receptacles. Rooms used only for temporary holding of soiled material may omit the flushing-rim clinical sink and work counters. However, if the flushing-rim clinical sink is omitted, other provisions for disposal of liquid waste shall be provided. The room shall not have direct connection with operating rooms or other sterile activity rooms. Soiled and clean workrooms or
▲ holding rooms shall be separated.

7.7.C7. Clean workroom or clean supply room.

▼ a. A clean workroom is required when clean materials are assembled within the surgical suite prior to use or following the decontamination cycle. It shall contain a work counter, a handwashing fixture, storage facilities for clean supplies, and a space to package reusable items. The storage for sterile supplies must be separated from this space. If the room is used only for storage and holding as part of a system for distribution of clean and sterile supply materials, the work counter and handwashing fixture may be omitted. Soiled and clean workrooms or holding rooms shall be separated.

b. Storage space for sterile and clean supplies should be adequate for the functional plan. The space should be moisture and temperature controlled and free from cross traffic.

c. An operating room suite design with a sterile core must provide for no cross traffic of staff and supplies from the decontaminated/soiled areas to the sterile/clean areas. The use of facilities outside the operating room for soiled/decontaminated processing and clean assembly and sterile processing will be designed to move the flow of goods and personnel from dirty to clean/sterile without compromising universal precautions or
▲ aseptic techniques in both departments.

7.7.C8. Medical gas storage facilities. Flammable anesthetics, if used, shall be stored in a separate room in accordance with Section 7.29. Main storage of medical gases may be outside or inside the facility. Provision shall be made for additional separate storage of reserve gas cylinders necessary to complete at least one day's procedures.

▼ **7.7.C9.** The anesthesia workroom for cleaning, testing, and storing anesthesia equipment shall contain work counter(s) and sink(s) and racks for cylinders. Provisions shall be made for separate storage of
▲ clean and soiled items.

7.7.C10. Equipment storage room(s) for equipment and supplies used in surgical suite.

7.7.C11. Staff clothing change areas. Appropriate areas shall be provided for male and female personnel (orderlies, technicians, nurses, and doctors) working within the surgical suite. The areas shall contain lockers, showers, toilets, lavatories equipped for handwashing, and space for donning scrub suits and booties. These areas shall be arranged to encourage a one-way traffic pattern so that personnel entering from outside the surgical suite can change and move directly into the surgical suite.

7.7.C12. Staff lounge and toilet facilities. Separate or combined lounges for male and female staff shall be provided. Lounge(s) shall be designed to minimize the need to leave the suite and to provide convenient access to the recovery room.

7.7.C13. Dictation and report preparation area. This may be accessible from the lounge area.

7.7.C14. Outpatient recovery. If the functional program includes outpatient surgery, provisions shall be made for separating outpatients into two categories, (Phase I) patients receiving general anesthesia and (Phase II) patients not subjected to general anesthesia. This requirement should be satisfied by separate rooms. Phase II shall provide privacy for each patient. A patient toilet room directly accessible

from outpatient recovery shall be provided. Smaller facilities with no more than two surgical procedure rooms may use the same space for (Phase II) recovery of patients not subjected to general anesthesia as that used for preoperative preparation.

7.7.C15. Outpatient surgery change areas. If the functional program defines outpatient surgery as part of the surgical suite, a separate area shall be provided where outpatients may change from street clothing into hospital gowns and be prepared for surgery. This would include a waiting room, locker(s), toilet(s), and clothing change or gowning area.

7.7.C16. Provisions shall be made for patient examination, interviews, preparation, testing, and obtaining vital signs of patients for outpatient surgery.

7.7.C17. Patient holding area. In facilities with two or more operating rooms, an area shall be provided to accommodate stretcher patients waiting for surgery. This holding area shall be under the visual control of the nursing staff.

7.7.C18. Storage areas for portable X-ray equipment, stretchers, fracture tables, warming devices, auxiliary lamps, etc. These areas shall be out of corridors and traffic.

▼ **7.7.C19.** Housekeeping facilities. Housekeeping facilities shall be provided for the exclusive use of the surgical suite. It shall be directly accessible from the suite and shall contain a service sink or floor receptor and provisions for storage of supplies and
▲ housekeeping equipment.

7.7.C20. Area for preparation and examination of frozen sections. This may be part of the general laboratory if immediate results are obtainable without unnecessary delay in the completion of surgery.

▼ **7.7.C21.** Ice machine. An ice machine shall be provided to provide ice for treatments and patient use. Ice intended for human consumption shall be from
▲ self-dispensing ice makers.

7.7.C22. Provisions for refrigerated blood bank storage.

▼ **7.7.C23.** Where applicable, appropriate provisions for refrigeration facilities for harvested organs.

7.7.C24. Provisions for pathological specimens storage prior to transfer to pathology section.

7.7.C25. See Section 9.5 of this document concerning the separate outpatient surgical unit.

7.7.C26. For general standards on detail and finishes, see Sections 7.28.A, 7.28.B, and Table 1.

7.7.C27. For elevators, see Section 7.30.A2-6.

7.7.C28. For mechanical considerations, see Section 7.31 and Tables 2 through 5.

7.7.C29. For electrical considerations, see Sections 7.32.A-I.

7.7.C30. For central services considerations, see ▲ Section 7.20.

7.8 Obstetrical Facilities

*7.8.A. (See Appendix A.)

7.8.B. Obstetrical Suite

7.8.B1. General

▼ The obstetrical unit shall be located and designed to prohibit nonrelated traffic through the unit. When delivery and operating rooms are in the same suite, access and service arrangements shall be such that neither staff nor patients need to travel through one area to reach the other. Except as permitted otherwise herein, existing facilities being renovated shall, as far as practicable, provide all the required support ▲ services.

7.8.B2. Postpartum Unit

a. Postpartum bedroom

▼ (1) A postpartum bedroom shall have a minimum of 100 square feet (9.29 square meters) of clear floor area per bed in multibed rooms and 120 square feet (11.15 square meters) of clear floor area in single-bed rooms. These areas shall be exclusive of toilet rooms, closets, alcoves, or vestibules. Where renovation work is undertaken, existing postpartum patient rooms shall have a minimum of 80 square feet (7.43 square meters) of clear floor area per bed in multiple-bed rooms and 100 square feet (9.29 square meters) in single-bed rooms.

(2) In multibed rooms there shall be a minimum clear distance of 4 feet (1.22 meters) between the foot of the bed and the opposite wall, 3 feet (0.91-meter) between the side of the bed and the nearest wall, and 4 feet (1.22 meters) between beds.

(3) The maximum number of beds per room shall be two. Note: In new construction, the maximum room capacity shall be two patients. Where renovation work is undertaken and the present capacity is four patients, maximum room capacity may be four patients.

(4) Each patient bedroom shall have a window or windows that can be opened from the inside. When the windows require the use of tools or keys, they shall be kept on the unit and readily accessible to staff.

(5) Each patient room shall have a nurse calling system for two-way voice communication.

(6) Handwashing facilities shall be provided in each patient bedroom. In multibed rooms the handwashing sink shall be located outside of the patients' cubical curtains so that it is accessible to staff.

(7) Each patient shall have access to a toilet room or bathroom without entering a general corridor. One such room shall serve no more than two beds and no more than two patient rooms. The lavatory may be omitted from a toilet room if each patient room served by the toilet contains a lavatory for handwashing.

b. The following support services for this unit shall be provided.

(1) A nurse station.

(2) A nurse office.

(3) Charting facilities.

(4) Toilet room for staff.

(5) Staff lounge.

(6) Lockable closets or cabinets for personal articles of staff.

(7) Consultation/conference room(s).

(8) Patients' lounge. The patients' lounge may be omitted if all rooms are single-bed rooms.

(9) Clean workroom or clean supply room. A clean workroom is required if clean materials are assembled within the obstetrical suite prior to use. It shall contain a work counter, a handwashing fixture, and storage facilities for clean and sterile supplies. If the room is used only for storage and holding as part of a system for distribution of clean and sterile supply materials, the work counter and handwashing fixtures may be omitted. Soiled and clean workrooms or holding rooms shall be separated and have no direct connection.

(10) Soiled workroom or soiled holding room for the exclusive use of the obstetrical suite. This room shall be separate from the clean workroom and shall have separate access doors. The soiled workroom shall contain a clinical sink (or equivalent flushing-rim fixture) and a handwashing fixture. The above fixtures shall both have a hot

and cold mixing faucet. The room shall have a work counter and space for separate covered containers for soiled linen and waste. Rooms used only for temporary holding of soiled material may omit the clinical sink and work counter. If the flushing-rim clinical sink is omitted, facilities for cleaning bedpans shall be provided elsewhere.

(11) Medication station. Provision shall be made for storage and distribution of drugs and routine medications. This may be done from a medicine preparation room or unit, from a self-contained medicine dispensing unit, or by another system. If used, a medicine preparation room or unit shall be under visual control of nursing staff. It shall contain a work counter, sink, refrigerator, and double-locked storage for controlled substances and shall have a minimum area of 50 square feet (4.65 square meters). Convenient access to handwashing facilities shall be provided. (Standard cup-sinks provided in many self-contained units are not adequate for handwashing.)

(12) Clean linen storage may be part of a clean workroom or a separate closet. When a close cart system is used, the cart may be stored in a alcove out of the path of normal traffic.

(13) Nourishment station shall contain sink, work counter, ice dispenser, refrigerator, cabinets, and equipment for serving hot or cold food. Space shall be included for temporary holding of unused or soiled dietary trays.

(14) Equipment storage room.

(15) Storage space for stretchers and wheelchairs. Storage space for stretchers and wheelchairs shall be provided in a strategic location, out of corridors and away from normal traffic.

(16) When bathing facilities are not provided in patient rooms, there shall be at least one shower and/or bathtub for each 6 beds or fraction thereof.

(17) Housekeeping room. A housekeeping room shall be provided for the exclusive use of the obstetrical suite. It shall be directly accessible from the suite and shall contain a service sink or floor receptor and provisions for storage of supplies and housekeeping equipment.

(18) Examination/treatment room and/or multipurpose diagnostic testing room shall have a minimum clear floor area of 120 square feet (11.15 square meters). When utilized as a multi-patient diagnostic testing room, a minimum clear floor area of 80 square feet (7.43 square meters) per patient shall be provided. An adjoining toilet room shall be provided for patient use.

(19) Emergency equipment storage shall be located in close proximity to the nurse station.

c. Infectious isolation room(s)

(1) One isolation room shall be provided for each 30 beds or major faction thereof. Each isolation room shall contain a clear floor area of 120 square feet (11.15 square meters) and a single bed. A minimum of one isolation room shall be provided regardless of the size of the unit. There shall be an anteroom of a minimum of 20 square feet (1.86 square meters), with facilities for handwashing, gowning, and storage of clean and soiled materials. One anteroom may serve not more than two isolation rooms.

(2) Each isolation room shall have an adjoining bathroom (with tub or shower).

7.8.B3. Caesarean/Delivery Suite

a. Caesarean/delivery room(s) shall have a minimum clear floor area of 360 square feet (33.45 square meters) with a minimum dimension of 16 feet (4.88 meters) exclusive of built-in shelves or cabinets. There shall be a minimum of one such room in every obstetrical unit.

b. Delivery room(s) shall have a minimum clear area of 300 square feet (27.87 square meters) exclusive of fixed cabinets and built-in shelves. An emergency communication system shall be connected with the obstetrical suite control station.

c. Infant resuscitation shall be provided within the caesarean/delivery room(s) and delivery rooms with a minimum clear floor area of 40 square feet (3.72 square meters) in addition to the required area of each room or may be provided in a separate but immediately accessible room with a clear floor area of 150 square feet (13.94 square meters). Six single or three duplex electrical outlets shall be provided for the infant in addition to the facilities required for the mother.

d. Labor room(s) (LDR rooms may be substituted.) In renovation projects, existing labor rooms may have a minimum clear area of 100 square feet (9.3 square meters) per bed.

Where LDRs or LDRPs are not provided, a minimum of two labor beds shall be provided for each caesarean/delivery room. In facilities that have only one caesarean/delivery room, two labor rooms shall be provided. Each room shall be designed for either one or two beds with a minimum clear area of 120 square feet (11.15 square meters) per bed. Each labor room shall contain a handwashing fixture and have access to a toilet room. One toilet room may serve two labor rooms. Labor rooms shall have controlled access with doors that are arranged for observation from a nursing station. At least one shower (which may be separate from the labor room if under staff control) for use of patients in labor shall be provided. Windows in labor rooms, if provided, shall be located, draped, or otherwise arranged, to preserve patient privacy from casual observation from outside the labor room.

e. Recovery room(s) (LDR rooms may be substituted.)

Each recovery room shall contain at least two beds and have a nurse station with charting facilities located to permit visual control of all beds. Each room shall include facilities for handwashing and dispensing medicine. A clinical sink with bedpan flushing device shall be available, as shall storage for supplies and equipment. There should be enough space for baby and crib and a chair for the support person. There should be the ability to maintain visual privacy of the new family.

f. Service Areas

(1) Individual rooms shall be provided as indicated in the following standards; otherwise, alcoves or other open spaces that do not interfere with traffic may be used. Services, except the soiled workroom and the housekeeping room, may be shared with the surgical facilities, if the functional program reflects this concept. Where shared, areas shall be arranged to avoid direct traffic between the delivery and operating rooms. The following services shall be provided:

(2) A control/nurse station located to restrict unauthorized traffic into the suite.

g. A supervisor's office or station.

h. A waiting room, with toilets, telephones, and drinking fountains conveniently located.

i. Sterilizing facilities with high-speed sterilizers convenient to all caesarean/delivery rooms. Sterilization facilities should be separate from the delivery area and adjacent to clean assembly. High-speed autoclaves should only be used in an emergency situation (i.e., a dropped instrument and no sterile replacement readily available). Sterilization facilities would not be necessary if the flow of materials were handled properly from a central service department based on the usage of the delivery room (DR).

j. A drug distribution station with handwashing facilities and provisions for controlled storage, preparation, and distribution of medication.

k. Scrub facilities for caesarean/delivery rooms. Two scrub positions shall be provided adjacent to entrance to each caesarean/delivery room. Scrub facilities should be arranged to minimize any splatter on nearby personnel or supply carts. In new construction, provide view windows at scrub stations to permit the observation of room interiors.

l. Soiled workroom or soiled holding room. This room shall be separate from the clean workroom and shall have separate access doors. The soiled workroom shall contain a clinical sink (or equivalent flushing-rim fixture). The room shall contain a handwashing fixture. The above fixtures shall both have a hot and cold mixing faucet. The room shall have a work counter and space for separate covered containers for soiled linen and waste. Rooms used only for temporary holding of soiled material may omit the clinical sink and work counter. If the flushing-rim clinical sink is eliminated, facilities for cleaning bedpans shall be provided elsewhere.

m. Fluid waste disposal: See l above.

▲ n. Clean workroom: See l above.

o. Anesthesia storage facilities. Storage space for service cylinders of medical gases shall be provided as needed. If flammable anesthetics are used, a separate room shall be provided for their storage in accordance with the details of Section 7.29.

▼ p. A clean sterile storage area readily available to the DR: size to be determined on level of usage, functions provided, and supplies from the hospital ▲ central distribution area.

q. An anesthesia workroom for cleaning, testing, and storing anesthesia equipment. It shall contain a work counter, sink, and provisions for separation of clean and soiled items.

r. Equipment storage room(s) for equipment and supplies used in the obstetrical suite.

▼ s. Staff clothing change areas. The clothing change area shall be designed to minimize physical contact between clean and contaminated personnel. The area shall contain lockers, showers, toilets, handwashing facilities, and space for donning and disposing scrub suits and booties.

t. Male and female support persons change area ▲ (designed as described above).

u. Lounge and toilet facilities for obstetrical staff convenient to delivery, labor, and recovery areas. In addition, on-call rooms for physician shall be provided.

v. Housekeeping room with a floor receptacle or service sink and storage space for housekeeping supplies and equipment.

w. An area for storing stretchers out of the path of normal traffic.

▼ **7.8.B4.** LDR and LDRP Facilities

When provided by the functional program, delivery procedures in accordance with birthing concepts may be performed in the LDR or LDRP rooms. LDR room(s) may be located in a separate LDR suite or as part of the Caesarean/Delivery suite. The postpartum unit may contain LDRP rooms. These rooms shall have a minimum of 250 square feet (23.23 square meters) of clear floor area with a minimum dimension of 13 feet (3.96 meters), exclusive of toilet room, closet, alcove, or vestibules. There should be enough space for crib and reclining chair for support person. An area within the room but distinct from the mother's area shall be provided for infant stabilization and resuscitation. See Table 5 in Section 7.31 for medical gas and electrical outlets. These outlets should be located in the room so that they are accessible to the mother's delivery area and infant resuscitation area. In renovation projects, existing LDR or LDRP rooms may have a minimum clear area of 200 square feet (18.58 square meters).

Each LDR or LDRP room shall be for single occupancy and have direct access to a private toilet with shower or tub. Each room shall be equipped with free-standing handwashing fixture (handwashing fixture with hands-free operation is acceptable for scrubbing). Examination lights may be portable, but must be immediately accessible.

a. Finishes shall be selected to facilitate cleaning and with resistance to strong detergents. Windows or doors within a normal sightline that would permit observation into the room shall be arranged or
▲ draped as necessary for patient privacy.

7.9 Emergency Service

(See Section 9.6 for the separate outpatient emergency unit.)

7.9.A. Definition
Levels of emergency care range from elementary initial emergency management to sophisticated definitive emergency care such as repair of heart wounds. For these standards, emergency services are described in these two broad categories: initial emergency management and definitive emergency management.

▼ **7.9.A1.** Initial emergency management is care provided to stabilize a victim's condition and to minimize potential for further injury during transport to an appropriate service. Patients may be brought to the "nearest hospital," which may or may not have all required services for definitive emergency management. It is important that the hospital, in those cases, be able to alleviate emergent illnesses and
▲ injuries and arrange for appropriate transfer.

*7.9.A2. Emergency care may range from the simple suturing of lacerations to full-scale medical procedures. Facilities that include personnel and equipment for definitive emergency care should provide for 24-hour service and complete emergency care leading to discharge to the patient's home or direct admission to the appropriate hospital.

7.9.B. General
The extent and type of emergency service to be provided will depend upon community needs and the availability of other services within the area. While initial emergency management must be available at every hospital, full-scale definitive emergency services may be impractical and/or an unnecessary duplication. All services need adequate equipment and 24-hour staffing to ensure no delay in essential treatment. The following standards are intended only as minimums. Additional facilities, as needed, shall be as required to satisfy the program.

Provisions for facilities to provide nonemergent treatment of outpatients are covered separately in Section 9.3.

7.9.C. Initial Emergency Management
At a minimum, each hospital shall have provisions for emergency treatment for staff, employees, and visitors, as well as for persons who may be unaware of or unable to immediately reach services in other facilities. This is not only for minor incidents that may require minimal care but also for persons with severe illness and injuries who must receive immediate emergency care and assistance prior to transport to other facilities.

Provisions for initial emergency management shall include:

7.9.C1. A marked entrance, at grade level, protected from the weather.

▼ **7.9.C2.** A treatment room with not less than 120 square feet (11.15 square meters) of clear area, exclusive of toilets, waiting area, and storage. Each treatment room shall contain an examination light, work counter, handwashing facilities, medical equipment, cabinets, medication storage, adequate electrical outlets above floor level, and counter space for writing. The treatment room may have additional space and provisions for several patients with cubicle curtains for privacy. Multiple-bed treatment rooms shall provide a minimum of 80 square feet (7.43 ▲ square meters) per patient cubicle.

7.9.C3. Storage out of traffic and under staff control for general medical/surgical emergency supplies, medications, and equipment such as ventilator, defibrillator, splints, etc.

▼ **7.9.C4.** Provisions for reception, control, and public ▲ waiting, including a public toilet.

7.9.C5. A patient toilet room convenient to the treatment room(s).

▼ **7.9.C6.** Communication hookup to the Poison ▲ Control Center and regional EMS system.

7.9.D. Definitive Emergency Care
When 24-hour emergency service is to be provided, the type, size, and number of the services shall be as defined in the functional program. As a minimum, the following shall be provided:

7.9.D1. Grade-level entrance sheltered from the weather with direct access from heliport (if included) and from public roads for ambulance and vehicle traffic. Entrance and driveway shall be clearly marked. If a raised platform is used for ambulance discharge, provide a ramp for pedestrian and wheelchair access.

7.9.D2. Paved emergency access to permit discharge of patients from automobiles and ambulances, and temporary parking convenient to the entrance.

7.9.D3. Reception, triage (see Table 5 in Section 7.31), and control station shall be located to permit staff observation and control of access to treatment area, pedestrian and ambulance entrances, and public waiting area.

7.9.D4. Wheelchair and stretcher storage shall be provided for arriving patients. This shall be out of traffic with convenient access from emergency entrances.

7.9.D5. Public waiting area with toilet facilities, drinking fountains, and telephones shall be provided.

7.9.D6. Communication center shall be convenient to nursing station and have radio, telephone, and intercommunication systems. (See Section 7.29.F.)

▼ **7.9.D7.** Examination and treatment room(s). Examination rooms shall have a minimum floor area of 120 square feet (11.15 square meters). The room shall contain work counter(s); cabinets; handwashing facilities; supply storage facilities; examination lights; and a desk, counter, or shelf space for writing. When treatment cubicles are in open multibed

areas, each cubicle shall have a minimum of 80 square feet (7.43 square meters) of clear floor space and shall be separated from adjoining cubicles by curtains. Handwashing facilities shall be provided for each four treatment cubicles or major fraction thereof in multiple-bed areas. For oxygen and vacuum, see Table 5 in Section 7.31. Treatment/examination rooms used for pelvic exams should allow for the foot of the examination table to face away from the door.

***7.9.D8.** Trauma/cardiac rooms for emergency procedures, including emergency surgery, shall have at least 250 square feet (23.23 square meters) of clear floor space. Each room shall have cabinets and emergency supply shelves, X-ray film illuminators, examination lights, and counter space for writing. Additional space with cubicle curtains for privacy may be provided to accommodate more than one patient at a time in the trauma room. Provisions shall be made for monitoring the patient. There shall be storage provided for immediate access to attire used for universal precautions. Doorways leading from the ambulance entrance to the cardiac trauma room shall be a minimum of 5 feet (1.52 meters) wide to simultaneously accommodate stretchers, equipment, and personnel. In renovation projects, existing cardiac/trauma rooms may have a clear area of 240 square feet (21 square meters), and doorways leading from the ambulance entrance to the room may be 4 feet (1.22 meters) wide.

7.9.D9. Provisions for orthopedic and cast work. These may be in separate room(s) or in the trauma room. They shall include storage for splints and other orthopedic supplies, traction hooks, X-ray film illuminators, and examination lights. If a sink is used for the disposal of plaster of Paris, a plaster trap shall be provided. The clear floor space for this area shall be dependent on the functional program and the procedures and equipment accommodated here.

7.9.D10. Scrub stations located in or adjacent and ▲ convenient to each trauma and/or orthopedic room.

7.9.D11. Convenient access to radiology and laboratory services.

▼ **7.9.D12.** Poison Control Center and EMS Communications Center may be a part of the staff ▲ work and charting area.

7.9.D13. Provisions for disposal of solid and liquid waste. This may be a clinical sink with bedpan flushing device within the soiled workroom.

▼ **7.9.D14.** Emergency equipment storage. Sufficient space shall be provided for emergency equipment that is under direct control of the nursing staff, such as a CPR cart, pumps, ventilators, patient monitoring equipment, and portable X-ray unit. This space shall be located in an area appropriate to the functional program easily accessible to staff but out of normal traffic patterns.

7.9.D15. A toilet room for patients. Where there are more than eight treatment areas, a minimum of two
▲ toilet facilities will be required.

7.9.D16. Storage rooms for clean, soiled, or used supplies.

▼ *a. Soiled workroom or soiled holding room for the exclusive use of the emergency service. This room shall be separate from the clean workroom and shall have separate access doors. The soiled workroom shall contain a clinical sink (or equivalent flushing-rim fixture). The room shall contain a lavatory (or handwashing fixture). The above fixtures shall both have a hot and cold mixing faucet. The room shall have a work counter and space for separate covered containers for soiled linen and waste. Rooms used only for temporary holding of soiled material may omit the clinical sink and work counter. If the flushing-rim clinical sink is eliminated, facilities for cleaning bedpans shall be provided elsewhere.

b. Clean workroom or clean supply room. If the room is used for preparing patient care items, it shall contain a work counter, a handwashing sink, and storage facilities for clean and sterile supplies. If the room is used only for storage and holding as part of a system for distribution of clean and sterile supply materials, the work counter and handwashing facilities may be omitted. Soiled and clean workrooms or holding rooms shall be separated and have no direct connection.

7.9.D17. Administrative center or nurses station for staff work and charting. This area shall have space for counters, cabinets, and medication storage, and shall have convenient access to handwashing facilities. It may be combined with or include centers for reception and communication or poison control. Preferably, the nurses station should permit visual observation of all traffic into the unit.

7.9.D18. Securable closets or cabinet compartments for the personal effects of emergency service personnel, located in or near the nurse station. At a minimum, these shall be large enough for purses and billfolds. Coats may be stored in closets or cabinets in the unit
▲ or in a central staff locker area.

7.9.D19. Convenient and private access to staff toilets, lounge, and lockers.

▼ **7.9.D20.** Housekeeping room. A housekeeping room shall be provided for the exclusive use of the emergency service. It shall be directly accessible from the unit and shall contain a service sink or floor receptor and provisions for storage of supplies and housekeeping equipment.

7.9.D21. Security Station

The non-selective 24-hour accessibility of the emergency department dictates that a security system reflecting local community needs be provided.

7.9.D22. Infectious Isolation Room

At least one infectious isolation room should be provided, with 120 square feet (11.15 square meters) of clear floor space and enclosed storage cabinets.

*7.9.D23. Bereavement Room. (See Appendix A.)

7.9.D24. Secured Holding Room

At least one holding/seclusion room shall be provided. This room shall allow for security, patient and
▲ staff safety, and soundproofing.

*7.9.E. Other Space Considerations. (See Appendix A.)

7.9.F. Details and Finishes; Ventilation and Mechanical; Electrical Standards
See Section 7.28 for details and finishes, Section 7.31 for ventilation and mechanical, and Section 7.32 for electrical standards.

7.10 Imaging Suite

7.10.A. General

▼ **7.10.A1.** Equipment and space shall be as necessary to accommodate the functional program. The imaging department provides diagnostic procedures. It includes fluoroscopy, radiography, mammography, tomography, computerized tomography scanning, ultrasound, magnetic resonance, angiography and other similar techniques. Layouts should be developed in compliance with manufacturer's recommendations, because area requirements may vary from machine to machine. Since technology changes frequently and from manufacturer to manufacturer, rooms can be sized larger to allow upgrading of equipment over a period of time.

7.10.A2. Most imaging requires radiation protection. A certified physicist representing the owner or appropriate state agency shall specify the type, location, and amount of radiation protection to be installed in accordance with the final approved department layout and equipment selections. Where protected alcoves with view windows are required, a minimum of 1 foot 6 inches (0.45 meter) between the view window and the outside partition edge shall be provided. Radiation protection requirements shall be incorporated into the specifications and the building plans.

7.10.A3. Beds and stretchers shall have ready access to and from other departments of the institution. Particular attention should be paid to the management of outpatients for preparation and observation. The emergency, surgery, cystoscopy, and outpatient clinics should be accessible to the imaging suite. Imaging should be located on the ground floor, if practical, because of equipment ceiling height requirements, close proximity to electrical services, and expansion considerations.

7.10.A4. Flooring shall be adequate to meet load requirements for equipment, patients, and personnel. Provision for wiring raceways, ducts or conduits should be made in floors, walls, and ceilings. Ceiling heights may be higher than normal. Ceiling mounted equipment should have properly designed rigid support structures located above the finished ceiling. A lay-in type ceiling should be considered for ease of installation, service, and remodeling.

7.10.B. Angiography

7.10.B1. Space shall be provided as necessary to accommodate the functional program. The procedure room should be a minimum of 400 square feet (37.16 square meters).

7.10.B2. A control room shall be provided as necessary to meet the needs of the functional program. A view window shall be provided to permit full view of the patient.

7.10.B3. A viewing area shall be provided and should be a minimum of 10 feet (3.05 meters) in length.

7.10.B4. A scrub sink located outside the staff entry to the procedure room shall be provided for use by staff.

7.10.B5. A patient holding area should be provided to accommodate two stretchers with additional spaces for additional procedure rooms.

7.10.B6. Storage for portable equipment and catheters shall be provided.

7.10.B7. Provision shall be made within the facility for extended post-procedure observation of outpatients.

7.10.C. Computerized Tomography (CT) Scanning

7.10.C1. CT scan rooms shall be as required to accommodate the equipment.

7.10.C2. A control room shall be provided which is designed to accommodate the computer and other controls for the equipment. A view window shall be provided to permit full view of the patient. The angle between the control and equipment centroid shall permit the control operator to see the patient's head.

*7.10.C3. (See Appendix A.)

7.10.C4. The control room shall be located to allow convenient film processing.

7.10.C5. A patient toilet shall be provided. It shall be convenient to the procedure room, and if directly accessible to the scan room, arranged so that a patient may leave the toilet without having to reenter the scan room.

7.10.D. Diagnostic X-ray

*7.10.D1. Radiography rooms shall be of a size to accommodate the functional program.

*7.10.D2. (See Appendix A.)

*7.10.D3. (See Appendix A.)

7.10.D4. Each X-ray room shall include a shielded control alcove. This area shall be provided with a view window designed to provide full view of the examination table and the patient at all times, including full view of the patient when the table is in the tilt position or the chest X-ray is being utilized. For mammography machines with built-in shielding for the operator, the alcove may be omitted when approved by the certified physicist or state radiation protection agency.

7.10.E. Magnetic Resonance Imaging (MRI)

7.10.E1. Space shall be provided as necessary to accommodate the functional program. The MRI room may range from 325 square feet (30.19 square meters) to 620 square feet (57.6 square meters) depending on the vendor and magnet strength.

7.10.E2. A control room shall be provided with full view of the MRI and should be a minimum of 100 square feet (9.29 square meters), but may be larger depending on the vendor and magnet size.

7.10.E3. A computer room shall be provided and could range from 150 square feet (13.94 square meters) to 380 square feet (35.30 square meters) depending on the vendor and magnet strength. Self-contained air conditioning supplement is normally required.

*7.10.E4. Cryogen storage may be required in areas where service to replenish supplies is not readily available.

7.10.E5. A darkroom may be required for loading cassettes and shall be located near the control room. This darkroom shall be outside the 10-gauss field.

7.10.E6. When spectroscopy is provided, caution should be exercised in locating it in relation to the magnetic fringe fields.

7.10.E7. Power conditioning and voltage regulation equipment as well as direct current (DC) may be required.

7.10.E8. Magnetic shielding may be required to restrict the magnetic field plot. Radio frequency shielding is required to attenuate stray radio frequencies.

7.10.E9. A patient hold area should be located near the MRI unit and should be large enough to accommodate stretchers.

7.10.E10. Venting of cryogen exhaust is required.

7.10.F. Ultrasound

7.10.F1. Space shall be provided as necessary to accommodate the functional program.

7.10.F2. A patient toilet, accessible from the procedure room and from the corridor, shall be provided.

7.10.G. Support Spaces
The following spaces are common to the imaging department and are minimum requirements unless stated otherwise:

7.10.G1. Patient Waiting Area.

The area shall be out of traffic, under staff control, and shall have seating capacity in accordance with the functional program. If the suite is routinely used for outpatients and inpatients at the same time, separate waiting areas shall be provided with screening for visual privacy between the waiting areas.

7.10.G2. Control Desk and Reception Area.

7.10.G3. Holding Area.

A convenient holding area under staff control shall be provided to accommodate inpatients on stretchers or beds.

7.10.G4. Patient Toilet Rooms.

Toilet rooms shall be provided convenient to the waiting rooms and shall be equipped with an emergency call system. Separate toilets shall be provided with direct access from each radiographic/fluoroscopic room so that a patient may leave the toilet without having to reenter the R&F room. Rooms used only occasionally for fluoroscopic procedures may utilize nearby patient toilets if they are located for immediate access.

7.10.G5. Patient Dressing Rooms.

Dressing rooms shall be provided convenient to the waiting areas and X-ray rooms. Each room shall include a seat or bench, mirror, and provisions for hanging patients' clothing and for securing valuables.

7.10.G6. Staff Facilities.

Toilets may be outside the suite but shall be convenient for staff use. In larger suites of three or more procedure rooms, toilets internal to the suite shall be provided. Staff lounge with lockers should be considered.

7.10.G7. Film Storage (Active).

A room with cabinets or shelves for filing patient
▲ film for immediate retrieval shall be provided.

7.10.G8. Film Storage (Inactive).

A room or area for inactive film storage shall be provided. It may be outside the imaging suite, but must be under imaging's administrative control and properly secured to protect films against loss or damage.

7.10.G9. Storage for Unexposed Film.

Storage facilities for unexposed film shall include protection of film against exposure or damage and shall not be warmer than the air of adjacent occupied spaces.

7.10.G10. Offices for Radiologist(s) and Assistant(s).

Offices shall include provisions for viewing, individual consultation, and charting of film.

7.10.G11. Clerical Offices/Spaces.

Office space shall be provided as necessary for the functional program.

▼ **7.10.G12.** Consultation Area.

An appropriate area for individual consultation with referring clinicians shall be provided.

7.10.G13. Contrast Media Preparation.

This area shall be provided with sink, counter, and storage to allow for mixing of contrast media. One preparation room, if conveniently located, may serve any number of rooms. Where pre-prepared media is used, this area may be omitted, but storage shall be provided for the media.

7.10.G14. Film Processing Room.

A darkroom shall be provided for processing film unless the processing equipment normally used does not require a darkroom for loading and transfer. When daylight processing is used, the dark room may be minimal for emergency and special uses. Film processing shall be located convenient to the procedure rooms and to the quality control area.

7.10.G15. Quality Control Area.

An area or room shall be provided near the processor for viewing film immediately after it is processed. All view boxes shall be illuminated to provide light of the same color value and intensity for appropriate comparison of several adjacent films.

7.10.G16. Cleanup Facilities.

Provisions for cleanup shall be located within the suite for convenient access and use. It shall include service sink or floor receptacle as well as storage space for equipment and supplies. If automatic film processors are used, a receptacle of adequate size with hot and cold water for cleaning the processor racks shall be provided.

7.10.G17. Handwashing Facilities.

Handwashing facilities shall be provided within each procedure room unless the room is used only for routine screening such as chest X-rays where the patient is not physically handled by the staff. Handwashing facilities shall be provided convenient to the MRI
▲ room, but need not be within the room.

7.10.G18. Clean Storage.

Provisions shall be made for the storage of clean supplies and linens. If conveniently located, storage may be shared with another department.

▼ **7.10.G19.** Soiled Holding.

Provisions shall be made for soiled holding. Separate provisions for contaminated handling and holding shall be made. Handwashing facilities shall be provided.

7.10.G20. Provision shall be made for locked stor-
▲ age of medications and drugs.

7.10.G21. Details and Finishes; Mechanical; Electrical.

See Section 7.28 for details and finishes; 7.31 for mechanical; and 7.32 for electrical.

▼ ***7.10.H. Cardiac Catheterization Lab (Cardiology).**
▲ (See Appendix A.)

7.11 Nuclear Medicine

7.11.A.
Equipment and space shall be provided as necessary to accommodate the functional program. Nuclear medicine includes positron emission tomography, which is not common to most facilities. It requires specialized planning for equipment.

▼ **7.11.B.**
A certified physicist representing the owner or state agency shall specify the type, location, and amount of radiation protection to be installed in accordance with final approved department layout and equipment selection. These specifications shall be incorporated
▲ into the plans.

7.11.C.
Support services, such as radiology and pathology, should be accessible to nuclear medicine. The emergency room and outpatient clinics should be in proximity.

▼ **7.11.D.**
Flooring should meet load requirements for equipment, patients, and personnel. Floors and walls should be constructed of materials that are easily decontaminated in case of radioactive spills. Walls should contain necessary support systems for either built-in or mobile oxygen and vacuum, and vents for radioactive gases. Provision for wiring raceways, ducts or conduits should be made in floors, walls, and ceilings. Ceilings may be higher than 8 feet (2.44 meters). Ceiling-mounted equipment should have properly designed rigid support structures located above the finished ceiling. A lay-in type ceiling should be considered for ease of service, installation, and remodeling.

7.11.E.
Space shall be provided as necessary to accommodate the functional program. Where the functional program calls for it, the nuclear medicine room shall accommodate the equipment, a stretcher, exercise equipment
▲ (treadmill and/or bicycle) and staff.

7.11.F.

If radiopharmaceutical preparation is performed on-site, an area adequate to house a radiopharmacy shall be provided with appropriate shielding. This area should include adequate space for storage of radionuclides, chemicals for preparation, dose calibrators, and record keeping. Floors and walls should be constructed of easily decontaminated materials. Vents and traps for radioactive gases should be provided if such are used. Hoods for pharmaceutical preparation shall meet applicable standards. If pre-prepared materials are used, storage and calculation area may be considerably smaller than that for on-site preparation. Space shall provide adequately for dose calibration, quality assurance, and record keeping. The area may still require shielding from other portions of the facilities.

▼ *7.11.G.*

Positron Emission Tomography (PET) (See Appendix A.)

7.11.H.

The nuclear medicine area, when operated separately from the imaging department, shall include the following:

7.11.H1. Services such as radiology and pathology should be accessible. The emergency room and outpatient clinics should be in proximity.

7.11.H2. Space shall be adequate to permit entry of stretchers, beds, and able to accommodate imaging equipment, electronic consoles, and if present, computer terminals.

7.11.H3. A darkroom on-site shall be available for film processing. The darkroom should contain protective storage facilities for unexposed film that guard the film against exposure or damage. If necessary, special refrigeration and humidity controls, separate from the ambient controls of adjacent occupied areas, should be provided.

7.11.H4. When the functional program requires a centralized computer area, it should be a separate room with access terminals available within the imaging rooms.

7.11.H5. Provisions for cleanup shall be located within the suite for convenient access and use. It shall include service sink or floor receptacle as well as storage space for equipment and supplies.

7.11.H6. Film storage with cabinets or shelves for filing patient film for immediate retrieval shall be provided.

▼ **7.11.H7.** Inactive film storage under the departmental administrative control and properly secured to protect film against loss or damage shall be provided.

7.11.H8. A consultation area with view boxes illuminated to provide light of the same color value and intensity for appropriate comparison of several adjacent films shall be provided. Space should be provided for computer access and display terminals if such are included in the program.

7.11.H9. Offices for physicians and assistants shall be provided and equipped for individual consultation, viewing, and charting of film.

7.11.H10. Clerical offices and spaces shall be provided as necessary for the program to function.

▼ **7.11.H11.** Waiting areas shall be provided out of traffic, under staff control, and shall have seating capacity in accordance with the functional program. If the department is routinely used for outpatients and inpatients at the same time, separate waiting areas shall be provided with screening or visual privacy between the waiting areas.

7.11.H12. A dose administration area as specified by the functional program, shall be provided and located near the preparation area. Since as much as several hours may elapse for the dose to take effect, the area shall provide for visual privacy from other areas. Thought should be given to entertainment and reading materials.

7.11.H13. A holding area for patients on stretchers or beds shall be provided out of traffic and under control of staff and may be combined with the dose administration area with visual privacy between the areas.

7.11.H14. Patient dressing rooms shall be provided convenient to the waiting area and procedure rooms. Each dressing room shall include a seat or bench, a mirror, and provisions for hanging patients' clothing and for securing valuables.

▼ **7.11.H15.** Toilet rooms shall be provided convenient to waiting and procedure rooms.

7.11.H16. Staff toilet(s) shall be provided convenient to the nuclear medicine laboratory.

7.11.H17. Handwashing facilities shall be provided within each procedure room.

7.11.H18. Control desk and reception area shall be provided.

7.11.H19. Storage area for clean linen with a handwashing facility shall be provided.

7.11.H20. Provisions shall be made for holding soiled material. Separate provisions shall be made for holding contaminated material.

7.11.H21. See Section 7.28 for details and finishes; 7.31 for mechanical; and 7.32 for electrical.

7.11.I. Radiotherapy Suite

7.11.I1. Rooms and spaces shall be provided as necessary to accommodate the functional program.

Equipment manufacturers recommendations should be sought and followed, since space requirements may vary from one machine to another and one manufacturer to another. The radiotherapy suite may contain one or both electron beam therapy and radiation therapy. Although not recommended, a simulation room may be omitted in small linear accelerator facilities where other positioning geometry is provided.

7.11.I2. Cobalt, linear accelerators, and simulation rooms require radiation protection. A certified physicist representing the owner or appropriate state agency shall specify the type, location, and amount of protection to be installed in accordance with final approved department layout and equipment selection. The architect shall incorporate these specifications into the hospital building plans.

7.11.I3. Cobalt rooms and linear accelerators shall be sized in accordance with equipment requirements and shall accommodate a stretcher for litter-borne patients. Layouts shall provide for preventing the escape of radioactive particles. Openings into the room, including doors, ductwork, vents, and electrical raceways and conduits, shall be baffled to prevent direct exposure to other areas of the facility.

*7.11.I4. Simulator, accelerator, and cobalt rooms shall be sized to accommodate the equipment with patient access on a stretcher, medical staff access to the equipment and patient, and service access.

7.11.I5. Flooring shall be adequate to meet load requirements for equipment, patients, and personnel. Provision for wiring raceways, ducts, or conduit should be made in floors and ceilings. Ceiling mounted equipment should have properly designed rigid support structures located above the finished ceiling. The ceiling height is normally higher than 8 feet (2.44 meters). A lay-in type of ceiling should be considered for ease of installation, service, and remodeling.

7.11.J. General Support Areas
The following areas shall be provided unless they are accessible from other areas such as imaging or OPD:

7.11.J1. A stretcher hold area adjacent to the treatment rooms, screened for privacy, and combined with a seating area for outpatients. The size of these areas will be dependent on the program for outpatients and inpatients.

7.11.J2. Exam rooms for each treatment room as specified by the functional program, each exam room to be a minimum of 100 square feet (9 square meters). Each exam room shall be equipped with a handwashing facility.

7.11.J3. Darkroom convenient to the treatment room(s) and the quality control area. Where daylight processing is used, the darkroom may be minimal for emergency use. If automatic film processors are used, a receptacle of adequate size with hot and cold water for cleaning the processor racks shall be provided either in the darkroom or nearby.

7.11.J4. Patient gowning area with provision for safe storage of valuables and clothing. At least one space should be large enough for staff assisted dressing.

7.11.J5. Business office and/or reception/control area.

7.11.J6. Housekeeping room equipped with service sink or floor receptor and large enough for equipment or supplies storage.

7.11.J7. Film file area.

7.11.J8. Film storage area for unprocessed film.

7.11.K. Optional Support Areas
The following areas may be required by the functional program:

7.11.K1. Quality control area with view boxes illuminated to provide light of the same color value and intensity.

7.11.K2. Computer control area normally located just outside the entry to the treatment room(s).

7.11.K3. Dosimetry equipment area.

7.11.K4. Hypothermia room (may be combined with an exam room).

7.11.K5. Consultation room.

7.11.K6. Oncologist's office (may be combined with consultation room).

7.11.K7. Physicist's office (may be combined with treatment planning).

7.11.K8. Treatment planning and record room.

7.11.K9. Work station/nutrition station.

7.11.L. Additional Support Areas for Linear Accelerator:

7.11.L1. Mold room with exhaust hood and handwashing facility.

7.11.L2. Block room with storage. The block room may be combined with the mold room.

7.11.M. Additional Support Areas for Cobalt Room:

▲ **7.11.M1.** Hot lab.

7.12 Laboratory Suite

Laboratory facilities shall be provided for the performance of tests in hematology, clinical chemistry, urinalysis, microbiology, anatomic pathology, cytology, and blood banking to meet the workload described in the functional program. Certain procedures may be performed on-site or provided through a contractual arrangement with a laboratory service acceptable to the authority having local jurisdiction.

Provisions shall be made for the following procedures to be performed on-site: blood counts, urinalysis, blood glucose, electrolytes, blood urea and nitrogen (BUN), coagulation, and transfusions (type and cross-match capability). Provisions shall also be included for specimen collection and processing.

The following physical facilities shall be provided within the hospital:

7.12.A.
Laboratory work counter(s) with space for microscopes, appropriate chemical analyzer(s), incubator(s), centrifuge(s), etc. shall be provided. Work areas shall include sinks with water and access to vacuum, gases, and air, and electrical services as needed.

7.12.B.
Refrigerated blood storage facilities for transfusions shall be provided. Blood storage refrigerator shall be equipped with temperature-monitoring and alarm signals.

7.12.C.
Lavatory(ies) or counter sink(s) equipped for handwashing shall be provided. Counter sinks may also be used for disposal of nontoxic fluids.

7.12.D.
Storage facilities, including refrigeration, for reagents, standards, supplies, and stained specimen microscope slides, etc. shall be provided.

7.12.E.
Specimen (blood, urine, and feces) collection facility shall be provided. Blood collection area shall have work counter, space for patient seating, and handwashing facilities. Urine and feces collection room shall be equipped with water closet and lavatory. This facility may be located outside the laboratory suite.

7.12.F.
Chemical safety provisions including emergency shower, eyeflushing devices, and appropriate storage for flammable liquids, etc., shall be made.

7.12.G.
Facilities and equipment for terminal sterilization of contaminated specimens before transport (autoclave or electric oven) shall be provided. (Terminal sterilization is not required for specimens that are incinerated on-site.)

7.12.H.
If radioactive materials are employed, facilities shall be available for long-term storage and disposal of these materials. No special provisions will normally be required for body waste products from most patients receiving low level isotope diagnostic material. Requirements of authorities having jurisdiction should be verified.

7.12.I.
Administrative areas including offices as well as space for clerical work, filing, and record maintenance shall be provided.

7.12.J.
Lounge, locker, and toilet facilities shall be conveniently located for male and female laboratory staff. These may be outside the laboratory area and shared with other departments.

The functional program shall describe the type and location of all special equipment that is to be wired, plumbed, or plugged in, and the utilities required to operate each.

Note: Refer to NFPA code requirements applicable to hospital laboratories, including standards clarifying that hospital units do not necessarily have the same fire safety requirements as commercial chemical laboratories.

7.13 Rehabilitation Therapy Department

7.13.A. General
Rehabilitation therapy is primarily for restoration of body functions and may contain one or several categories of services. If a formal rehabilitative therapy service is included in a project, the facilities and equipment shall be as necessary for the effective function of the program. Where two or more rehabilitative services are included, items may be shared, as appropriate.

7.13.B. Common Elements
Each rehabilitative therapy department shall include the following, which may be shared or provided as separate units for each service:

> **7.13.B1.** Office and clerical space with provision for filing and retrieval of patient records.

> **7.13.B2.** Reception and control station(s) with visual control of waiting and activities areas. (This may be combined with office and clerical space.)

7.13.B3. Patient waiting area(s) out of traffic with provision for wheelchairs.

7.13.B4. Patient toilets with handwashing facilities accessible to wheelchair patients.

7.13.B5. Space(s) for storing wheelchairs and stretchers out of traffic while patients are using the services. These spaces may be separate from the service area but must be conveniently located.

7.13.B6. A conveniently accessible housekeeping room and service sink for housekeeping use.

7.13.B7. Locking closets or cabinets within the vicinity of each work area for securing staff personal effects.

7.13.B8. Convenient access to toilets and lockers.

7.13.B9. Access to a demonstration/conference room.

7.13.C. Physical Therapy
If physical therapy is part of the service, the following, at least, shall be included:

▼ **7.13.C1.** Individual treatment area(s) with privacy screens or curtains. Each such space shall have not less than 60 square feet (5.57 square meters) of clear
▲ floor area.

7.13.C2. Handwashing facilities for staff either within or at each treatment space. (One handwashing facility may serve several treatment stations.)

7.13.C3. Exercise area and facilities.

7.13.C4. Clean linen and towel storage.

7.13.C5. Storage for equipment and supplies.

7.13.C6. Separate storage for soiled linen, towels, and supplies.

7.13.C7. Patient dressing areas, showers, and lockers. These shall be accessible and usable by the handicapped.

7.13.C8. Provisions shall be made for thermotherapy, diathermy, ultrasonics, and hydrotherapy when required by the functional program.

7.13.D. Occupational Therapy
If this service is provided, the following, at least, shall be included:

7.13.D1. Work areas and counters suitable for wheelchair access.

7.13.D2. Handwashing facilities.

7.13.D3. Storage for supplies and equipment.

7.13.E. Prosthetics and Orthotics
If this service is provided, the following, at least, shall be included:

7.13.E1. Workspace for technicians.

7.13.E2. Space for evaluating and fitting, with provision for privacy.

7.13.E3. Space for equipment, supplies, and storage.

7.13.F. Speech and Hearing
If this service is provided, the following, at least, shall be included:

7.13.F1. Space for evaluation and treatment.

7.13.F2. Space for equipment and storage.

7.14 Respiratory Therapy Service

The type and extent of respiratory therapy service in different institutions vary greatly. In some, therapy is delivered in large sophisticated units, centralized in a specific area; in others, basic services are provided only at patients' bedsides. If respiratory service is provided, the following elements shall be included as a minimum, in addition to those elements stipulated in Sections 7.13.B1, 7, 8, and 9:

7.14.A. Storage for Equipment and Supplies

▼ **7.14.B.** Space and Utilities for Cleaning and Sanitizing Equipment. Provide physical separation of the space for receiving and cleaning soiled materials from the space
▲ for storage of clean equipment and supplies.

7.14.C.
Respiratory services shall be conveniently accessible on a 24-hour basis to the critical care units.

7.14.D.
If respiratory services such as testing and demonstration for outpatients are part of the program, additional facilities and equipment shall be provided as necessary for the appropriate function of the service, including but not limited to:

7.14.D1. Patient waiting area with provision for wheelchairs.

7.14.D2. A reception and control station.

7.14.D3. Patient toilets and handwashing facilities.

7.14.D4. Room(s) for patient education and demonstration.

7.15 Morgue

These facilities shall be accessible through an exterior entrance and shall be located to avoid the need for transporting bodies through public areas.

7.15.A.

The following elements shall be provided when autopsies are performed in the hospital:

7.15.A1. Refrigerated facilities for body holding.

7.15.A2. An autopsy room containing the following:

a. A work counter with a sink equipped for handwashing.

b. A storage space for supplies, equipment, and specimens.

c. An autopsy table.

▶ d. A deep sink for washing of specimens.

7.15.A3. A housekeeping service sink or receptor for cleanup and housekeeping.

7.15.B.

If autopsies are performed outside the facility, a well-ventilated, temperature-controlled, body-holding room shall be provided.

7.16 Pharmacy

7.16.A. General

The size and type of services to be provided in the pharmacy will depend upon the type of drug distribution system used, number of patients to be served, and extent of shared or purchased services. This shall be described in the functional program. The pharmacy room or suite shall be located for convenient access, staff control, and security. Facilities and equipment shall be as necessary to accommodate the functions of the program. (Satellite facilities, if provided, shall include those items required by the program.) As a minimum, the following elements shall be included:

7.16.B. Dispensing

7.16.B1. A pickup and receiving area.

7.16.B2. An area for reviewing and recording.

▼ **7.16.B3.** An extemporaneous compounding area that includes a sink and sufficient counter space for drug preparation. Floor drainage may also be required,
▲ depending on the extent of compounding conducted.

7.16.B4. Work counters and space for automated and manual dispensing activities.

7.16.B5. An area for temporary storage, exchange, and restocking of carts.

7.16.B6. Security provisions for drugs and personnel in the dispensing counter area.

7.16.C. Manufacturing

7.16.C1. A bulk compounding area.

7.16.C2. Provisions for packaging and labeling.

7.16.C3. A quality-control area.

7.16.D. Storage (may be cabinets, shelves, and/or separate rooms or closets)

7.16.D1. Bulk storage.

7.16.D2. Active storage.

7.16.D3. Refrigerated storage.

7.16.D4. Volatile fluids and alcohol storage constructed according to applicable fire safety codes for the substances involved.

7.16.D5. Secure storage for narcotics and controlled drugs.

7.16.D6. Storage for general supplies and equipment not in use.

7.16.E. Administration

7.16.E1. Provision for cross-checking of medication and drug profiles of individual patients.

7.16.E2. Poison control, reaction data, and drug information centers.

7.16.E3. A separate room or area for office function including desk, filing, communication, and reference.

7.16.E4. Provisions for patient counseling and instruction (may be in a room separate from the pharmacy).

7.16.E5. A room for education and training (may be in a multipurpose room shared with other departments).

7.16.F. Other

7.16.F1. Handwashing facilities shall be provided within each separate room where open medication is handled.

7.16.F2. Provide for convenient access to toilet and locker.

7.16.F3. If unit dose procedure is used, provide additional space and equipment for supplies, packaging, labeling, and storage, as well as for the carts.

7.16.F4. If IV solutions are prepared in the pharmacy, provide a sterile work area with a laminar-flow workstation designed for product protection. The laminar-flow system shall include a nonhydroscopic filter rated at 99.97 percent (HEPA), as tested by DOP tests, and have a visible pressure gauge for detection of filter leaks or defects.

7.16.F5. Provide for consultation and patient education when the functional program requires dispensing of medication to outpatients.

7.17 Dietary Facilities

▼ **7.17.A. General**

Food service facilities and equipment shall conform with these standards and with the standards of the National Sanitation Foundation and other appropriate codes and shall provide food service for staff, visitors, inpatients, and outpatients as may be appropriate.

Consideration may also be required for meals to VIP suites, and for cafeterias for staff, ambulatory patients, and visitors as well as providing for nourishments and snacks between scheduled meal service.

Patient food preparation areas shall be located in an area adjacent to delivery, interior transportation, storage, etc.

Finishes in the dietary facility shall be selected to ensure cleanability and the maintenance of sanitary
▲ conditions.

7.17.B. Functional Elements

If on-site conventional food service preparation is used, the following in size and number appropriate for approved function shall be provided:

▼ **7.17.B1.** Receiving/control stations. Provide an area for the receiving and control of incoming dietary supplies. This area shall be separated from the general receiving area and shall contain the following: a control station and a breakout for loading, uncrating, and weighing supplies.

7.17.B2. Storage spaces. They shall be convenient to the receiving area and shall be located to exclude traffic through the food preparation area to reach them. Storage spaces for bulk, refrigerated, and frozen foods shall be provided. A minimum of four days' supplies shall be stocked. (In remote areas, this number may be increased to accommodate length of delivery in emergencies.)

Food storage components shall be grouped for convenient access from receiving and to the food preparation areas.

All food shall be stored clear of the floor. Lowest shelf shall be not less than 12 inches (30 centimeters) above the floor or shall be closed in and sealed tight for ease of cleaning.

7.17.B3. Cleaning supplies storage. Provide a separate storage room for the storage of non-food items such as cleaning supplies that might contaminate edibles.

7.17.B4. Additional storage rooms. They shall be provided as necessary for the storage of cooking wares, extra trays, flatware, plastic and paper products, and portable equipment.

7.17.B5. Food preparation work spaces. Provide work spaces for food preparation, cooking, and baking. These areas shall be as close as possible to the user (i.e., tray assembly and dining). Provide additional spaces for thawing and portioning.

7.17.B6. Assembly and distribution. Provide a patient tray assembly area and locate within close proximity to the food preparation and distribution areas.

7.17.B7. Food service carts. A cart distribution system shall be provided with spaces for storage, loading, distribution, receiving, and sanitizing of the food service carts. The cart traffic shall be designed to eliminate any danger of cross-circulation between outgoing food carts and incoming, soiled carts, and the cleaning and sanitizing process. Cart circulation shall not be through food processing areas.

7.17.B8. Dining area. Provide dining space(s) for ambulatory patients, staff, and visitors. These spaces shall be separate from the food preparation and distribution areas.

7.17.B9. Vending services. If vending devices are used for unscheduled meals, provide a separate room that can be accessed without having to enter the main dining area. The vending room shall contain coin-operated machines, bill changers, a handwashing fixture, and a sitting area. Facilities for the servicing and sanitizing of the machines shall be provided as part of the food service program of the facility.

7.17.B10. Area for receiving, scraping, and sorting soiled tableware shall be adjacent to ware washing and separate from food preparation areas.

7.17.B11. Ware washing facilities. They shall be designed to prevent contamination of clean wares with soiled wares through cross-traffic. The clean wares shall be transferred for storage or use in the dining area without having to pass through food preparation areas. The final rinse water shall be at least 180°F.

7.17.B12. Pot washing facilities including multi-compartmented sinks of adequate size for intended use shall be provided convenient to using service. Supplemental heat for hot water to clean pots and pans may be by booster heater or by steam jet.

Mobil carts or other provisions should be made for drying and storage of pots and pans.

7.17.B13. Waste storage room. A food waste storage room shall be conveniently located to the food preparation and ware washing areas but not within the food preparation area. It shall have direct access to the hospital's waste collection and disposal facilities.

7.17.B14. Handwashing. Fixtures that are operable without the use of hands shall be located conveniently accessible at locations throughout the unit.

7.17.B15. Office spaces. Offices for the use of the food service manager shall be provided. In smaller facilities, this space may be located in an area that is part of the food preparation area.

7.17.B16. Toilets and locker spaces. Spaces shall be provided for the exclusive use of the dietary staff. They shall not open directly into the food preparation areas, but must be in close proximity to them.

7.17.B17. Housekeeping rooms. They shall be provided for the exclusive use of the dietary department and shall contain the following: a floor sink and space for mops, pails, and supplies. Where hot water or steam is used for general cleaning, additional space within the room shall be provided for the storage of hoses and nozzles.

7.17.B18. Icemaking equipment. It shall be of type that is convenient for service and easily cleaned. It shall be provided for both drinks and food products (self-dispensing equipment), and for general use (storage-bin type equipment).

7.17.B19. Commissary or contract services from other areas. Items above may be reduced as appropriate. Provide for protection of food delivered to insure freshness, retention of hot and cold, and avoidance of contamination. If delivery is from outside sources, provide protection against weather. Provisions must be made for thorough cleaning and sanitizing of equipment to avoid mix of soiled and clean.

7.17.C. Equipment

Mechanical devices shall be heavy duty, suitable for use intended, and easily cleaned. Where equipment is movable provide heavy duty locking casters. If equipment is to have fixed utility connections, the equipment should not be equipped with casters. Walk-in coolers, refrigerators, and freezers shall be insulated at floor as well as at walls and top. Coolers and refrigerators shall be capable of maintaining a temperature down to freezing. Freezers shall be capable of maintaining a temperature of 20 degrees below 0 F. Coolers, refrigerators, and freezers shall be thermostatically controlled to maintain desired temperature settings in increments of 2 degrees or less. Interior temperatures shall be indicated digitally so as to be visible from the exterior. Controls shall include audible and visible high and low temperature alarm. Time of alarm shall be automatically recorded.

Walk-in units may be lockable from outside but must have release mechanism for exit from inside at all times. Interior shall be lighted. All shelving shall be corrosion resistant, easily cleaned, and constructed and anchored to support a loading of at least 100 pounds per linear foot.

All cooking equipment shall be equipped with automatic shut off devices to prevent excessive heat buildup.

Under-counter conduits, piping, and drains shall be arranged to not interfere with cleaning of floor below or of the equipment.

7.17.D. Plumbing

Provide condensate drains for chiller coils of type that may be cleaned as needed without disassembly. (Unless specifically required by local authorities, traps are not required for condensate drains.) Provide air gap where condensate drains empty into floor drains. Provide heater elements for condensate lines in freezer or other areas where freezing may be a problem.

Floor drains and/or floor sinks shall be of type that can be easily cleaned by removal of cover. Provide floor drains or floor sinks at all "wet" equipment (as ice machines) and as required for wet cleaning of floors. Provide removable stainless steel mesh in addition to grilled drain cover to prevent entry of large particles of waste which might cause stoppages. Location of floor drains and floor sinks shall be coordinated to avoid conditions where locations of equipment make removal of covers for cleaning difficult. No plumbing lines may be exposed overhead or on walls where possible accumulation of dust or soil may create a cleaning problem or where leaks would create a potential for food contamination.

All handwashing facilities shall be usable without need for hand contact.

Grease traps shall be of capacity required and shall be accessible from outside of the building without need to interrupt any services.

7.17.E. Hoods and Venting Equipment

Hoods and venting equipment shall meet the requirements of NFPA 96.

7.18 Administration and Public Areas

The following shall be provided:

7.18.A. Entrance
This shall be at grade level, sheltered from inclement weather, and accessible to the handicapped.

7.18.B. Lobby
This shall include:

7.18.B1. A counter or desk for reception and information.

7.18.B2. Public waiting area(s).

7.18.B3. Public toilet facilities.

7.18.B4. Public telephones.

7.18.B5. Drinking fountain(s).

7.18.C. Interview Space(s)
These shall include provisions for private interviews relating to social service, credit, and admissions.

7.18.D. Admissions Area
For initial admission of inpatients, the area shall include:

7.18.D1. A separate waiting area for patients and accompanying persons.

7.18.D2. A work counter or desk for staff.

7.18.D3. A storage area for wheelchairs, out of the path of normal traffic.

7.18.E. General or Individual Office(s)
These shall be provided for business transactions, medical and financial records, and administrative and professional staff.

7.18.F. Multipurpose Room(s)
These shall be provided for conferences, meetings, and health education purposes, and include provisions for the use of visual aids. One multipurpose room may be shared by several services.

7.18.G. Storage for Office Equipment and Supplies

7.18.H. Quality Assurance and Utilization Review Area

7.19 Medical Records

Rooms, areas, or offices for the following personnel and/or functions shall be provided:

7.19.A. Medical Records Administrator/Technician

7.19.B. Review and Dictation

7.19.C. Sorting, Recording, or Microfilming Records

7.19.D. Record Storage

7.20 Central Services

The following shall be provided:

▼ **7.20.A. Separate Soiled and Clean Work Areas**

7.20.A1. Soiled Workroom

This room shall be physically separated from all other areas of the department. Workspace should be provided to handle the cleaning and initial sterilization/disinfection of all medical/surgical instruments and equipment. Work tables, sinks, flush type devices, and washer/sterilizer decontaminators. Pass-through doors and washer/sterilizer decontaminators should deliver into clean processing area/work-
▲ rooms.

*** 7.20.A2.** Clean Assembly/Workroom

This workroom shall contain handwashing facilities, workspace, and equipment for terminal sterilizing of medical and surgical equipment and supplies. Clean and soiled work areas should be physically separated.

7.20.B. Storage Areas

7.20.B1. Clean/Sterile Medical/Surgical Supplies

▼ A room for breakdown should be provided for manufacturers' clean/sterile supplies (clean processing area should not be in this area but adjacent). Storage for packs etc., shall include provisions for ventilation, humidity, and temperature control.

7.20.C. Administrative/Changing Room
If required by the functional program, this room should be separate from all other areas and provide for staff to change from street clothes into work attire. Lockers, sink, and showers should be made available within the
▲ immediate vicinity of the department.

7.20.D. Storage Room for Patient Care and Distribution Carts
▼ This area should be adjacent, easily available to clean and sterile storage, and close to main distribution point
▲ to keep traffic to a minimum and ease of work flow.

7.21 General Stores

In addition to supply facilities in individual departments, a central storage area shall also be provided. General stores may be located in a separate building on-site with provisions for protection against inclement weather during transfer of supplies.

The following shall be provided:

7.21.A. Off-street Unloading Facilities

7.21.B. Receiving Area

7.21.C. General Storage Room(s)

General storage room(s) with a total area of not less than 20 square feet (1.86 square meters) per inpatient bed shall be provided. Storage may be in separate, concentrated areas within the institution or in one or more individual buildings on-site. A portion of this storage may be provided off-site.

7.21.D. Additional Storage Room(s)

Additional storage areas for outpatient facilities shall be provided in an amount not less than 5 percent of the total area of the outpatient facilities. This may be combined with and in addition to the general stores or be located in a central area within the outpatient department. A portion of this storage may be provided off-site.

7.22 Linen Services

7.22.A. General

Each facility shall have provisions for storing and processing of clean and soiled linen for appropriate patient care. Processing may be done within the facility, in a separate building on- or off-site, or in a commercial or shared laundry.

7.22.B.

Facilities and equipment shall be as required for cost effective operation as described in the functional program. At a minimum, the following elements shall be included:

7.22.B1. A separate room for receiving and holding soiled linen until ready for pickup or processing.

7.22.B2. A central, clean linen storage and issuing room(s), in addition to the linen storage required at individual patient units.

7.22.B3. Cart storage area(s) for separate parking of clean- and soiled-linen carts out of traffic.

▼ **7.22.B4.** A clean linen inspection and mending room or area. If not provided elsewhere, a clean linen inspection, delinting, folding, assembly and packaging area should be provided as part of the linen services. Mending should be provided for in the linen services department. A space for tables, shelving, ▲ and storage should be provided.

7.22.B5. Handwashing facilities in each area where unbagged, soiled linen is handled.

7.22.C.

If linen is processed outside the building, provisions shall also be made for:

7.22.C1. A service entrance, protected from inclement weather, for loading and unloading of linen.

7.22.C2. Control station for pickup and receiving.

7.22.D.

If linen is processed in a laundry facility which is part of the project (within or as a separate building), the following shall be provided in addition to that of Section 7.22.B:

7.22.D1. A receiving, holding, and sorting room for control and distribution of soiled linen. Discharge from soiled linen chutes may be received within this room or in a separate room.

7.22.D2. Laundry processing room with commercial type equipment which can process at least a seven day supply within the regular scheduled work week. This may require a capacity for processing a seven day supply in a 40-hour week.

7.22.D3. Storage for laundry supplies.

7.22.D4. Employee handwashing facilities in each room where clean or soiled linen is processed and handled.

7.22.D5. Arrangement of equipment that will permit an orderly work flow and minimize cross-traffic that might mix clean and soiled operations.

7.22.D6. Conveniently accessible staff lockers, showers, and lounge.

7.23 Facilities for Cleaning and Sanitizing Carts

Facilities shall be provided to clean and sanitize carts serving the central service department, dietary facilities, and linen services. These facilities may be centralized or departmentalized.

7.24 Employee Facilities

Lockers, lounges, toilets, etc. should be provided for employees and volunteers. These should be in addition to, and separate from, those required for medical staff and public.

7.25 Housekeeping Rooms

In addition to the housekeeping rooms required in certain departments, sufficient housekeeping rooms shall be provided throughout the facility as required to maintain a clean and sanitary environment. Each shall contain a floor receptor or service sink and storage space for housekeeping equipment and supplies. There shall not be less than one housekeeping room for each floor.

7.26 Engineering Service and Equipment Areas

The following shall be provided as essential for effective service and maintenance functions:

▼ **7.26.A.**

Room(s) or separate building(s) for boilers, mechanical, and electrical equipment, except:

7.26.A1. Roof-top air conditioning and ventilation equipment installed in weatherproof housings.

7.26.A2. Standby generators where the engine and appropriate accessories (i.e., batteries) are properly heated and enclosed in a weatherproof housing.

7.26.A3. Cooling towers and heat rejection equipment.

7.26.A4. Electrical transformers and switchgear where required to serve the facility and where installed in a weatherproof housing.

7.26.A5. Medical gas parks and equipment.

7.26.A6. Air cooled chillers where installed in a weatherproof housing.

7.26.A7. Trash compactors and incinerators. Site lighting, post indicator valves, and other equipment
▲ normally installed on the exterior of the building.

7.26.B.

Engineer's office with file space and provisions for protected storage of facility drawings, records, manuals, etc.

7.26.C.

General maintenance shop(s) for repair and maintenance.

7.26.D.

Storage room for building maintenance supplies. Storage for solvents and flammable liquids shall comply with applicable NFPA codes.

7.26.E.

Separate area or room specifically for storage, repair, and testing of electronic and other medical equipment. The amount of space and type of utilities will vary with the type of equipment involved and types of outside contracts used.

7.26.F.

Yard equipment and supply storage areas shall be located so that equipment may be moved directly to the exterior without interference with other work.

7.27 Waste Processing Services

7.27.A. Storage and Disposal

▼ Facilities shall be provided for sanitary storage and treatment or disposal of waste using techniques acceptable to the appropriate health and environmental authorities. The functional program shall stipulate the categories and volumes of waste for disposal and shall
▲ stipulate the methods for disposal of each.

7.27.B. Incinerator

An incinerator shall be provided for the complete destruction of pathological waste. The incinerator may be shared by two or more nearby institutions. It may be acceptable in some jurisdictions to omit the incinerator if arrangements can be made with a licensed local service to pick up and incinerate pathological wastes.

7.27.B1. Incinerators may also be used to dispose of other hospital waste where local regulations permit. All incinerators shall be designed and equipped for the actual quantity and type of waste to be destroyed and should meet all applicable air pollution regulations.

7.27.B2. Incinerators with fifty-pounds-per-hour or greater capacities shall be in a separate room or outdoors; those with lesser capacities may be located in a separate area within the facility boiler room. Rooms and areas containing incinerators shall have adequate space and facilities for incinerator charging and cleaning, as well as necessary clearances for work and maintenance. Provisions shall be made for operation, temporary storage, and disposal of materials so that odors and fumes do not drift back into occupied areas. Existing approved incinerator installations, which are not in separate rooms or outdoors, may remain unchanged provided they meet the above criteria.

7.27.B3. The design and construction of incinerators and trash chutes shall comply with NFPA 82.

▼ ***7.27.B4.** See Appendix A. (Heat recovery.)

***7.27.B5.** See Appendix A. (Environmental guide-
▲ lines.)

7.27.C. Nuclear Waste Disposal

See *Code of Federal Regulations,* title X, parts 20 and 35, concerning the handling and disposal of nuclear materials in health care facilities.

7.28 General Standards for Details and Finishes

If approved by the authorities having jurisdiction, retained portions of existing facilities that are not required to be totally modernized due to financial or other hardships may, as a minimum, comply with applicable requirements of the Existing Health Care Occupancies Section of NFPA 101. However, a plan of correction for these portions should also be developed and implemented.

Details and finishes in new construction projects, including additions and alterations, shall comply with the following (see Section 1.2 concerning existing facilities where total compliance is structurally impractical):

▶ **7.28.A. Details**

7.28.A1. Compartmentation, exits, fire alarms, automatic extinguishing systems, and other fire prevention and fire protection measures, including that within existing facilities, shall comply with NFPA 101, with the following stipulation. The Fire-Safety Evaluation System (FSES) of appendix C shall not be used as a substitute for the basic NFPA 101 design criteria for new construction or major renovation in existing facilities. (The FSES is intended as an evaluation tool for fire safety only.) See Section 1.5 for exceptions. *Note: For most projects it is essential that third-party reimbursement requirements also be followed. Verify where these may be in excess of standards in this document.*

▼ **7.28.A2.** Corridors in outpatient suites and in areas not commonly used for patient bed or stretcher transportation may be reduced in width to 5 feet (1.52
▲ meters).

7.28.A3. Location of items such as drinking fountains, telephone booths, vending machines, and portable equipment shall not restrict corridor traffic or reduce the corridor width below the model standard.

7.28.A4. Rooms which contain bathtubs, sitz baths, showers, and/or water closets for inpatient use shall be equipped with doors and hardware permitting emergency access from the outside. When such rooms have only one opening or are small, the doors shall open outward or in a manner that will avoid pressing a patient who may have collapsed within the room. Similar considerations may be desirable for certain outpatient services.

7.28.A5. If required by the program, door hardware on patient toilet rooms in psychiatric nursing units may be designed to allow staff to control access.

▼ **7.28.A6.** The minimum door size for inpatient bedrooms in new work shall be 3 feet 8 inches (1.11 meters) wide and 7 feet (2.13 meters) high to provide clearance for movement of beds and other equipment. Existing doors of not less than 2 feet 10 inches (86.36 centimeters) wide may be considered for acceptance where function is not adversely affected and replacement is impractical. Doors to other rooms used for stretchers (including hospital wheeled-bed stretchers) and/or wheelchairs shall have a minimum width of 2 feet 10 inches (86.36 centimeters). Where used in these Guidelines, door width and height shall be the nominal dimension of the door leaf, ignoring projections of frame and stops. *Note: While these standards are intended for access by patients and patient equipment, size of
▲ office furniture, etc., shall also be considered.*

7.28.A7. All doors between corridors, rooms, or spaces subject to occupancy, except elevator doors, shall be of the swing type. Openings to showers, baths, patient toilets, ICU patient compartments with the break-away feature, and other such areas not leading to fire exits may be exempt from this standard.

7.28.A8. Doors, except those to spaces such as small closets not subject to occupancy, shall not swing into corridors in a manner that might obstruct traffic flow or reduce the required corridor width. (Large walk-in-type closets are considered inhabitable spaces.)

7.28.A9. Windows and outer doors that frequently may be left open shall be equipped with insect screens.

7.28.A10. Patient rooms or suites in new construction intended for 24-hour occupancy shall have windows or vents that can be opened from the inside to vent noxious fumes and smoke products and to bring in fresh air in emergencies. Operation of such windows shall be restricted to inhibit possible escape or suicide. Where the operation of windows or vents requires the use of tools or keys, these shall be on the same floor and easily accessible to staff. Windows in existing buildings designed with approved engineered smoke-control systems may be of fixed construction.

▼ **7.28.A11.** Glass doors, lights, sidelights, borrowed lights, and windows located within 12 inches (30.48 centimeters) of a door jamb (with a bottom-frame height of less than 60 inches or 1.52 meters above the finished floor) shall be constructed of safety glass, wired glass, or plastic, break-resistant material that creates no dangerous cutting edges when broken. Similar materials shall be used for wall openings in active areas such as recreation and exercise rooms, unless otherwise required for fire safety.

Safety glass-tempered or plastic glazing materials shall be used for shower doors and bath enclosures. Plastic and similar materials used for glazing shall comply with the flame-spread ratings of NFPA 101. Safety glass or plastic glazing materials, as noted above, shall also be used for interior windows and doors, including those in pediatric and psychiatric unit corridors. In renovation projects, only glazing within 18 inches (46 centimeters) of the floor must be changed to safety glass, wire glass, or plastic,
▲ break-resistant material.

Note: Provisions of this paragraph concern safety from hazards of breakage. NFPA 101 contains additional requirements for glazing in exit corridors, etc., especially in buildings without sprinkler systems.

7.28.A12. Linen and refuse chutes shall meet or exceed the following standards:

   a. Service openings to chutes shall comply with NFPA 101.

   b. The minimum cross-sectional dimension of gravity chutes shall be 2 feet (60.96 centimeters).

   c. Chute discharge into collection rooms shall comply with NFPA 101.

   d. Chutes shall meet the provisions as described in NFPA 82.

7.28.A13. Dumbwaiters, conveyors, and material-handling systems shall not open directly into a corridor or exit, but shall open into a room enclosed by construction with a fire resistance rating of not less than one hour and with class C, ¾-hour labeled fire doors. Service entrance doors to vertical shafts containing dumbwaiters, conveyors, and material handling systems shall be not less than class B, 1½-hour fire doors. Where horizontal conveyors and material-handling systems penetrate fire-rated walls or partitions, such openings must be provided with class B 1½-hour labeled fire doors for 2-hour walls and class C ¾-hour labeled fire doors for 1-hour walls or partitions.

7.28.A14. Thresholds and expansion joint covers shall be flush with the floor surface to facilitate the use of wheelchairs and carts. Expansion and seismic joints shall be constructed to restrict the passage of smoke.

7.28.A15. Grab bars shall be provided in all patient toilets, showers, bathtubs, and sitz baths at a wall clearance of 1½ inches (3.81 centimeters). Bars, including those which are part of such fixtures as soap dishes, shall be sufficiently anchored to sustain a concentrated load of 250 pounds (113.4 kilograms).

7.28.A16. Location and arrangement of fittings for handwashing facilities shall permit their proper use and operation. Particular care should be given to the clearances required for blade-type operating handles.

7.28.A17. Mirrors shall not be installed at handwashing fixtures in food preparation areas, nurseries, clean and sterile supply areas, scrub sinks, or other areas where asepsis control would be lessened by hair combing.

7.28.A18. Provisions for hand drying shall be included at all handwashing facilities except scrub sinks. These provisions shall be paper or cloth units enclosed to protect against dust or soil and to insure single-unit dispensing. Hot air dryers are permitted provided that installation precludes possible contamination by recirculation of air.

7.28.A19. Lavatories and handwashing facilities shall be securely anchored to withstand an applied vertical load of not less than 250 pounds (113.4 kilograms) on the fixture front.

7.28.A20. Radiation protection requirements for X-ray and gamma ray installations shall conform with NCRP Report Nos. 33 and 49 and all applicable local requirements. Provision shall be made for testing completed installations before use. All defects must be corrected before approval. Testing is to be coordinated with local authorities to prevent duplication.

7.28.A21. The minimum ceiling height shall be 7 feet 10 inches (2.39 meters), with the following exceptions:

   a. Boiler rooms shall have ceiling clearances not less than 2 feet 6 inches (76.20 centimeters) above the main boiler header and connecting piping.

   b. Ceilings in radiographic, operating and delivery rooms, and other rooms containing ceiling-mounted equipment or ceiling-mounted surgical light fixtures shall be of sufficient height to accommodate the equipment or fixtures and their normal movement.

▼ c. Ceilings in corridors, storage rooms, and toilet rooms shall be not less than 7 feet 8 inches (2.34 meters) in height. Ceiling heights in small, normally
▲ unoccupied spaces may be reduced.

   d. Suspended tracks, rails, and pipes located in the traffic path for patients in beds and/or on stretchers, including those in inpatient service areas, shall be not less than 7 feet (2.13 meters) above the floor. Clearances in other areas may be 6 feet 8 inches (2.03 meters).

▼ e. Where existing structures make the above ceiling clearance impractical, clearances shall be as required to avoid injury to individuals up to ▲ 6 feet 4 inches (1.93 meters) tall.

f. Seclusion treatment rooms shall have a minimum ceiling height of 9 feet (2.74 meters).

7.28.A22. Recreation rooms, exercise rooms, equipment rooms, and similar spaces where impact noises may be generated shall not be located directly over patient bed areas or delivery and operating suites, unless special provisions are made to minimize such noise.

7.28.A23. Rooms containing heat-producing equipment, such as boiler or heater rooms or laundries, shall be insulated and ventilated to prevent the floor surface above and/or the adjacent walls of occupied areas from exceeding a temperature of 10°F (6°C) above ambient room temperature.

7.28.A24. The noise reduction criteria shown in Table 1 shall apply to partitions, floors, and ceiling construction in patient areas.

7.28.B. Finishes

▼ **7.28.B1.** Cubicle curtains and draperies shall be noncombustible or flame-retardant, and shall pass both the large and small scale tests of NFPA 701 and ▲ NFPA 13 when applicable.

7.28.B2. Materials and certain plastics known to produce noxious gases when burned shall not be used for mattresses, upholstery, and other items insofar as practical. (Typical "hard" floor coverings such as vinyl, vinyl composition, and rubber normally do not create a major fire or smoke problem.)

7.28.B3. Floors in areas and rooms in which flammable anesthetic agents are stored or administered shall comply with NFPA 99. Conductive flooring may be omitted in anesthetizing areas where a written resolution is signed by the hospital board stating that no flammable anesthetic agents will be used and appropriate notices are permanently and conspicuously affixed to the wall in each such area and room.

7.28.B4. Floor materials shall be easily cleanable and appropriately wear-resistant for the location. Floors in areas used for food preparation or food assembly shall be water-resistant. Floor surfaces, including tile joints, shall be resistant to food acids. In all areas subject to frequent wet-cleaning methods, floor materials shall not be physically affected by germicidal cleaning solutions. Floors subject to traffic while wet (such as shower and bath areas, kitchens, and similar work areas) shall have a non-slip surface.

Table 1
Sound Transmission Limitations in General Hospitals

	Airborne sound transmission class (STC)[a]	
	Partitions	Floors
New construction		
Patient room to patient room	45	40
Public space to patient room[b]	55	40
Service areas to patient room[c]	65	45
Patient room access corridor[d]	45	45
Existing construction		
Patient room to patient room	35	40
Public space to patient room[b]	40	40
Service areas to patient room[c]	45	45

a Sound transmission class (STC) shall be determined by tests in accordance with methods set forth in ASTM E90 and ASTM E413. *Where partitions do not extend to the structure above, sound transmission through ceilings and composite STC performance must be considered.*

b Public space includes corridors (except patient room access corridors), lobbies, dining rooms, recreation rooms, treatment rooms, and similar space.

c Service areas include kitchens, elevators, elevator machine rooms, laundries, garages, maintenance rooms, boiler and mechanical equipment rooms, and similar spaces of high noise. Mechanical equipment located on the same floor or above patient rooms, offices, nurses stations, and similar occupied space shall be effectively isolated from the floor.

d Patient room access corridors contain composite walls with doors/windows and have direct access to patient rooms.

▼ **7.28.B5.** In new construction or major renovation work, the floors and wall bases of operating and delivery rooms used for caesarean sections shall be monolithic and joint free. The floors and wall bases of kitchens, soiled workrooms, and other areas subject to frequent wet cleaning shall also be homogenous, but may have tightly sealed joints. ▲

7.28.B6. Wall finishes shall be washable. In the vicinity of plumbing fixtures, wall finishes shall be smooth and water-resistant.

▼ In dietary and food preparation areas, wall construction, finish, and trim, including the joints between the walls and the floors, shall be free of insect- and rodent-harboring spaces.

In operating rooms, delivery rooms for caesarean sections, isolation rooms, and sterile processing rooms, wall finishes shall be free of fissures, open joints, or crevices that may retain or permit passage
▲ of dirt particles.

7.28.B7. Floors and walls penetrated by pipes, ducts, and conduits shall be tightly sealed to minimize entry of rodents and insects. Joints of structural elements shall be similarly sealed.

▼ **7.28.B8.** Ceilings, including exposed structure in areas normally occupied by patients or staff in food-preparation and food-storage areas, shall be cleanable with routine housekeeping equipment. Acoustic and lay-in ceiling, where used, shall not interfere with infection control.

In dietary areas and in other areas where dust fallout may present a problem, provide suspended ceilings.

In operating rooms, delivery rooms for caesarean sections, isolation rooms, and sterile processing rooms, provide ceilings that contain a minimum number of fissures, open joints, or crevices and minimize retention or passage of dirt particles.

In psychiatric patient rooms, toilets, and seclusion rooms, ceiling construction shall be monolithic to inhibit possible escape or suicide. Ceiling-mounted air and lighting devices shall be security type. Ceiling-mounted fire prevention sprinkler heads
▲ shall be of the concealed type.

7.28.B9. Rooms used for protective isolation shall not have carpeted floors and shall have monolithic ceilings.

7.29 Design and Construction, Including Fire-Resistive Standards

7.29.A. Design
Every building and portion thereof shall be designed and constructed to sustain all live and dead loads, including seismic and other environmental forces, in accordance with accepted engineering practices and standards as prescribed by local jurisdiction or by one of the model building codes. (See Section 1.1.A.)

7.29.B. Construction
Construction shall comply with the applicable requirements of NFPA 101, the standards contained herein, and the requirements of authorities having jurisdiction. If there are no applicable local codes, one of the recognized model building codes shall be used (see Section 1.5).

Note: NFPA 101 generally covers fire/safety requirements only, whereas most model codes also apply to structural elements. The fire/safety items of NFPA 101 would take precedence over other codes in case of conflict. Appropriate application of each would minimize problems. For example, some model codes require closers on all patient doors. NFPA 101 recognizes the potential fire/safety problems of this requirement and stipulates that if closers are used for patient room doors, smoke detectors should also be provided within each affected patient room.

7.29.C. Freestanding Buildings
Separate freestanding buildings for the boiler plant, laundry, shops, general storage or other nonpatient contact areas shall be built in accordance with applicable building codes for such occupancy.

7.29.D. Interior Finishes
Interior finishing materials shall comply with the flame-spread limitations and the smoke-production limitations indicated in NFPA 101. This does not apply to minor quantities of wood or other trim (see NFPA 101) or to wall covering less than four mil thick applied over a noncombustible base.

7.29.E. Insulation Materials
Building insulation materials, unless sealed on all sides and edges with noncombustible material, shall have a flame-spread rating of 25 or less and a smoke-developed rating of 150 or less when tested in accordance with NFPA 258.

7.29.F. Provisions for Disasters (See also Section 1.4.)

▼ **7.29.F1.** An emergency-radio communication system shall be provided in each facility. This system shall operate independently of the building's service and emergency power systems during emergencies. The system shall have frequency capabilities to communicate with state emergency communication networks. Additional communication capabilities will be required of facilities containing a formal community emergency-trauma service or other specialty services (such as regional pediatric critical care
▲ units) that utilize staffed patient transport units.

7.29.F2. Unless specifically approved, hospitals shall not be built in areas subject to damage or inaccessibility due to natural floods. Where facilities may be subject to wind or water hazards, provision shall be made to ensure continuous operation.

7.30 Elevators

7.30.A. General

▼ All hospitals having patient facilities (such as bedrooms, dining rooms, or recreation areas) or critical services (such as operating, delivery, diagnostic, or therapy) located on other than the grade-level entrance floor shall have electric or hydraulic elevators. Installation and testing of elevators shall comply with ANSI A17.1. (See ASCE 7-88 (revised 1991) for seismic design and
▲ control systems requirements for elevators.)

7.30.A1. In the absence of an engineered traffic study the following guidelines for number of elevators shall apply:

a. At least one hospital-type elevator shall be installed when 1 to 59 patient beds are located on any floor other than the main entrance floor.

b. At least two hospital-type elevators shall be installed when 60 to 200 patient beds are located on floors other than the main entrance floor, or where the major inpatient services are located on a floor other than those containing patient beds. (Elevator service may be reduced for those floors providing only partial inpatient services.)

c. At least three hospital-type elevators shall be installed where 201 to 350 patient beds are located on floors other than the main entrance floor, or where the major inpatient services are located on a floor other than those containing patient beds. (Elevator service may be reduced for those floors which provide only partial inpatient services.)

d. For hospitals with more than 350 beds, the number of elevators shall be determined from a study of the hospital plan and the expected vertical transportation requirements.

7.30.A2. Hospital-type elevator cars shall have inside dimensions that accommodate a patient bed with attendants. Cars shall be at least 5 feet (1.52 meters) wide by 7 feet 6 inches (2.29 meters) deep. Car doors shall have a clear opening of not less than 4 feet (1.22 meters) wide and 7 feet (2.13 meters) high.

Note: Additional elevators installed for visitors and material handling may be smaller than noted above, within restrictions set by standards for handicapped access.

7.30.A3. Elevators shall be equipped with a two-way automatic level-maintaining device with an accuracy of + ¼ inch (+ 0.64 centimeters).

▼ **7.30.A4.** Each elevator, except those for material handling, shall be equipped with a two-way special service switch for staff use for bypassing all landing button calls and traveling directly to any floor.

7.30.A5. Elevator call buttons and controls shall not
▲ be activated by heat or smoke. Light beams, if used for operating door reopening devices without touch, shall be used in combination with door-edge safety devices and shall be interconnected with a system of smoke detectors. This is so that the light control feature will be overridden or disengaged should it encounter smoke at any landing.

▼ **7.30.A6.** See ASCE 7-88 (revised 1991) for seismic
▲ design and control systems requirements for elevators.

7.30.B. Field Inspection and Tests

Inspections and tests shall be made and the owner shall be furnished with written certification stating that the installation meets the requirements set forth in this section as well as all applicable safety regulations and codes.

7.31 Mechanical Standards

7.31.A. General

7.31.A1. The mechanical system should be designed for overall efficiency and life cycle costing. Details for cost-effective implementation of design features are interrelated and too numerous (as well as too basic) to list individually. Recognized engineering procedures shall be followed for the most economical and effective results. A well-designed system can generally achieve energy efficiency at minimal additional cost and simultaneously provide improved patient comfort. Different geographic areas may have climatic and use conditions that favor one system over another in terms of overall cost and efficiency. In no case shall patient care or safety be sacrificed for conservation (see Appendix B).

▼ Mechanical, electrical, and HVAC equipment may be located either internally, externally, or in separate
▲ buildings.

7.31.A2. Remodeling and work in existing facilities may present special problems. As practicality and funding permit, existing insulation, weather stripping, etc., should be brought up to standard for maximum economy and efficiency. Consideration shall be given to additional work that may be needed to achieve this.

7.31.A3. Facility design consideration shall include site, building mass, orientation, configuration, fenestration, and other features relative to passive and active energy systems.

7.31.A4. Insofar as practical, the facility should include provisions for recovery of waste cooling and heating energy (ventilation, exhaust, water and steam discharge, cooling towers, incinerators, etc.).

7.31.A5. Facility design consideration shall include recognized energy-saving mechanisms such as variable-air-volume systems, load shedding, programmed controls for unoccupied periods (nights and weekends, etc.) and use of natural ventilation, site and climatic conditions permitting. Systems with excessive installation and/or maintenance costs that negate long-range energy savings should be avoided (see Appendix B).

7.31.A6. Air-handling systems shall be designed with an economizer cycle where appropriate to use outside air. (Use of mechanically circulated outside air does not reduce need for filtration.)

It may be practical in many areas to reduce or shut down mechanical ventilation during appropriate climatic and patient-care conditions and to use open windows for ventilation.

7.31.A7. Major changes have been made to previous ventilation standards to permit maximum use of simplified systems, such as the variable-air-volume (VAV) supply. However, care must be taken in design to avoid possibility of large temperature differentials, high velocity supply, excessive noise, air stagnation, etc. Air supply and exhaust in rooms for which no minimum total air change rate is noted may vary down to zero in response to room load. For rooms listed in Table 2, where VAV systems are permitted, minimum total air change shall be within limits noted. Temperature control shall also comply with these standards. To maintain asepsis control, airflow supply and exhaust should generally be controlled to ensure movement of air from "clean" to "less clean" areas, especially in critical areas.

▼ **7.31.A8.** Prior to acceptance of the facility, all mechanical systems shall be tested, balanced, and operated to demonstrate to the owner or his designated representative that the installation and performance of these systems conform to design intent. Test results ▲ shall be documented for maintenance files.

7.31.A9. Upon completion of the equipment-installation contract, the owner shall be furnished with a complete set of manufacturers' operating, maintenance, and preventive maintenance instructions, a parts lists, and complete procurement information including equipment numbers and descriptions. Operating staff persons shall also be provided with instructions for properly operating systems and equipment. Required information shall include energy ratings as needed for future conservation calculations.

7.31.B. Thermal and Acoustical Insulation

▼ **7.31.B1.** Insulation within the building shall be provided to conserve energy, protect personnel, prevent vapor condensation, and reduce noise and vibration.

7.31.B2. Insulation on cold surfaces shall include an exterior vapor barrier. (Material that will not absorb or transmit moisture will not require a separate vapor ▲ barrier.)

7.31.B3. Insulation, including finishes and adhesives on the exterior surfaces of ducts and equipment, shall have a flame-spread rating of 25 or less and a smoke-developed rating of 50 or less as determined by an independent testing laboratory in accordance with NFPA 255. The smoke-development rating for pipe insulation shall not exceed 150. This includes mechanical refrigeration and distribution equipment and hot water distribution equipment such as valves, pumps, chillers, etc.

▼ **7.31.B4.** Remodeling of lined duct systems destroys the integrity of the liner sealant. However, if linings are used in nonsensitive hospital areas, they shall meet ASTM C1071. These linings (including coatings, adhesives, and exterior surface insulation on pipes and ducts in spaces used as air supply plenums) shall have a flame-spread rating of 25 or less and a smoke-developed rating of 50 or less, as determined by an independent testing laboratory in ▲ accordance with NFPA 255.

7.31.B5. Duct linings exposed to air movement should not be used in ducts serving operating rooms, delivery rooms, LDR rooms, nurseries, and critical care units. Where its use cannot be avoided, terminal filters of at least 90 percent efficiency shall be installed downstream of all lining material. This requirement shall not apply to mixing boxes and acoustical traps that have special coverings over such lining.

7.31.B6. Existing accessible insulation within areas of facilities to be modernized shall be inspected, repaired, and/or replaced, as appropriate.

▼ **7.31.B7.** No lined duct work will be installed down- ▲ stream of humidification.

7.31.C. Steam and Hot Water Systems

7.31.C1. Boilers shall have the capacity, based upon the net ratings published by the Hydronics Institute or another acceptable national standard, to supply the normal heating, hot water, and steam requirements of all systems and equipment. Their number and arrangement shall accommodate facility needs despite the breakdown or routine maintenance of any one boiler. The capacity of the remaining boiler(s) shall be sufficient to provide hot water service for clinical, dietary, and patient use; steam for sterilization and dietary purposes; and heating for operating, delivery, birthing, labor, recovery, intensive care, nursery, and general patient rooms. However, reserve capacity for facility space heating is not required in geographic areas where a design dry-bulb temperature of 25°F (-4°C) or more represents not less than 99 percent of the total hours in any one heating month as noted in ASHRAE's *Handbook of Fundamentals,* under the "Table for Climatic Conditions for the United States."

7.31.C2. Boiler accessories including feed pumps, heat-circulating pumps, condensate return pumps, fuel oil pumps, and waste heat boilers shall be connected and installed to provide both normal and standby service.

7.31.C3. Supply and return mains and risers for cooling, heating, and steam systems shall be equipped with valves to isolate the various sections of each system. Each piece of equipment shall have valves at the supply and return ends.

7.31.D. Air Conditioning, Heating, and Ventilation Systems

7.31.D1. The ventilation rates shown in Table 2 shall be used only as model standards; they do not preclude the use of higher, more appropriate rates. All rooms and areas in the facility used for patient care shall have provisions for ventilation. Though natural window ventilation for nonsensitive areas and patient rooms may be employed, weather permitting, availability of mechanical ventilation should be considered for use in interior areas and during periods of temperature extremes. Fans serving exhaust systems shall be located at the discharge end and shall be readily serviceable. Exhaust systems may be combined to enhance the efficiency of recovery devices required for energy conservation.

a. Facility design should utilize energy-conserving mechanisms, including recovery devices, variable air volume, load shedding, and systems to shut down or reduce ventilation of unoccupied areas, insofar as patient care is not compromised. When appropriate, mechanical ventilation should employ an economizer cycle that uses outside air to reduce heating- and cooling-system loads. Filtering requirements shall be met if outside air is used as part of the mechanical ventilation

system. Innovative design that provides for additional energy conservation while meeting standards for acceptable patient care should be considered (see Appendix B).

b. Fresh air intakes shall be located at least 25 feet (7.62 meters) from exhaust outlets of ventilating systems, combustion equipment stacks, medical-surgical vacuum systems, plumbing vents, or areas that may collect vehicular exhaust or other noxious fumes. (Prevailing winds and/or proximity to other structures may require greater clearances.) Plumbing and vacuum vents that terminate at a level above the top of the air intake may be located as close as 10 feet (3.05 meters). The bottom of outdoor air intakes serving central systems shall be as high as practical, but at least 6 feet (1.83 meters) above ground level, or, if installed above the roof, 3 feet (91 centimeters) above roof level. Exhaust outlets from areas that may be contaminated shall be above roof level and arranged to minimize recirculation of exhaust air into the building.

c. The ventilation systems shall be designed and balanced according to the requirements shown in Table 2 and in the applicable notes. (Also see note 8 of Table 2 for reductions and shutdown of ventilation systems during room vacancy.)

d. In new construction and major renovation work, air supply for operating and delivery rooms shall be from ceiling outlets near the center of the work area. This will most effectively control air movement. Return air shall be from the floor level. Each operating and delivery room shall have at least two return-air inlets located as remotely from each other as practical. (Design should consider turbulence and other factors of air movement to minimize fall of particulates onto sterile surfaces.) Where extraordinary procedures, such as organ transplants, justify special designs, installation shall properly meet performance needs as determined by applicable standards. These special designs should be reviewed on a case-by-case basis.

▼ e. Air supply for nurseries, LDRP rooms, and rooms used for invasive procedures shall be at or near the ceiling. Return or exhaust air inlets shall be near the floor level. Exhaust grills for anesthesia evacuation and other special applications shall
▲ be permitted to be installed in the ceiling.

f. Each space routinely used for administering inhalation anesthesia shall be equipped with a

continued on page 54

Table 2

Ventilation Requirements for Areas Affecting Patient Care in Hospitals and Outpatient Facilities[1]

Area designation	Air movement relationship to adjacent area[2]	Minimum air changes of outdoor air per hour[3]	Minimum total air changes per hour[4]	All air exhausted directly to outdoors[5]	Recirculated by means of room units[6]	Relative humidity[7] (%)	Design temperature[8] (degrees F)
SURGERY AND CRITICAL CARE							
Operating/surgical cystoscopic rooms[9]	Out	3	15	—	No	50-60	70-75
Delivery room[9]	Out	3	15	—	No	45-60	70-75
Recovery room[9]	—	2	6	—	No	30-60	70
Critical and intensive care	—	2	6	—	No	30-60	70-75
Treatment room[10]	—	—	6	—	—	—	75
Trauma room[10]	Out	3	15	—	No	45-60	70-75
Anesthesia gas storage	—	—	8	Yes	—	—	—
NURSING							
Patient room	—	1	2	—	—	—	70-75
Toilet room	In	—	10	Yes	—	—	—
Newborn nursery suite	—	2	6	—	No	30-60	75
Protective isolation[11]	Out	1	6	—	No	—	70-75
Infectious isolation[12]	In	1	6	Yes	No	—	70-75
Isolation alcove or anteroom[11,12]	In/Out	—	10	Yes	No	—	—
Labor/delivery/recovery	—	—	2	—	—	—	70-75
Labor/delivery/recovery/postpartum	—	—	2	—	—	—	70-75
Patient corridor	—	—	2	—	—	—	—
ANCILLARY							
Radiology[13]							
X-ray (surgical/critical care and catheterization)	Out	3	15	—	No	45-60	70-75
X-ray (diagnostic & treat.)	—	—	6	—	—	—	75
Darkroom	In	—	10	Yes	No	—	—
Laboratory							
General[14]	—	—	6	—	—	—	—
Biochemistry[14]	Out	—	6	—	No	—	—
Cytology	In	—	6	Yes	No	—	—
Glass washing	In	—	10	Yes	—	—	—
Histology	In	—	6	Yes	No	—	—
Microbiology[14]	In	—	6	Yes	No	—	—
Nuclear medicine[13]	In	—	6	Yes	No	—	—

Table 2 Notes

1 The ventilation rates in this table cover ventilation for comfort, as well as for asepsis and odor control in areas of acute care hospitals that directly affect patient care and are determined based on health care facilities being predominantly "no smoking" facilities. Where smoking may be allowed, ventilation rates will need adjustments. Refer to ASHRAE Standard 62-1989, *Ventilation for Acceptable Indoor Air Quality*, and *ASHRAE Handbook of Fundamentals*, latest edition. Areas where specific ventilation rates are not given in the table shall be ventilated in accordance with these ASHRAE publications. Specialized patient care areas, including organ transplant units, burn units, specialty procedure rooms, etc., shall have additional ventilation provisions for air quality control as may be appropriate. OSHA standards and/or NIOSH criteria require special ventilation requirements for employee health and safety within health care facilities.

2 Design of the ventilation system shall, insofar as possible, provide that air movement is from "clean to less clean" areas. However, continuous compliance may be impractical with full utilization of some forms of variable air volume and load shedding systems that may be used for energy conservation. Areas that do require positive and continuous control are noted with "out" or "in" to indicate the required direction of air movement in relation to the space named. Rate of air movement may, of course, be varied as needed within the limits required for positive control. Where indication of air movement direction is enclosed in parentheses, continuous directional control is required only when the specialized equipment or device is in use or where room use may otherwise compromise the intent of movement from clean to less clean. Air movement for rooms indicated in the table with dashes and nonpatient areas may vary as necessary to satisfy the requirements of those spaces. Additional adjustments may be needed when space is unused or unoccupied and air systems are deenergized or reduced.

3 To satisfy exhaust needs, replacement air from outside is necessary. Table 2 does not attempt to describe specific amounts of outside air to be supplied to individual spaces except for certain areas such as those listed. Distribution of the outside air, added to the system to balance required exhaust, shall be as required by good engineering practice.

4 Number of air changes may be reduced when the room is unoccupied if provisions are made to ensure that the number of air changes indicated is reestablished any time the space is being utilized. Adjustments shall include provisions so that the

Table 2 *(continued)*

Ventilation Requirements for Areas Affecting Patient Care in Hospitals and Outpatient Facilities[1]

Area designation	Air movement relationship to adjacent area[2]	Minimum air changes of outdoor air per hour[3]	Minimum total air changes per hour[4]	All air exhausted directly to outdoors[5]	Recirculated by means of room units[6]	Relative humidity[7] (%)	Design temperature[8] (degrees F)
Laboratory *(continued)*							
Pathology	In	—	6	Yes	No	—	—
Serology	Out	—	6	—	No	—	—
Sterilizing	In	—	10	Yes	—	—	—
Autopsy room	In	—	12	Yes	No	—	—
Nonrefrigerated body-holding room[15]	In	—	10	Yes	Yes	—	70
Pharmacy	—	—	4	—	—	—	—
DIAGNOSTIC AND TREATMENT							
Examination room	—	—	6	—	—	—	75
Medication room	—	—	4	—	—	—	—
Treatment room	—	—	6	—	—	—	75
Physical therapy and hydrotherapy	In	—	6	—	—	—	75
Soiled workroom or soiled holding	In	—	10	Yes	No	—	—
Clean workroom or clean holding	—	—	4	—	—	—	—
STERILIZING AND SUPPLY							
ETO-sterilizer room[16]	In	—	10	Yes	No	—	75
Sterilizer equipment room[16]	In	—	10	Yes	—	—	—
Central medical and surgical supply							
Soiled or decontamination room	In	—	6	Yes	No	—	—
Clean workroom and sterile							
storage	Out	—	4	—	No	(Max) 70	75
SERVICE							
Food preparation center[17]	—	—	10	—	No	—	—
Warewashing	In	—	10	Yes	No	—	—
Dietary day storage	In	—	2	—	—	—	—
Laundry, general	—	—	10	Yes	—	—	—
Soiled linen (sorting and storage)	In	—	10	Yes	No	—	—
Clean linen storage	—	—	2	—	—	—	—
Soiled linen and trash chute room	In	—	10	Yes	No	—	—
Bedpan room	In	—	10	Yes	Yes	—	—
Bathroom	—	—	10	—	—	—	75
Janitor's closet	In	—	10	Yes	No	—	—

direction of air movement shall remain the same when the number of air changes is reduced. Areas not indicated as having continuous directional control may have ventilation systems shut down when space is unoccupied and ventilation is not otherwise needed.

5   Air from areas with contamination and/or odor problems shall be exhausted to the outside and not recirculated to other areas. Note that individual circumstances may require special consideration for air exhaust to outside, e.g., an intensive care unit in which patients with pulmonary infection are treated, and rooms for burn patients.

6   Because of cleaning difficulty and potential for buildup of contamination, recirculating room units shall not be used in areas marked "No." Isolation and intensive care unit rooms may be ventilated by reheat induction units in which only the primary air supplied from a central system passes through the reheat unit. Gravity-type heating or cooling units such as radiators or convectors shall not be used in operating rooms and other special care areas.

7   The ranges listed are the minimum and maximum limits where control is specifically needed.

8   Dual temperature indications (such as 70-75) are for an upper and lower variable range at which the room temperature must be controlled. A single figure indicates a heating or cooling capacity of at least the indicated temperature. This is usually applicable when patients may be undressed and require a warmer environment. Nothing in these guidelines shall be construed as precluding the use of temperatures lower than those noted when the patients' comfort and medical conditions make lower temperatures desirable. Unoccupied areas such as storage rooms shall have temperatures appropriate for the function intended.

9   National Institute of Occupational Safety and Health (NIOSH) Criteria Documents regarding Occupational Exposure to Waste Anesthetic Gases and Vapors, and Control of Occupational Exposure to Nitrous Oxide indicate a need for both local exhaust (scavenging) systems and general ventilation of the areas in which the respective gases are utilized.

10   The term *trauma room* as used here is the operating room space in the emergency department or other trauma reception area that is used for emergency surgery. The first aid room and/or "emergency room" used for initial treatment of accident victims may be ventilated as noted for the "treatment room."

continued on next page

11 The protective isolation rooms described in these guidelines are those that might be utilized for patients with a high susceptibility to infection from leukemia, burns, bone marrow transplant, or acquired immunodeficiency syndrome and that require special consideration for which air movement relationship to adjacent areas would be positive rather than negative. For protective isolation the patient room shall be positive to both anteroom and toilet. Anteroom shall be negative to corridor. HEPA filters should be used on air supply. Where requirements for both infectious and protective isolation are reflected in the anticipated patient load, ventilation shall be modified as necessary. Variable supply air and exhaust systems that allow maximum isolation room space flexibility with reversible air movement direction would be acceptable only if appropriate adjustments can be ensured for different types of isolation occupancies. Control of the adjustments shall be under the supervision of the medical staff.

12 The infectious isolation rooms described in these guidelines are those that might be utilized in the average community hospital. The assumption is made that most isolation procedures will be for infectious patients and that the room should also be suitable for normal private patient use when not needed for isolation. This compromise obviously does not provide for ideal isolation. The design should consider types and numbers of patients who might need this separation within the facility. When need is indicated by the program, it may be desirable to provide more complete control with a separate anteroom as an air lock to minimize potential for airborne particulates from the patients' area reaching adjacent areas. Isolation room shall be negative to anteroom and positive to toilet. Anteroom shall be negative to corridor.

13 Large hospitals may have separate departments for diagnostic and therapeutic radiology and nuclear medicine. For specific information on radiation precautions and handling of nuclear materials, refer to appropriate publications of the National Radiation Safety Council and Nuclear Regulatory Commission. Special requirements are imposed by the U.S. Nuclear Regulatory Commission (Regulatory Guide 10.8-1980) regarding use of Xenon-133 gas.

14 When required, appropriate hoods and exhaust devices for the removal of noxious gases shall be provided (see Section 7.31.D1o and NFPA 99).

15 A nonrefrigerated body-holding room would be applicable only for health care facilities in which autopsies are not performed on-site, or the space is used only for holding bodies for short periods prior to transferring.

16 Specific OSHA regulations regarding ethylene oxide (ETO) use have been promulgated. 29 CRF Part 1910.1047 includes specific ventilation requirements including local exhaust of the ETO sterilizer area. Also see Section 7.31.D1r.

17 Food preparation centers shall have ventilation systems that have an excess air supply for "out" air movements when hoods are not in operation. The number of air changes may be reduced or varied to any extent required for odor control when the space is not in use. See Section 7.31.D1 for designation of hoods.

continued from page 51

scavenging system to vent waste gases. If a vacuum system is used, the gas-collecting system shall be arranged so that it does not disturb patients' respiratory systems. Gases from the scavenging system shall be exhausted directly to the outside. The anesthesia evacuation system may be combined with the room exhaust system, provided that the part used for anesthesia gas scavenging exhausts directly to the outside and is not part of the recirculation system. Separate scavenging systems are not required for areas where gases are used only occasionally, such as the emergency room, offices for routine dental work, etc. Acceptable concentrations of anesthetizing agents are unknown at this time. The absence of specific data makes it difficult to set specific standards. However, any scavenging system should be designed to remove as much of the gas as possible from the room environment. It is assumed that anesthetizing equipment will be selected and maintained to minimize leakage and contamination of room air.

g. The bottoms of ventilation (supply/return) openings shall be at least 3 inches (7.62 centimeters) above the floor.

h. All central ventilation or air conditioning systems shall be equipped with filters with efficiencies equal to, or greater than, those specified in Table 3. Where two filter beds are required, filter bed no. 1 shall be located upstream of the air conditioning equipment and filter bed no. 2 shall be downstream of any fan or blowers. Filter efficiencies, tested in accordance with ASHRAE 52-76, shall be average. Filter frames shall be durable and proportioned to provide an airtight fit with the enclosing ductwork. All joints between filter segments and enclosing ductwork shall have gaskets or seals to provide a positive seal against air leakage. A manometer shall be installed across each filter bed having a required efficiency of 75 percent or more, including hoods requiring HEPA filters.

▼*i. Duct humidifiers shall be located at least 15 feet (1.39 meters) in front of the final filters or be fitted with water removal devices that do not allow any water droplets to reach the filter. Humidifiers shall be connected to airflow proving switches that prevent humidification unless the required volume of airflow is present or high limit humidistats are provided. All duct takeoffs should be sufficiently downstream of the humidifier to ensure complete moisture dissemination. Reservoir-type water spray humidifiers shall not
▲ be used.

j. Air-handling duct systems shall meet the requirements of NFPA 90A and those contained herein.

k. Ducts that penetrate construction intended for X-ray or other ray protection shall not impair the effectiveness of the protection.

l. Fire and smoke dampers shall be constructed, located, and installed in accordance with the requirements of NFPA 101 and 90A. Fans, dampers, and detectors shall be interconnected so that damper activation will not damage ducts. Maintenance access shall be provided at all dampers. All damper locations should be shown on drawings. Dampers should be activated by fire or smoke sensors, not by fan cutoff alone. Switching systems for restarting fans may be installed for fire department use in venting smoke after a fire has been controlled. However, provisions should be made to avoid possible damage to the system due to closed dampers. When smoke partitions are required, heating, ventilation, and air conditioning zones shall be coordinated with compartmentation insofar as practical to minimize need to penetrate fire and smoke partitions.

m. Hoods and safety cabinets should not be used for normal exhaust of a space. If air change standards in Table 2 do not provide sufficient air for proper operation of exhaust hoods and safety cabinets (when in use), supplementary makeup air (filtered and preheated) should be provided around these units to maintain the required airflow direction and exhaust velocity. Supplementary makeup air will avoid dependence upon infiltration from outdoor and/or from contaminated areas. Makeup systems for hoods shall be arranged to minimize "short circuit" of air movement and to avoid reduction in air velocity at the point of contaminant capture.

n. Laboratory hoods shall meet the following general standards:

i. Have an average face-velocity of at least 75 feet per minute (0.38 meters per second).

ii. Be connected to an exhaust system to the outside which is separate from the building exhaust system.

iii. Have an exhaust fan located at the discharge end of the system.

iv. Have an exhaust duct system of noncombustible corrosion-resistant material as needed to meet the planned usage of the hood.

Table 3

Filter Efficiencies for Central Ventilation and Air Conditioning Systems in General Hospitals and Psychiatric Facilities

Area designation	No. filter beds	Filter bed no. 1	Filter bed no. 2
All areas for inpatient care, treatment, and diagnosis, and those areas providing direct service or clean supplies such as sterile and clean processing, etc.	2	25	90
Protective isolation room	2	25	90
Laboratories	1	80	—
Administrative, bulk storage, soiled holding areas, food preparation areas, and laundries	1	25	—

Note: Additional roughing or prefilters should be considered to reduce maintenance required for main filters. Ratings shall be based on ASHRAE 52-76.

o. Laboratory hoods shall meet the following special standards:

i. Fume hoods, and their associated equipment in the air stream, intended for use with perchloric acid and other strong oxidants, shall be constructed of stainless steel or other material consistent with special exposures, and be provided with a water wash and drain system to permit periodic flushing of duct and hood. Electrical equipment intended for installation within such ducts shall be designed and constructed to resist penetration by water. Lubricants and seals shall not contain organic materials. When perchloric acid or other strong oxidants are only transferred from one container to another, standard laboratory fume hoods and the associated equipment may be used in lieu of stainless steel construction. Fume hoods intended for use with radioactive isotopes shall be constructed of stainless steel or other material suitable for the particular exposure and shall comply with NFPA 801, *Facilities for Handling Radioactive Materials.*

Note: Radioactive isotopes used for injections, etc., without probability of airborne particulates or gases may be processed in a clean-workbench-type hood where acceptable to the Nuclear Regulatory Commission.

ii. In new construction and major renovation work, each hood used to process infectious or radioactive materials shall have a minimum face velocity of 150 feet per minute (0.76 meters per second) with suitable static-pressure-operated dampers and alarms to alert staff of fan shutdown. Each shall also have filters with a 99.97 percent efficiency (based on the DOP, dioctyl-phthalate test method) in the exhaust stream, and be designed and equipped to permit the safe removal, disposal, and replacement of contaminated filters. Filters shall be as close to the hood as practical to minimize duct contamination. Hoods that process radioactive materials shall meet the requirements of the Nuclear Regulatory Commission.

p. Exhaust hoods in food preparation centers shall comply with NFPA 96. All hoods over cooking ranges shall be equipped with grease filters, fire extinguishing systems, and heat-actuated fan controls. Cleanout openings shall be provided every 20 feet (6.10 meters) in the horizontal exhaust duct systems serving these hoods. (Horizontal runs of ducts serving range hoods should be kept to a minimum.)

q. The ventilation system for anesthesia storage rooms shall conform to the requirements of NFPA 99, including the gravity option. Mechanically operated air systems are optional in this room.

r. The space that houses ethylene oxide (ETO) sterilizers should be designed to:

i. Provide a dedicated local exhaust system with adequate capture velocity (i.e., with a minimum capture of 200 feet per minute [1.02 meters per second]) to allow for the most effective installation of an air handling system, i.e., exhaust over sterilizer door, atmospheric exhaust vent for safety valve, exhaust at sterilizer, drain and exhaust for the aerator, and multiple load station.

ii. Provide exhaust in ETO source areas such as service/aeration areas.

iii. Ensure that general airflow is away from sterilizer operator(s).

iv. Provide a dedicated exhaust duct system for ETO. The exhaust outlet to the atmosphere should be at least 25 feet (7.62 meters) away from any air intake.

v. Meet OSHA requirements.

s. Boiler rooms shall be provided with sufficient outdoor air to maintain equipment combustion rates and to limit workstation temperatures.

t. Gravity exhaust may be used, where conditions permit, for nonpatient areas such as boiler rooms, central storage, etc.

u. The energy-saving potential of variable air volume systems is recognized and these standards herein are intended to maximize appropriate use of that system. Any system utilized for occupied areas shall include provisions to avoid air stagnation in interior spaces where thermostat demands are met by temperatures of surrounding areas (see Appendix B).

v. Special consideration shall be given to the type of heating and cooling units, ventilation outlets, and appurtenances installed in patient-occupied areas of psychiatric units. The following shall apply:

i. All air grilles and diffusers shall be of a type that prohibits the insertion of foreign objects.

ii. All convector or HVAC enclosures exposed in the room shall be constructed with rounded corners and shall have enclosures fastened with tamper-proof screws.

iii. HVAC equipment shall be of a type that minimizes the need for maintenance within the room.

7.31.E. Plumbing and Other Piping Systems.
Unless otherwise specified herein, all plumbing systems shall be designed and installed in accordance with *National Standard Plumbing Code*, chapter 14, Medical Care Facility Plumbing Equipment.

7.31.E1. The following standards shall apply to plumbing fixtures:

a. The material used for plumbing fixtures shall be nonabsorptive and acid-resistant.

b. Water spouts used in lavatories and sinks shall have clearances adequate to avoid contaminating utensils and the contents of carafes, etc.

c. All fixtures used by medical and nursing staff and all lavatories used by patients and food handlers shall be trimmed with valves that can be operated without hands (single-lever devices may be used). Blade handles used for this purpose shall not exceed 4-1/2 inches (11.43 centimeters) in length. Handles on scrub sinks and clinical sinks shall be at least 6 inches (15.24 centimeters) long.

d. Clinical sinks shall have an integral trap wherein the upper portion of the water trap provides a visible seal.

▼ e. Showers and tubs shall have nonslip walking ▲ surfaces.

7.31.E2. The following standards shall apply to potable water supply systems:

a. Systems shall be designed to supply water at sufficient pressure to operate all fixtures and equipment during maximum demand. Supply capacity for hot- and cold-water piping shall be determined on the basis of fixture units, using recognized engineering standards. When the ratio of plumbing fixtures to occupants is proportionally more than required by the building occupancy and is in excess of 1,000 plumbing fixture units, a diversity factor is permitted.

b. Each water service main, branch main, riser, and branch to a group of fixtures shall have valves. Stop valves shall be provided for each fixture. Appropriate panels for access shall be provided at all valves where required.

c. Vacuum breakers shall be installed on hose bibbs and supply nozzles used for connection of hoses or tubing in laboratories, housekeeping sinks, bedpan-flushing attachments, and autopsy tables, etc.

d. Bedpan-flushing devices (may be cold water) shall be provided in each inpatient toilet room; however, installation is optional in psychiatric and alcohol-abuse units where patients are ambulatory.

e. Potable water storage vessels (hot and cold) not intended for constant use shall not be installed.

7.31.E3. The following standards shall apply to hot water systems:

a. The water-heating system shall have sufficient supply capacity at the temperatures and amounts indicated in Table 4. Water temperature is measured at the point of use or inlet to the equipment.

▼ b. Hot-water distribution systems serving patient care areas shall be under constant recirculation to provide continuous hot water at each hot water outlet. The temperature of hot water for showers and bathing shall be appropriate for comfortable use but ▲ shall not exceed 110°F (43°C) (see Table 4).

7.31.E4. The following standards shall apply to drainage systems:

a. Drain lines from sinks used for acid waste disposal shall be made of acid-resistant material.

b. Drain lines serving some types of automatic blood-cell counters must be of carefully selected material that will eliminate potential for undesirable chemical reactions (and/or explosions) between sodium azide wastes and copper, lead, brass, and solder, etc.

Table 4
Hot Water Use

	Clinical	Dietary[1]	Laundry
Liters per second per bed*	.0033	.0020	.0021
Gallons per hour per bed*	3	2	2
Temperature (°C)**	43	49	71**
Temperature (°F)**	110	120	160**

1 Provisions shall be made to provide 180°F (82°C) rinse water at warewasher. (May be by separate booster.)

* Quantities indicated for design demand of hot water are for general reference minimums and shall not substitute for accepted engineering design procedures using actual number and types of fixtures to be installed. Design will also be affected by temperatures of cold water used for mixing, length of run and insulation relative to heat loss, etc. As an example, total quantity of hot water needed will be less when temperature available at the outlet is very nearly that of the source tank and the cold water used for tempering is relatively warm.

**Provisions shall be made to provide 160°F (71°C) hot water at the laundry equipment when needed. (This may be by steam jet or separate booster heater.) However, it is emphasized that this does not imply that all water used would be at this temperature. Water temperatures required for acceptable laundry results will vary according to type of cycle, time of operation, and formula of soap and bleach as well as type and degree of soil. Lower temperatures may be adequate for most procedures in many facilities but the higher 160°F (71°C) should be available when needed for special conditions.

Table 5
Station Outlets for Oxygen, Vacuum (Suction), and Medical Air Systems

Section	Location	Oxygen	Vacuum	Med. Air
7.2.A	Patient Rooms (Medical and Surgical)	1 (one outlet accessible to each bed)	1 (one outlet) accessible to each bed)	—
7.2.B10	Examination/Treatment (Medical, Surgical, and Postpartum Care)	1	1	—
7.2.C/7.2.D	Isolation (Infectious and Protective) (Medical and Surgical)	1	1	—
7.2.E	Security Room (Medical, Surgical, and Postpartum)	1	1	—
7.3.A	Critical Care (General)	2	2	1
7.3.A14	Isolation (Critical)	2	2	1
7.3.B	Coronary Critical Care	2	2	1
7.3.C	Cardiac Critical Care	2	2	1
7.3.D	Pediatric Critical Care	2	2	1
7.3.E	Newborn Intensive Care	3	4	3
7.4.B	Newborn Nursery (Full-Term)	1	1	1
7.5.A	Pediatric and Adolescent	1	1	1
7.5.B	Pediatric Nursery	1	1	1
7.6.A	Psychiatric Patient Rooms	—	—	—
7.6.C	Psychiatric Isolation	—	—	—
7.6.D	Seclusion Treatment Room	—	—	—
7.7.A1	General Operating Room	2	4	2
7.7.A2	Cardio, Ortho, Neurological	2	4	2
7.7.A.3	Orthopedic Surgery	2	4	2
7.7.A4	Surgical Cysto and Endo	1	3	2
7.7.B	Post-Anesthetic Care Unit	1	1	1
7.7.C9	Anesthesia Workroom	1 per workstation	—	1 per workstation
7.7.C14	Outpatient Recovery	1	1	1
7.8.B2	Postpartum Bedroom	1	1	—
7.8.B2(c)	Postpartum Isolation Room	1	1	—
7.8.B3	Caesarean/Delivery Room	2	4	2
7.8.B3(d)	Labor Room	1	1	1
7.8.B3(e)	Recovery Room	1	1	1
7.8.B4	Labor/Delivery/Recovery (LDR)	2	3	2
7.8.B4	Labor/Delivery/Recovery/Postpartum (LDRP)	2	3	2
7.9.C2	Initial Emergency Management per bed	1	1	1
7.9.D3	Triage Area (Definitive Emergency Care)	1	1	—
7.9.D7	Definitive Emergency Care Exam/Treatment Rooms	1	1	1
7.9.D7	Definitive Emergency Care Holding Area	1	1	—
7.9.D8	Trauma/Cardiac Room(s)	2	2	1
7.9.D9	Orthopedic and Cast Room	1	1	1
7.9.D22	Isolation Room (Emergency Service)	1	1	1
7.10.H	Cardiac Catheterization Lab	1	3	2
7.15.A2	Autopsy Room	—	1 per workstation	1 per workstation

c. Insofar as possible, drainage piping shall not be installed within the ceiling or exposed in operating and delivery rooms, nurseries, food preparation centers, food serving facilities, food storage areas, central services, electronic data processing areas, electric closets, and other sensitive areas. Where exposed, overhead drain piping in these areas is unavoidable, special provisions shall be made to protect the space below from leakage, condensation, or dust particles.

d. Floor drains shall not be installed in operating, delivery, and cystoscopic rooms.

e. Drain systems for autopsy tables shall be designed to positively avoid splatter or overflow onto floors or back siphonage and for easy cleaning and trap flushing.

f. Building sewers shall discharge into community sewerage. Where such a system is not available, the facility shall treat its sewage in accordance with local and state regulations.

g. Kitchen grease traps shall be located and arranged to permit easy access without the need to enter food preparation or storage areas.

h. Where plaster traps are used, provisions shall be made for appropriate access and cleaning.

7.31.E5. The installation of nonflammable medical gas and air systems shall comply with the requirements of NFPA 99. (See Table 5 for rooms requiring station outlets.) When any piping or supply of medical gases is installed, altered, or augmented, the altered zone shall be tested and certified as required by NFPA 99.

7.31.E6. Clinical vacuum system installations shall be in accordance with NFPA 99. (See Table 5 for rooms which require station outlets.)

Note: Cautionary comments of NFPA 99 may be especially applicable when a vacuum system is being considered for scavenging of anesthetizing gases.

7.31.E7. All piping, except control-line tubing, shall be identified. All valves shall be tagged, and a valve schedule shall be provided to the facility owner for permanent record and reference.

▼ **7.31.E8.** Where the functional program includes hemodialysis, continuously circulated filtered cold ▲ water shall be provided.

7.32 Electrical Standards

7.32.A. General

7.32.A1. All material and equipment, including conductors, controls, and signaling devices, shall be installed in compliance with applicable sections of NFPA 70 and NFPA 99. All materials shall be listed as complying with approved established standards.

7.32.A2. The electrical installations, including alarm, nurses call and communication systems, shall be tested to demonstrate that equipment installation and operation is appropriate and functional. A written record of performance tests on special electrical systems and equipment shall show compliance with applicable codes and standards. Grounding continuity shall be tested as described in NFPA 99.

▼ **7.32.A3.** Shielded isolation transformers, voltage regulators, filters, surge suppressors, or other safeguards shall be provided as required where power line disturbances are likely to affect data processing and/ ▲ or automated laboratories or diagnostic equipment.

7.32.A4. Design of the electrical systems shall include provisions for avoiding power-factor deviations below established norms.

7.32.B. Switchboards and Power Panels

Switchboards and power panels shall comply with NFPA 70. The main switchboard shall be located in an area separate from plumbing and mechanical equipment and shall be accessible to authorized persons only. The switchboards shall be convenient for use, readily accessible for maintenance, away from traffic lanes, and located in a dry, ventilated space free of corrosive or explosive fumes, gases, or any flammable material. Overload protection devices shall operate properly at ambient room temperatures.

7.32.C. Panelboards

Panelboards serving normal lighting and appliance circuits shall be located on the same floor as the circuits they serve. Panelboards serving critical branch emergency circuits shall be located on each floor that has major users (operating rooms, delivery suite, intensive care, etc.). Panelboards serving life safety emergency circuits may also serve floors above and/or below for secondary users (general patient areas, administration, laboratory, X-ray, etc.).

7.32.D. Lighting

▼ **7.32.D1.** The Illuminating Engineering Society of North America (IES) has developed recommended lighting levels for health care facilities. The reader should refer to the *IES Lighting Handbook* (1987, volume 2, Applications) and *Lighting for Health Care Facilities* (1985) and to Appendix B (Energy Conservation Considerations) for additional infor-▲ mation.

Three types of interior lighting systems are available and should be maximized when designing lighting. They are direct, indirect, and task lighting. Site lighting, a specialty, requires design skill to create an efficient system. In general, the use of light colors and reflective surfaces can affect lighting efficiency.

a. Direct lighting has been the standard design for years and will remain so for some time. Its performance has been dramatically increased in recent years through the improvement of luminaries and the use of more efficient light sources.

b. Indirect lighting utilizes the reflectance characteristics of the ceiling and walls to disperse the light, resulting in less glare and higher visual comfort. Calculations are best accomplished by computers. The most popular sources for indirect lighting are metal halide and high-pressure sodium.

c. Task lighting reduces general area lighting needs by applying light to a specific task. This system of lighting results in the greatest energy savings by focusing light only in required spaces. Emphasis should be given to task lighting design that is independently controlled for use on an as-needed basis.

d. Site lighting should be high- and/or low-pressure sodium or metal halides. Calculations of footcandles and layouts are best accomplished by computer for maximization of light efficiency.

7.32.D2. Approaches to buildings and parking lots, and all occupied spaces within buildings shall have fixtures for lighting.

7.32.D3. Patient rooms shall have general lighting and night lighting. A reading light shall be provided for each patient. Flexible light arms, if used, shall be mechanically controlled to prevent the bulb from contacting the bed linen. At least one night light fixture in each patient room shall be controlled at the room entrance. All light controls in patient areas shall be quiet-operating. Lighting for intensive care bed areas shall permit staff observation of the patient but minimize glare.

▼ **7.32.D4.** Operating and delivery rooms shall have general lighting in addition to special lighting units provided at surgical and obstetrical tables. General lighting and special lighting shall be on separate ▲ circuits.

7.32.D5. Nursing unit corridors shall have general illumination with provisions for reducing light levels at night.

▼ **7.32.D6.** Light intensity for staff and patient needs should generally comply with health care guidelines set forth in the IES publications. Consideration should be given to controlling intensity to prevent harm to the patients' eyes (i.e., retina damage in premature infants and cataracts due to ultraviolet light).

Many procedures are available to satisfy requirements, but the design should consider light quality as well as quantity for effectiveness and efficiency. While light levels in the IES publication are referenced herein, those publications include other useful guidance and recommendations which the designer is encouraged to follow.

7.32.D7. Light intensity of required emergency lighting shall generally comply with standards in the IES ▲ publication, *Lighting for Health Care Facilities.*

7.32.E. Receptacles (Convenience Outlets)

▼ **7.32.E1.** Receptacles for pediatric and psychiatric units shall be in accordance with NFPA 70.

7.32.E2. Each operating room and delivery room shall have at least six receptacles at anesthetizing locations. Where mobile X-ray equipment requiring special electrical considerations is used, additional receptacles distinctively marked for X-ray use shall be provided. (See NFPA 70, article 517 for receptacle requirements when capacitive discharge or battery-operated, mobile X-ray units are used.) Each OR should have at least 16 simplex or 8 duplex receptacles at the height of 36 inches (0.91 meter). In addition, special receptacles for X-ray, laser or other equipment requiring special plugs or voltage shall be provided in accordance with the functional plan.

7.32.E3. Each patient room shall have duplex-grounded receptacles. There shall be one at each side of the head of each bed; one for television, if used; and one on every other wall. Receptacles may be omitted from exterior walls where construction makes installation impractical. Nurseries shall have at least two duplex-grounded receptacles for each bassinet. Critical care areas as defined in NFPA 70, article 517, including pediatric and newborn intensive care, shall have at least seven duplex outlets at the head of each bed, crib, or bassinet. Trauma and resuscitation rooms shall have eight duplex outlets located convenient to head of each bed. Emergency department examination and treatment rooms shall have a minimum of six duplex outlets located convenient to the head of each bed. Approximately 50 percent of critical and emergency care outlets shall be connected to emergency system power and be so labeled.

7.32.E4. Duplex-grounded receptacles for general use shall be installed approximately 50 feet (15.24 meters) apart in all corridors and within 25 feet (7.62 meters) of corridor ends. Receptacles in pediatric unit corridors shall be of the tamper-resistant type or protected by 5 milliampere ground-fault circuit interrupters (GFCI). Single-polarized receptacles marked for use of X-ray only shall be installed in corridors of patient areas so that mobile equipment may be used anywhere within a patient room using a cord length of 50 feet (15.24 meters) or less. If the same mobile X-ray unit is used in operating rooms and in nursing areas, receptacles for X-ray use shall permit the use of one plug in all locations. *Where capacitive discharge or battery-powered X-ray units are used,* ▲ *separate polarized receptacles are not required.*

7.32.E5. Electrical receptacle coverplates or electrical receptacles supplied from the emergency system shall be distinctively colored or marked for identification. If color is used for identification purposes, the same color should be used throughout the facility.

7.32.F. Equipment Installation in Special Areas

7.32.F1. At inhalation anesthetizing locations, all electrical equipment and devices, receptacles, and wiring shall comply with applicable sections of NFPA 99 and NFPA 70.

7.32.F2. Fixed and mobile X-ray equipment installations shall conform to articles 517 and 660 of NFPA 70.

7.32.F3. The X-ray film illuminator unit or units for displaying at least two films simultaneously shall be installed in each operating room, specified emergency treatment rooms, and X-ray viewing room of the radiology department. All illuminator units within one space or room shall have lighting of uniform intensity and color value.

▼ **7.32.F4.** Ground-fault circuit interrupters shall comply with NFPA 70. *When ground-fault circuit interrupters (GFCI) are used in critical areas, provisions shall be made to insure that other essential equip-* ▲ *ment is not affected by activation of one interrupter.*

7.32.F5. In areas such as critical care units and special nurseries where a patient may be treated with an internal probe or catheter connected to the heart, the ground system shall comply with applicable sections of NFPA 99 and NFPA 70.

7.32.G. Nurses Calling System.

7.32.G1. In patient areas, each patient room shall be served by at least one calling station for two-way voice communication. Each bed shall be provided with a call device. Two call devices serving adjacent beds may be served by one calling station. Calls shall activate a visible signal in the corridor at the patient's door, in the clean workroom, in the soiled workroom, and at the nursing station of the nursing unit. In multicorridor nursing units, additional visible signals shall be installed at corridor intersections. In rooms containing two or more calling stations, indicating lights shall be provided at each station. Nurses calling systems at each calling station shall be equipped with an indicating light which remains lighted as long as the voice circuit is operating.

7.32.G2. A nurses emergency call system shall be provided at each inpatient toilet, bath, sitz bath, and shower room. This system shall be accessible to a collapsed patient lying on the floor. Inclusion of a pull cord will satisfy this standard.

The emergency call system shall be designed so that a signal activated at a patient's calling station will initiate a visible and audible signal distinct from the regular nurse calling system that can be turned off only at the patient calling station. The signal shall activate an enumerator panel at the nurse station, a visible signal in the corridor at the patient's door, and at other areas defined by the functional program. Provisions for emergency calls will also be needed in outpatient and treatment areas where patients may be subject to incapacitation.

7.32.G3. In areas such as critical care where patients are under constant visual surveillance, the nurses call system may be limited to a bedside button or station that activates a signal readily seen at the control station.

▼ **7.32.G4.** A staff emergency assistance system for staff to summon additional assistance shall be provided in each operating, delivery, recovery, emergency examination and/or treatment area, and in critical care units, nurseries, special procedure rooms, stress-test areas, triage, out-patient surgery, admission and discharge areas, and areas for mental patients including seclusion and security rooms, anterooms and toilet rooms serving them, communal toilet and bathing facility rooms, dining, activity, therapy, exam, and treatment rooms. This system shall annunciate at the nurse station with back-up to another staffed area
▲ from which assistance can be summoned.

7.32.H. Emergency Electric Service

7.32.H1. An emergency electrical source shall be provided and connected to certain circuits to provide lighting and power during an interruption of the normal electric supply. Where stored fuel is required, storage capacity shall permit continuous operation for at least 24 hours. Fuel storage for electricity generation shall be separate from heating fuels. If the use of heating fuel for diesel engines is considered after the required 24-hour supply has been exhausted, positive valving and filtration shall be provided to avoid entry of water and/or contaminants. In areas where the electrical service is found to be unreliable, consideration should be given to the use of dual-fuel generator units.

7.32.H2. The source(s) of this emergency electric service shall be:

a. An emergency generating set for facilities whose normal service is supplied by one or more central station transmission lines.

b. An emergency generating set or a central station transmission line for facilities whose normal electrical supply is generated on the premises.

7.32.H3. The required emergency generating set, including the prime mover and generator, shall be located on the premises and shall conform to NFPA 99 and NFPA 110.

7.32.H4. As required in NFPA 99 and NFPA 70, emergency electricity shall be provided to all services that must continue to function during any failure of the normal power source including the fire pump, if installed. As a minimum, each patient bed and treatment space shall have access to a receptacle on the critical branch of the emergency power system. Where access is by extension cords, length required shall not exceed 50 feet (15.24 meters). See NFPA 99 for special care areas.

7.32.H5. Local codes and regulations may have additional requirements.

7.32.H6. Exhaust systems (including locations, mufflers, and vibration isolators) for internal combustion engines shall be designed and installed to minimize objectionable noise. Where a generator is routinely used to reduce peak loads, protection of patient areas from excessive noise may become a critical issue.

7.32.H7. Emergency generator sets shall have adequate clearances for access and maintenance and shall be provided with appropriate ventilation for cooling and elimination of fumes. Mechanisms for intake air shall be arranged to resist entry of rain and/or snow.

▼ **7.32.I. Fire Alarm System**
The fire alarm and detector system shall be in compli-
▲ ance with NFPA 101 and NFPA 72.

8. NURSING FACILITIES

8.1 General Conditions

8.1.A. Applicability

▼ This section covers freestanding facilities or a distinct part of a general acute-care hospital, and represents minimum requirements for new construction and shall not be applied to existing facilities unless major construction renovations (see Section 1.2.A) are undertaken.

Note: For requirements regarding swing beds see
▲ *Section 7.1.E.*

8.1.B. Ancillary Services

When the nursing facility is part of, or contractually linked with, another facility, services such as dietary, storage, pharmacy, and laundry may be shared insofar as practical. In some cases, all ancillary service requirements will be met by the principal facility and the only modifications necessary will be within the nursing facility. In other cases, programmatic concerns and requirements may dictate separate services.

8.1.C. Hospital Conversions

While there are similarities in the spatial arrangement of hospitals and nursing facilities, the service requirements of long-term care residents will require additional special design considerations. When a section of an acute-care facility is converted, it may be necessary to reduce the number of beds to provide space for long-term care services. Design shall maximize opportunities for ambulation and self-care, and minimize the negative aspects of institutionalization.

8.1.D. Site

▼ See Sections 3.1 and 3.3 for requirements regarding
▲ location and environmental pollution control.

8.1.E. Roads

▼ Roads shall be provided within the property for access to the main entrance and service areas. Fire department access shall be provided in accordance with local requirements. The property or campus shall be marked
▲ to identify emergency services or departments.

8.1.F. Parking

▼ In the absence of local requirements, each nursing facility shall have parking space to satisfy the needs of residents, employees, staff, and visitors. The facility shall
▲ provide a minimum of one space for every four beds.

8.1.G. Program of Functions

The sponsor for each project shall provide a functional program for the facility (see Section 1.1.F of this document).

8.1.H. Services

Each nursing facility shall, as a minimum, contain the elements described herein. However, when the project calls for the sharing or purchase of services, appropriate modifications or deletions in space requirements may be made.

8.2 Nursing Unit

Each nursing unit shall comply with the following:

8.2.A. Number of Beds

▼ In the absence of local requirements, consideration should be given to restricting the size of the nursing unit to 60 beds or a maximum travel distance from the nurses station to a resident room door of 150 feet
▲ (45.72 meters).

8.2.B. Resident Rooms

Each resident room shall meet the following requirements:

▼ **8.2.B1.** Maximum room occupancy in renovations (less than 50 percent change) shall be four residents; two residents in new construction.

8.2.B2. In new construction, minimum room areas (exclusive of toilets, closets, lockers, wardrobes, alcoves, or vestibules) shall be 120 square feet (11.15 square meters) in single bed rooms and 100 square feet (9.29 square meters) per bed in multiple-bed rooms. In renovations, minimum room areas (exclusive of toilets, closets, lockers, wardrobes, alcoves, or vestibules) shall be 100 square feet (9.29 square meters) in single bed rooms and 80 square feet (7.43 square meters) per bed in multiple-bed rooms. In multiple-bed rooms, clearance shall allow for the movement of beds and equipment without disturbing residents. The dimensions and arrangement of rooms should be such that there is a minimum of 3 feet (0.91 meter) between the sides and foot of the bed and any wall, other fixed obstruction, or other bed. *If function is not impaired*, minor encroachments such as columns, lavatories, and door swings may be ignored in determining space requirements.

8.2.B3. Each room shall have a window that meets the requirements of Section 8.8.A5.

8.2.B4. A nurses calling system shall be provided. Each bed shall be provided with a call device. Two call devices serving adjacent beds may be served by one calling station. Calls shall activate a visible signal in the corridor at the resident's door or other appropriate location. In multicorridor nursing units, additional visible signals shall be installed at corridor intersections.

A nurses emergency call system shall be provided at each inpatient toilet, bath, sitz bath, and shower room. This system shall be accessible to a collapsed resident lying on the floor. Inclusion of a pull cord will satisfy this standard.

The emergency call system shall be designed so that a signal activated at a resident's calling station will initiate a visible and audible signal distinct from the regular nurse calling system that can be turned off only at the resident calling station. The signal shall activate an annunciator panel at the nurses station or other appropriate location, a visible signal in the corridor at the resident's door, and at other areas defined ▲ by the functional program.

8.2.B5. Handwashing facilities shall be provided in each resident room. They may be omitted from single-bed or two-bed rooms when such is located in an adjoining toilet room serving that room only.

▼ **8.2.B6.** Each resident shall have access to a toilet room without having to enter the corridor area. One toilet room shall serve no more than four beds and no more than two resident rooms. The toilet room shall contain a water closet, a lavatory, and the door should swing outward. The lavatory may be omitted from a toilet room if each resident room served by that toilet contains a lavatory for handwashing.

8.2.B7. Each resident bedroom shall have a wardrobe, locker, or closet with minimum clear dimensions of 1 foot 10 inches (55.88 centimeters) depth by 1 foot 8 inches (50.80 centimeters); with a shelf and clothes rod to permit a vertically clear hanging space of 5 feet (1.52 meters) for full length garments. (The shelf may be omitted if the unit provides at least two drawers and capacity for storing ▲ extra blankets, pillows, etc.)

8.2.B8. Visual privacy shall be provided for each resident in multiple-bed rooms. Design for privacy shall not restrict resident access to the toilet, lavatory, or room entrance.

8.2.B9. Beds shall be no more than two deep from windows in new construction and three deep from windows in renovated construction.

8.2.B10. Provision should be made for wheelchairs within the room.

8.2.C. Service Areas

The size and features of each service area will depend upon the number and types of residents served. Although identifiable spaces are required for each indicated function, consideration will be given to multiple-use design solutions that provide equal, though unspecified, areas. Service areas may be arranged and located to serve more than one nursing unit, but at least one such service area shall be provided on each nursing floor unless noted otherwise. Except where the words *room* or *office* are used, service may be provided in a multipurpose area. The following service areas shall be located in or be readily accessible to each nursing unit:

▼ **8.2.C1.** Nurses station. This shall have space for charting, storage, and administrative activities.

8.2.C2. Toilet room(s) with handwashing facilities for staff shall be provided and may be unisex.

8.2.C3. Lockable closets, drawers, or compartments shall be provided for safekeeping of staff personal effects such as handbags, etc.

8.2.C4. Staff lounge area(s) shall be provided and may be shared by more than one nursing unit or ▲ service.

8.2.C5. Clean utility room. If the room is used for work, it shall contain a counter and handwashing facilities.

▼ **8.2.C6.** Soiled utility or soiled holding room. This shall contain a clinical sink or equivalent flushing-rim fixture, handwashing facilities, and waste receptacle.

8.2.C7. Medication station. Provision shall be made for 24-hour distribution of medications. A medicine preparation room, a self-contained medicine dispensing unit, or other system may be used for this purpose. The medicine preparation room, if used, shall be visually controlled from the nurses station. It shall contain a work counter, sink, refrigerator, and locked storage for controlled drugs. It shall have a minimum area of 50 square feet (4.65 square meters). A self-contained medicine dispensing unit, if used, may be located at the nurses station, in the clean workroom, in an alcove, or in other space convenient for staff control. (Standard "cup" sinks provided in many self-contained units are not adequate for handwashing.)

8.2.C8. Clean linen storage. A separate closet or designated area shall be provided. If a closed-cart system is used, storage may be in an alcove where staff control can be assured.

8.2.C9. Nourishment station. This should contain a work counter, refrigerator, storage cabinets, and a sink for serving nourishments between meals. Ice for residents' consumption shall be provided by ice-maker units (which may serve more than one nourishment station). The nourishment station shall include space for trays and dishes used for nonscheduled meal service. Handwashing facilities shall be in or immediately accessible from the nourishment station.

8.2.C10. Storage space for wheelchairs shall be located away from normal traffic.

8.2.C11. Resident bathing facilities. A minimum of one bathtub or shower shall be provided for every 20 beds (or a major fraction thereof) not otherwise served by bathing facilities in resident rooms. Residents shall have access to at least one bathtub per floor. Each tub or shower shall be in an individual room or enclosure with space for private use of the bathing fixture, for drying and dressing. At least one shower on each floor shall be at least 4 feet (1.22 meters) square without curbs and be designed for use by a wheelchair resident.

8.2.C12. Bedpan cleaning facilities shall be provided on each nursing floor in addition to those in the residents' toilet room. Such facilities may be located in ▲ the soiled utility or holding room.

8.2.D. Resident Toilet Facilities

A separate toilet shall be provided that is directly accessible to each multifixture central bathing area without requiring entry into the general corridor. This may also serve as the required toilet training facility.

8.3 Resident Support Areas

8.3.A. Area Need

▼ In new construction, the total area set aside for dining, resident lounges, and recreation areas shall be at least 35 square feet (3.25 square meters) per bed with a minimum total area of at least 225 square feet (20.90 square meters). At least 20 square feet (1.86 square meters) per bed shall be available for dining. Additional space may be required for outpatient day care programs.

For renovations, at least 14 square feet (1.30 square meters) per bed shall be available for dining. Additional space may be required for outpatient day care programs. ▲

8.3.B. Storage

▼ Storage space(s) for supplies, resident needs, and recreation shall be provided. This area shall be on-site but not necessarily in the same building as the resident ▲ room, provided access is convenient.

8.4 Rehabilitation Therapy

Each nursing facility which provides physical and/or occupational therapy services for rehabilitating long-term care residents shall have areas and equipment that conform to program intent. Where the nursing facility is part of a general hospital or other facility, services may be shared as appropriate.

8.4.A. Physical and Occupational Therapy Provisions (Inpatient/Outpatient):

As a minimum, the following shall be located on-site, convenient for use:

8.4.A1. Space for files, records, and administrative activities.

8.4.A2. Provisions for wheelchair residents.

8.4.A3. Storage for supplies and equipment.

8.4.A4. Handwashing facilities within the therapy unit.

8.4.A5. Space and equipment for carrying out each of the types of therapy that may be prescribed.

8.4.A6. Provisions for resident privacy.

8.4.A7. Housekeeping rooms, in or near unit.

8.4.A8. Resident toilet room(s), usable by wheelchair residents.

8.4.B. Physical and Occupational Therapy for Outpatients

If the program includes outpatient treatment, additional provisions shall include:

8.4.B1. Convenient facility access usable by the handicapped.

8.4.B2. Lockers for storing patients' clothing and personal effects.

8.4.B3. Outpatient facilities for dressing.

8.4.B4. Shower(s) for patients' use.

8.5 Barber/Beauty Area

Facilities and equipment for resident hair care and grooming shall be provided separate from the resident rooms. These may be part of another area, such as the daily activity room, provided that location and scheduling preserve patient dignity.

8.6. General Services

The following services shall be provided:

8.6.A. Dietary Facilities

▼ Food service facilities and equipment shall conform with these standards and any local food and sanitation standards and other appropriate codes and shall provide food service for staff, visitors, inpatients, and outpatients as may be appropriate.

Consideration may also be required for meals to VIP suites, and for cafeterias for staff, ambulatory patients, and visitors as well as providing for nourishments and snacks between scheduled meal service.

Location of patient food preparation area shall be on a single floor and for efficient access and function with adjacency to delivery, interior transportation storage, etc. (Additional food preparation areas may be utilized for remote areas used for substations and short order functions.)

The dietary facility shall be easy to clean and to maintain in a sanitary condition.

At the completion of equipment purchase, operating and maintenance manuals of all items of equipment shall be bound into a folder for permanent record and delivered to the owner. These shall include dimensions, connection and power requirements, maintenance requirements, operating instructions, parts lists, and
▲ sources of service.

8.6.B. Functional Elements

▼ If the dietary department is on-site, the following facilities, in the size and number appropriate for the type of food service selected, shall be provided:

8.6.B1. A control station for receiving and controlling food supplies.

8.6.B2. Storage space, including cold storage, for at least a 4-day supply of food. (Facilities in remote areas may require proportionally more food storage facilities.)

8.6.B3. Food preparation facilities. Conventional food preparation systems require space and equipment for preparing, cooking, and baking. Convenience food service systems using frozen prepared meals, bulk packaged entrees, individual packaged portions, or those using contractual commissary services, require space and equipment for thawing, portioning, cooking, and/or baking.

8.6.B4. Handwashing facility(ies) located in the food preparation area.

8.6.B5. Facilities for assembly and distribution of patient meals.

8.6.B6. Dining space for residents and staff.

8.6.B7. Warewashing space located in a room or an alcove separate from the food preparation and serving area. Commercial-type warewashing equipment shall be provided. Space shall also be provided for receiving, scraping, sorting, and stacking soiled tableware and for transferring clean tableware to the using areas. Convenient handwashing facilities shall be available.

8.6.B8. Potwashing facilities.

8.6.B9. Storage areas and sanitizing facilities for cans, carts, and mobile-tray conveyors.

8.6.B10. Waste storage facilities located in a separate room easily accessible to the outside for direct pick-up or disposal.

8.6.B11. Office(s) or desk spaces for dietitian(s) and/or a dietary service manager.

8.6.B12. Toilet for dietary staff convenient to the kitchen area.

8.6.B13. A housekeeping room located within the dietary department. This shall include a floor receptor or service sink and storage space for housekeeping equipment and supplies.

8.6.B14. Icemaking facilities. These may be located in the food preparation area or in a separate room, but must be easily cleanable and convenient to the dietary function.

8.6.C. Administrative Areas

The following shall be provided:

8.6.C1. Entrance

This shall be at grade level, sheltered from inclement weather, and accessible to the handicapped.

8.6.C2. Administrative/Lobby Area

This shall include:

a. A counter or desk for reception and information.

b. Public waiting area(s).

c. Public toilet facilities.

d. Public telephone(s).

e. Drinking fountain(s).

8.6.C3. General or Individual Office(s)

These shall be provided for business transactions, admissions, social services, medical and financial records, and administrative and professional staff. There shall be included provisions for private interviews.

8.6.C4. Multipurpose Room(s)

There shall be a multipurpose room for conferences, meetings, and health education purposes as required by the functional program; it shall include provisions for the use of visual aids. One multipurpose room may be shared by several services.

8.6.C5. Storage for Office Equipment and Supplies

8.6.D. Clerical files and staff office space shall be provided as needed.

8.6.E. Linen Services

8.6.E1. General

Each facility shall have provisions for storing and processing of clean and soiled linen for appropriate resident care. Processing may be done within the facility, in a separate building on- or off-site, or in a commercial or shared laundry. At a minimum, the following elements shall be included:

a. A separate room for receiving and holding soiled linen until ready for pickup or processing.

b. A central, clean linen storage and issuing room(s), in addition to the linen storage required at individual resident units.

c. Provisions shall be made for parking of clean and soiled linen carts separately and out of traffic.

d. Handwashing facilities in each area where unbagged, soiled linen is handled.

8.6.E2. If linen is processed off-site, provisions shall also be made for:

a. A service entrance, protected from inclement weather, for loading and unloading of linen.

b. Control station for pickup and receiving.

8.6.E3. If linen is processed in a laundry facility which is part of the site (within or as a separate building), the following shall be provided in addition to that of Section 8.6.E:

a. A receiving, holding, and sorting room for control and distribution of soiled linen. Discharge from soiled linen chutes may be received within this room or in a separate room.

b. Laundry processing room with commercial-type equipment which can process at least a seven day supply within the regular scheduled work week.

c. Storage for laundry supplies.

d. Arrangement of equipment that will permit an orderly work flow and minimize cross-traffic that might mix clean and soiled operations.

8.6.F. Housekeeping Rooms
Housekeeping rooms shall be provided throughout the facility as required to maintain a clean and sanitary environment. Each shall contain a floor receptor or service sink and storage space for housekeeping equipment and supplies. There shall not be less than one housekeeping room for each floor.

8.6.G. Engineering Service and Equipment Areas
The following shall be provided as necessary for effective service and maintenance functions:

8.6.G1. Room(s) or separate building(s) for boilers, mechanical, and electrical equipment.

8.6.G2. Provisions for protected storage of facility drawings, records, manuals, etc.

8.6.G3. General maintenance area for repair and maintenance.

8.6.G4. Storage room for building maintenance supplies. Storage for solvents and flammable liquids shall comply with applicable NFPA codes.

8.6.G5. Yard equipment and supply storage areas shall be located so that equipment may be moved directly to the exterior.

8.6.G6. General storage space(s) shall be provided for equipment such as intravenous stands, inhalators, air mattresses, walkers, etc., medical supplies, housekeeping supplies, and equipment.

8.7 Waste Storage and Disposal

Facilities shall be provided for sanitary storage and treatment or disposal of waste using techniques acceptable to the appropriate health and environmental ▲ authorities.

8.8 Details and Finishes

Nursing facilities require features that encourage ambulation of long-term residents. Potential hazards to the infirm, such as sharp corners, highly polished floors, and loose carpets, should be avoided.

Alterations shall not diminish the level of compliance with these standards below that which existed prior to the alteration. However, features in excess of those for new constructions are not required to be maintained.

8.8.A. Details

8.8.A1. The placement of drinking fountains, public telephones, and vending machines shall not restrict corridor traffic or reduce the corridor width below the minimum stipulated in NFPA 101.

8.8.A2. Doors to all rooms containing bathtubs, sitz baths, showers, and water closets for resident use shall be equipped with privacy hardware that permits emergency access without keys. When such rooms have only one entrance or are small, the doors shall open outward.

▼ **8.8.A3.** Each room intended for use by wheelchair-confined residents, staff, or employees, including all residents toilets and bathing facilities, shall have one door whose width is in compliance with UFAS or ADA. Resident room doors, exit doors, etc., shall ▲ comply with NFPA 101.

8.8.A4. Windows and outer doors that may be left open shall have insect screens.

8.8.A5. Resident rooms or suites in new construction shall have operable windows or vents that open from the inside. Operation of such windows shall be restricted to inhibit possible resident escape or suicide. Where the operation of windows or vents requires the use of tools or keys, these shall be located on the same floor at a prominent staff-controlled location. For existing construction only, windows in buildings designed with approved engineered-smoke-control systems may be of fixed construction.

8.8.A6. Doors, sidelights, borrowed lights, and windows glazed to within 18 inches (45.72 centimeters) of the floor shall be constructed of safety glass, wire glass, or plastic glazing material that resists breaking and creates no dangerous cutting edges when broken. Similar materials shall be used in wall openings in activity areas (such as recreation rooms and exercise rooms) unless fire safety codes require otherwise. Glazing for shower doors and tub enclosures shall be safety glass or plastic.

▼ **8.8.A7.** Thresholds and expansion joint covers shall be designed to facilitate use of wheelchairs and carts and to prevent tripping. Expansion and seismic joints shall be constructed to restrict the passage of fire ▲ and/or smoke.

8.8.A8. Grab bars shall be installed in all resident toilets, showers, tubs, and sitz baths. For wall-mounted grab bars, a 1½-inch (3.81 centimeter) clearance from walls is required. Bars, including those which are part of fixtures such as soap dishes, shall have the strength to sustain a concentrated load of 250 pounds (113.4 kilograms).

8.8.A9. Handrails shall be provided on both sides of all corridors normally used by residents. A clearance of 1½ inches (3.81 centimeters) shall be provided between the handrail and the wall. Rail ends shall be finished to minimize potential for personal injury.

8.8.A10. Handwashing facilities shall be constructed with sufficient clearance for blade-type operating handles as may be required.

8.8.A11. Lavatories and handwashing facilities shall be securely anchored.

8.8.A12. Each resident handwashing facility shall have a mirror. Mirror placement shall allow for convenient use by both wheelchair occupants and/or ambulatory persons. Tops and bottoms may be at levels usable by individuals either sitting or standing, or additional mirrors may be provided for wheelchair occupants. One separate full-length mirror may serve for wheelchair occupants.

8.8.A13. Provisions for hand drying shall be included at all handwashing facilities. These shall be paper or cloth towels enclosed to protect against dust or soil and to insure single-unit dispensing.

8.8.A14. The minimum ceiling height shall be 7 feet 10 inches (2.39 meters) with the following exceptions:

a. Boiler rooms shall have ceiling clearances of at least 2 feet 6 inches (76.20 centimeters) above the main boiler header and connecting pipe.

b. Rooms containing ceiling-mounted equipment shall have the required ceiling height to ensure proper functioning of that equipment.

c. Ceilings in corridors, storage rooms, and toilet rooms shall be at least 7 feet 8 inches (2.34 meters). Ceilings in normally unoccupied spaces may be reduced to 7 feet (2.13 meters).

d. Building components and suspended tracks, rails, and pipes located along the path of normal traffic shall be not less than 7 feet (2.13 meters) above the floor.

e. Where existing conditions make the above impractical, clearances shall be sufficient to avoid injury to individuals up to 6 feet 4 inches (1.93 meters) tall.

8.8.A15. Rooms containing heat-producing equipment (such as boiler rooms, heater rooms, and laundries) shall be insulated and ventilated to prevent the floors of occupied areas overhead and the adjacent walls from exceeding a temperature of 10°F (6°C) above the ambient room temperature of such occupied areas.

8.8.B. Finishes

8.8.B1. Cubicle curtains and draperies shall be non-combustible or flame-retardant as prescribed in both the large- and small-scale tests in NFPA 701.

▼ **8.8.B2.** Materials provided by the facility for finishes and furnishings, including mattresses and upholstery, ▲ shall comply with NFPA 101.

8.8.B3. Floor materials shall be readily cleanable and appropriate for the location. Floors in areas used for food preparation and assembly shall be water-resistant. Floor surfaces, including tile joints, shall be resistant to food acids. In all areas subject to frequent wet-cleaning methods, floor materials shall not be physically affected by germicidal cleaning solutions. Floors subject to traffic while wet (such as shower and bath areas, kitchens, and similar work areas) shall have a slip-resistant surface. Carpet and padding in resident areas shall be stretched taut and free of loose edges or wrinkles that might create hazards or interfere with the operation of wheelchairs, walkers, wheeled carts, etc.

8.8.B4. Wall bases in areas subject to routine wet cleaning shall be coved, integrated with the floor, and tightly sealed.

8.8.B5. Wall finishes shall be washable and, if near plumbing fixtures, shall be smooth and moisture-resistant. Finish, trim, walls, and floor constructions in dietary and food storage areas shall be free from rodent- and insect-harboring spaces.

8.8.B6. Floor and wall openings for pipes, ducts, and conduits shall be tightly sealed to resist fire and smoke and to minimize entry of pests. Joints of structural elements shall be similarly sealed.

8.8.B7. The finishes of all exposed ceilings and ceiling structures in resident rooms and staff work areas shall be readily cleanable with routine housekeeping equipment. Finished ceilings shall be provided in dietary and other areas where dust fallout might create a problem.

8.9 Construction Features

All parts of the nursing facility shall be designed and constructed to sustain dead and live loads in accordance with local and national building codes and accepted engineering practices and standards, including requirements for seismic forces and applicable sections of NFPA 101.

8.10 Elevators

8.10.A. General
All buildings having patient use areas on more than one floor shall have electric or hydraulic elevator(s).

8.10.A1. In the absence of an engineered traffic study the following guidelines for number of elevators shall apply (these standards may be inadequate for moving large numbers of people in a short time; adjustments should be made as appropriate):

a. At least one hospital-type elevator shall be installed where patient beds are located on any floor other than the main entrance floor.

b. When 60 to 200 patient beds are located on floors other than the main entrance floor, at least two elevators, one of which shall be of the hospital-type, shall be installed.

c. When 201 to 350 patient beds are located on floors other than main entrance floor, at least three elevators, one of which shall be of the hospital-type, shall be installed.

d. For facilities with more than 350 patient beds above the main entrance floor, the number of elevators shall be determined from a facility plan study and from the estimated vertical transportation requirements.

e. When the skilled nursing unit is part of a general hospital, elevators may be shared and the standards of Section 7.30 shall apply.

8.10.A2. Cars of hospital-type elevators shall have inside dimensions that accommodate a patient bed with attendants. Cars shall be at least 5 feet (1.52 meters) wide by 7 feet 6 inches (2.29 meters) deep. The car door shall have a clear opening of not less than 3 feet 8 inches (1.12 meters). Other elevators required for passenger service shall be constructed to accommodate wheelchairs.

8.10.A3. Elevators shall be equipped with an automatic two-way leveling device with an accuracy of +¼ inch (0.7 centimeters).

8.10.A4. The controls, alarm buttons, and telephones in elevators shall be accessible to wheelchair patients.

8.10.A5. Elevator call buttons shall not be activated by heat or smoke. If employed, light beam door activators shall be used in combination with door-edge safety devices and shall be connected to a system of smoke detectors. This is so that the light control feature will disengage or be overridden if it encounters smoke at any landing.

8.10.B. Field Inspection and Tests

Inspections and tests shall be made and the owner shall be furnished with written certification stating that the installation meets the standards set forth in this section as well as all applicable safety regulations and codes.

8.11 Mechanical Standards

8.11.A. General

8.11.A1. The mechanical system should be subject to general review for overall efficiency and life-cycle cost. Details for cost-effective implementation of design features are interrelated and too numerous (as well as too basic) to list individually. Recognized engineering procedures shall be followed for the most economical and effective results. A well-designed system can generally achieve energy efficiency with minimal additional cost and simultaneously provide improved resident comfort. In no case shall resident care or safety be sacrificed for conservation.

8.11.A2. Remodeling and work in existing facilities may present special problems. Consideration shall be given to additional work that may be needed.

8.11.A3. Facility design considerations shall include site, building, orientation, and configuration.

8.11.A4. As appropriate, controls for air-handling systems shall be designed with an economizer cycle to use outside air for cooling and/or heating.

8.11.A5. To maintain asepsis control, airflow supply and exhaust should generally be controlled to ensure movement of air from "clean" to "less clean" areas.

8.11.A6. Prior to acceptance of the facility, all mechanical systems shall be tested, balanced, and operated to demonstrate to the design engineer or his representative that the installation and performance of these systems conform to design intent. Test results shall be documented for maintenance files.

8.11.A7. Upon completion of the equipment installation contract, the owner shall be furnished with a complete set of manufacturers' operating, maintenance, and preventive maintenance instructions, a parts list, and complete procurement information, including equipment numbers and descriptions. Operating staff persons shall also be provided with instructions for properly operating systems and equipment. Required information shall include energy ratings as needed for future conservation calculations.

8.11.B. Thermal and Acoustical Insulation

8.11.B1. Insulation within the building shall be provided to conserve energy, protect personnel, prevent vapor condensation, and reduce noise and vibration.

8.11.B2. Insulation on cold surfaces shall include an exterior vapor barrier. (Material that will not absorb or transmit moisture will not require a separate vapor barrier.)

8.11.B3. Insulation, including finishes and adhesives on the exterior surfaces of ducts and equipment, shall have a flame-spread rating of 25 or less and a smoke-developed rating of 50 or less as determined by an independent testing laboratory in accordance with NFPA 255. The smoke-development rating for pipe insulation shall not exceed 150. This includes mechanical refrigeration and distribution equipment and hot water distribution equipment such as valves, pumps, chillers, etc.

▼ **8.11.B4.** If duct linings are used, they shall meet the erosion test method described in ASTM C1071. These linings (including coatings, adhesives, and exterior surface insulation of pipes and ducts in spaces used as air supply plenums) shall have a flame-spread rating of 25 or less and a smoke-developed rating of 50 or less, as determined by an independent testing laboratory in accordance with NFPA 255. Duct lining may not be installed down-
▲ stream of humidifiers.

8.11.B5. In facilities undergoing major renovations, existing accessible insulation shall be inspected, repaired, and/or replaced as appropriate.

8.11.C. Steam and Hot Water Systems

8.11.C1. Boilers shall have the capacity, based on the net ratings published by the Hydronics Institute or another acceptable national standard, to supply not less than 70 percent of the normal requirements of all systems and equipment. Their number and arrangement shall accommodate facility needs despite the breakdown or routine maintenance of any one boiler. The capacity of the remaining boiler(s) shall be sufficient to provide hot water service for clinical, dietary, and resident use; steam for dietary purposes; and heating for general resident rooms. However, reserve capacity for facility space heating is not required in geographic areas where a design dry-bulb temperature of 25°F (-4°C) or more represents not less than 99 percent of the total hours in any one heating month as noted in ASHRAE's *Handbook of Fundamentals*, under the "Table for Climatic Conditions for the United States."

8.11.C2. Boiler accessories, including feed pumps, heat-circulating pumps, condensate return pumps, fuel oil pumps, and waste heat boilers, shall be connected and installed to provide both normal and standby service.

8.11.C3. Supply and return mains and risers for cooling, heating, and steam systems shall be equipped with valves to isolate the various sections of each system. Each piece of equipment shall have valves at the supply and return ends, except for vacuum condensate returns, which do not require valves at each piece of equipment.

8.11.D. Air Conditioning, Heating, and Ventilation Systems

▼ **8.11.D1.** The ventilation rates shown in Table 6, as applicable, shall be used only as model standards; they do not preclude the use of higher, more appropriate rates. All rooms and areas in the facility shall have provision for positive ventilation. Though natural window ventilation may be utilized where weather and outside air quality permit, use of mechanical ventilation should be considered for interior areas and during periods of temperature extremes. Non-central air-handling systems, e.g., through-the-wall fan coil units, may be utilized. Fans serving exhaust systems shall be located at the discharge end and shall be readily serviceable. Exhaust systems may be combined to enhance the efficiency of recovery devices required for energy conservation.

a. When appropriate, mechanical ventilation should employ an economizer cycle that uses outside air to reduce heating-and-cooling-system loads. Filtering will be necessary when outside air is used as part of the mechanical ventilation system. Innovative design that provides for additional energy conservation while meeting the intent of these standards for acceptable resident care should be considered.

b. Fresh air intakes shall be located at least 25 feet (7.62 meters) from exhaust outlets of ventilating systems, combustion equipment stacks, medical-surgical vacuum systems, plumbing vents, or areas that may collect vehicular exhaust or other noxious fumes. (Prevailing winds and/or proximity to other structures may require greater clearances.) The bottom of outdoor air intakes serving central ventilating systems shall be as high as practical, but at least 6 feet (1.83 meters) above ground level, or, if installed above roof, 3 feet (0.91 meter) above roof level. Exhaust outlets from areas that may be contaminated shall be above roof level and arranged to minimize recirculation of exhaust air into the building.

▲

c. The ventilation systems shall be designed and balanced to provide directional flow as shown in Table 6.

▼ d. All central ventilation or air conditioning systems shall be equipped with filters with efficiencies equal to, or greater than, those specified in Table 7. Filter efficiencies, tested in accordance with ASHRAE Standard 52-76, shall be average. Filter frames shall be durable and proportioned to provide an airtight fit with the enclosing duct work. All joints between filter segments and the enclosing ductwork shall have gaskets or seals ▲ to provide a positive seal against air leakage.

e. Air-handling duct systems shall meet the requirements of NFPA 90A and those contained herein.

f. Fire and smoke dampers shall be constructed, located, and installed in accordance with the requirements of NFPA 101 and 90A. Fans, dampers, and detectors shall be interconnected so that damper activation will not damage ducts. Maintenance access shall be provided at all dampers. All damper locations should be shown on drawings. Dampers should be activated by fire or smoke sensor, not by fan cutoff alone.

Switching systems for restarting fans may be installed for fire department use in evacuating smoke after a fire has been controlled. However, provisions should be made to avoid possible damage to the system because of closed dampers.

When smoke partitions are required, heating, ventilating, and air conditioning zones shall be coordinated with compartmentation insofar as practical to minimize the need to penetrate fire and smoke partitions.

continued on page 73

Table 6

Pressure Relationships and Ventilation of Certain Areas of Nursing Homes[1]

Area designation	Air movement relationship to adjacent area[2]	Minimum air changes of outdoor air per hour[3]	Minimum total air changes per hour[4]	All air exhausted directly to outdoors[5]	Recirculated by means of room units[6]	Relative humidity[7] (%)	Design temperature[8] (degrees F)
PATIENT CARE							
Patient room	—	2	2	—	—	50-60	70-75
Patient area corridor	—	—	2	—	—	45-60	—
Toilet room	In	—	10	Yes	—	—	—
DIAGNOSTIC AND TREATMENT							
Examination	—	2	6	—	—	—	75
Physical therapy	In	2	6	—	—	—	75
Occupational therapy	In	2	6	—	—	—	75
Soiled workroom or soiled holding	In	2	10	Yes	No	—	—
Clean workroom or clean holding	Out	2	4	—	—	(Max.) 70	75
STERILIZING AND SUPPLY							
Sterilizer exhaust room[9]	In	—	10	Yes	No	—	—
Linen and trash chute room	In	—	10	Yes	No	—	—
Laundry, general	—	2	10	Yes	No	—	—
Soiled linen sorting and storage	In	—	10	Yes	No	—	—
Clean linen storage	Out	—	2	Yes	No	—	—
SERVICE							
Food preparation center[10]	—	2	10	Yes	Yes	—	—
Warewashing room	In	—	10	Yes	Yes	—	—
Dietary day storage	—	—	2	Yes	No	—	—
Janitor closet	In	—	10	Yes	No	—	—
Bathroom	In	—	10	Yes	No	—	75

Table 6 Notes

1 The ventilation rates in this table cover ventilation for comfort, as well as for asepsis and odor control in areas of acute care hospitals that directly affect patient care and are determined based on health care facilities being predominantly "no smoking" facilities. Where smoking may be allowed, ventilation rates will need adjustments. Refer to ASHRAE *Standard 62-1989, Ventilation for Acceptable Indoor Air Quality,* and *ASHRAE Handbook of Fundamentals,* latest edition. Areas where specific ventilation rates are not given in the table shall be ventilated in accordance with these ASHRAE publications. Specialized patient care areas, including organ transplant units, burn units, specialty procedure rooms, etc., shall have additional ventilation provisions for air quality control as may be appropriate. OSHA standards and/or NIOSH criteria require special ventilation requirements for employee health and safety within health care facilities.

2 Design of the ventilation system shall, insofar as possible, provide that air movement is from "clean to less clean" areas. However, continuous compliance may be impractical with full utilization of some forms of variable air volume and load shedding systems that may be used for energy conservation. Areas that do require positive and continuous control are noted in the table with "Out" or "In" to indicate the required direction of air movement in relation to the space named. Rate of air movement may, of course, be varied as needed within the limits required for positive control. Where indication of air movement direction is enclosed in parentheses, continuous directional control is required only when the specialized equipment or device is in use or where room use may otherwise compromise the intent of movement from clean to less clean. Air movement for rooms indicated in the table with dashes and nonpatient areas may vary as necessary to satisfy the requirements of those spaces. Additional adjustments may be needed when space is unused or unoccupied and air systems are deenergized or reduced.

3 To satisfy exhaust needs, replacement air from outside is necessary. Table 2 does not attempt to describe specific amounts of outside air to be supplied to individual spaces except for certain areas such as those listed. Distribution of

continued on next page

the outside air, added to the system to balance required exhaust, shall be as required by good engineering practice.

4. Number of air changes may be reduced when the room is unoccupied if provisions are made to ensure that the number of air changes indicated is reestablished any time the space is being utilized. Adjustments shall include provisions so that the direction of air movement shall remain the same when the number of air changes is reduced. Areas not indicated as having continuous directional control may have ventilation systems shut down when space is unoccupied and ventilation is not otherwise needed.

5. Air from areas with contamination and/or odor problems shall be exhausted to the outside and not recirculated to other areas. Note that individual circumstances may require special consideration for air exhaust to outside, e.g., an intensive care unit in which patients with pulmonary infection are treated, and rooms for burn patients.

6. Because of cleaning difficulty and potential for buildup of contamination, recirculating room units shall not be used in areas marked "No." Isolation and intensive care unit rooms may be ventilated by reheat induction units in which only the primary air supplied from a central system passes through the reheat unit. Gravity-type heating or cooling units such as radiators or convectors shall not be used in operating rooms and other special care areas.

7. The ranges listed are the minimum and maximum limits where control is specifically needed.

8. Dual temperature indications (such as 70-75) are for an upper and lower variable range at which the room temperature must be controlled. A single figure indicates a heating or cooling capacity of at least the indicated temperature. This is usually applicable when patients may be undressed and require a warmer environment. Nothing in these guidelines shall be construed as precluding the use of temperatures lower than those noted when the patients' comfort and medical conditions make lower temperatures desirable. Unoccupied areas such as storage rooms shall have temperatures appropriate for the function intended.

9. Specific OSHA regulations regarding ethylene oxide (ETO) use have been promulgated. 29 CRF Part 1910.1047 includes specific ventilation requirements including local exhaust of the ETO sterilizer area. Also see Section 7.31.D1r.

10. Food preparation centers shall have ventilation systems that have an excess air supply for "out" air movements when hoods are not in operation. The number of air changes may be reduced or varied to any extent required for odor control when the space is not in use. See Section 7.31.D1 for designation of hoods.

continued from page 71

▼ g. Non-central air-handling systems, e.g., through-the-wall coil units, should be equipped with filters rated at 80 percent arrestance or more.

8.11.E. Plumbing and Other Piping Systems

Unless otherwise specified herein, all plumbing systems shall be designed and installed in accordance with the *National Standard Plumbing Code,* chapter 14, "Medical Care Facility Plumbing Equipment."

8.11.E1. The following standards shall apply to plumbing fixtures:

a. The material used for plumbing fixtures shall be nonabsorptive and acid-resistant.

b. Water spouts used in lavatories and sinks shall have clearances adequate to avoid contaminating utensils and the contents of carafes, etc.

c. All fixtures used by medical and nursing staff and all lavatories used by food handlers shall be trimmed with valves that can be operated without hands (single-lever devices may be used). Blade handles used for this purpose shall not exceed 4½ inches (11.43 centimeters) in length. Handles on scrub sinks and clinical sinks shall be at least 6 inches (15.24 centimeters) long.

d. Clinical sinks shall have an integral trap wherein the upper portion of the water trap provides a visible seal.

e. Showers and tubs shall have a slip-resistant surface.

8.11.E2. The following standards shall apply to potable water supply systems:

a. Systems shall be designed to supply water at sufficient pressure to operate all fixtures and equipment during maximum demand. Supply capacity for hot- and cold-water piping shall be determined on the basis of fixture units, using recognized engineering standards. When the ratio of plumbing fixtures to occupants is proportionally more than required by the building occupancy and is in excess of 1,000 plumbing fixture units, a diversity factor is permitted.

b. Each water service main, branch main, riser, and branch to a group of fixtures shall have valves. Stop valves shall be provided for each fixture. Appropriate panels for access shall be provided at all valves where required.

c. Backflow preventers (vacuum breakers) shall be installed on hose bibs and supply nozzles used for connection of hoses or tubing in laboratories, housekeeping sinks, and bedpan-flushing attachments, etc.

d. Potable water storage vessels (hot and cold) not intended for constant use shall not be installed.

8.11.E3. The following standards shall apply to hot water systems:

a. The water-heating system shall have sufficient supply capacity at the temperatures and amounts indicated in Table 8. Water temperature is measured at the point of use or inlet to the equipment.

b. Hot-water distribution systems serving resident care areas shall be under constant recirculation to provide continuous hot water at each hot water outlet. The temperature of hot water for showers and bathing shall be appropriate for comfortable use but shall not exceed 110°F (43°C).

8.11.E4. The following standards shall apply to drainage systems:

a. Insofar as possible, drainage piping shall not be installed within the ceiling or exposed in food preparation centers, food serving facilities, food storage areas, central services, electronic data processing areas, electric closets, and other sensitive areas. Where exposed overhead drain piping in these areas is unavoidable, special provisions shall be made to protect the space below from leakage, condensation, or dust particles.

b. Building sewers shall discharge into community sewerage. Where such a system is not available, the facility shall treat its sewage in accordance with local and state regulations.

c. Kitchen grease traps shall be located and arranged to permit easy access.

8.11.E5. Any installation of nonflammable medical gas, air, or clinical vacuum systems shall comply with the requirements of NFPA 99. When any piping or supply of medical gases is installed, altered, or augmented, the altered zone shall be tested and certified as required by NFPA 99.

8.11.E6. All piping, except control-line tubing, shall be identified. All valves shall be tagged, and a valve schedule shall be provided to the facility owner for
▲ permanent record and reference.

8.12 Electrical Standards

8.12.A. General

8.12.A1. All material and equipment, including conductors, controls, and signaling devices, shall be installed to provide a complete electrical system in accordance with NFPA 70 and NFPA 99.

8.12.A2. All electrical installations and systems shall be tested to verify that the equipment has been installed and that it operates as designed.

▼ **8.12.A3.** Electrical systems for nursing facilities shall comply with applicable sections of NFPA 70.

8.12.A4. Lighting shall be engineered to the specific application. Table 9 may be used as a guideline.

a. The Illuminating Engineering Society of North America (IES) has developed recommended lighting budget figures for footcandle levels and
▲ watts per square foot.

▼ b. Approaches to buildings and parking lots, and all occupied spaces within buildings shall have fixtures for lighting.

c. Resident rooms shall have general lighting and night lighting. A reading light shall be provided for each resident. Flexible light arms, if used, shall be mechanically controlled to prevent the bulb from contacting the bed linen. At least one night light fixture in each patient room shall be controlled at the room entrance. All light controls in resident areas shall be quiet-operating.

d. Nursing unit corridors shall have general illumination with provisions for reducing light levels at night.

e. Excessive contrast in lighting levels that make effective sight adaptation difficult should be minimized.

8.12.A5. Receptacles (Convenience Outlets)

a. Each resident room shall have duplex-grounded receptacles. There shall be one at each side of the head of each bed and one on every other wall. Receptacles may be omitted from exterior walls where construction makes installation impractical.

b. Duplex-grounded receptacles for general use shall be installed approximately 50 feet (15.24 meters) apart in all corridors and within 25 feet (7.62 meters) of corridor ends.

c. Electrical receptacle coverplates or electrical receptacles supplied from the emergency system shall be distinctively colored or marked for identification. If color is used for identification purposes, the same color should be used throughout the facility.

d. Ground-fault-interrupters shall comply with NFPA 70.

8.12.B. Emergency Electrical Service

8.12.B1. As a minimum, nursing facilities or sections thereof shall have emergency electrical systems as required in NFPA 101 and Chapter 16 of ▲ NFPA 99.

8.12.B2. When the nursing facility is a distinct part of an acute-care hospital, it may use the emergency generator system for required emergency lighting and power, if such sharing does not reduce hospital services. Life support systems and their respective areas shall be subject to applicable standards of Section 7.32.

▼ **8.12.B3.** An emergency electrical source shall provide lighting and/or power during an interruption of the normal electric supply. Where stored fuel is required, storage capacity shall permit continuous operation for at least 24 hours. Fuel storage for electricity generation shall be separate from heating fuels. If the use of heating fuel for diesel engines is considered after the required 24-hour supply has been exhausted, positive valving and filtration shall be provided to avoid entry of water and/or contaminants.

8.12.B4. The source(s) of required emergency electric services shall be in accordance with Chapter 16 of NFPA 99.

8.12.B5. A required emergency generating set, including a prime mover and generator, shall be located on the premises and shall conform to NFPA 99 and NFPA 110.

8.12.B6. Local codes and regulations may have additional requirements.

8.12.B7. Exhaust systems (including locations, mufflers, and vibration isolators) for internal combustion engines shall be designed and installed to minimize objectionable noise. Where a generator is routinely used to reduce peak loads, protection of patient areas from excessive noise may become a critical issue.

8.12.C. Fire Alarm System
Fire alarm and detection systems shall be provided in ▲ compliance with NFPA 101, NFPA 72, and NFPA 72E.

Table 7

Filter Efficiencies for Central Ventilation and Air Conditioning Systems in Nursing Facilities

Area Designation	Mininum number of filter beds	Filter efficiencies (%)	
		Filter bed no. 1	Filter bed no. 2
All areas for inpatient care, treatment, and/or diagnosis, and those areas providing direct service or clean supplies	2	25	80
Administrative, bulk storage, soiled holding, laundries, food preparation areas	1	25	

Note: Filter efficiency ratings are based on ASHRAE Standard 52-76.

Table 8

Hot Water Use

	Resident Care Areas	Dietary[1]	Laundry
Liters per second per bed*	0.0033	0.0020	0.0021
Gallons per hour per bed*	3	2	2
Temperature (Centigrade)**	43	49	71**
Temperature (Fahrenheit)**	110 (max.)	120 (min.)	160 (min.)**

1 Provisions may be made to provide 180° Fahrenheit (82°C) rinse water at warewasher (may be by separate booster).

* Quantities indicated for design demand of hot water are for general reference minimums and shall not substitute for accepted engineering design procedures using actual number and types of fixtures to be installed. Design will also be affected by temperatures of cold water used for mixing, length of run, and insulation relative to heat loss, etc. As an example, total quantity of hot water needed will be less when temperature available at the outlet is very nearly that of the source tank and the cold water used for tempering is relatively warm.

** However, it is emphasized that this does not imply that all water used would be at this temperature. Water temperatures required for acceptable laundry results will vary according to type of cycle, time of operation, and formula of soap and bleach as well as type and degree of soil. Lower temperatures may be adequate for most procedures in many facilities but higher temperatures should be available when needed for special conditions.

Nursing Facilities

Table 9

Illumination Values for Nursing Facilities

Area/Activity[2]	Lux[1,2,4]	Footcandles[1,2,4]
Barber/Beauty area	500	50
Corridors		
Nursing areas—day	200	20
Nursing areas—night	100	10
Dietary	500	50
Elevators	150	15
Examination room	500	50
Employee lounge	500	50
Employee locker room	200	20
Linens		
Sorting soiled linen	300	30
Central (clean) linen supply	300	30
Linen rooms/closets	100	10
Janitor closet	150	15
Lobby		
General	200	20
Receptionist	300	30
Administrative spaces		
General office	500	50
Medical records	500	50
Conference/interview area/room	500	50
Mechanical/electrical room/space	300	30
Nursing station		
General	300	30
Desk	500	50
Medication area	500	50
Nourishment center	500	50
Corridors—day	200	20
Corridors—night	100	10
Occupational therapy		
Work area, general	300	30
Work benches/tables	500	50
Resident room		
General[5]	150	15
Reading/bed	300	30
Toilet	300	30
Physical therapy	300	30
Resident lounge		
General	150	15
Reading	300	30
Resident dining	300	30
Speech therapy	300	30
Stairways	150	15
Storage, general	200	20
Toilet/shower/bath	300	30
Utility, clean and soiled	300	30
Waiting area		
General	200	20
Reading	300	30

Table 9 Notes

1 The illuminance values in the table are taken from the IES Lighting Handbook Application volume. The values in the table are from the mid or high range found in the IES Handbook.

2 Illuminance valves are given in lux with an approximate equivalence in footcandles and so such are intended as target (nominal) value with deviations expected.

3 The area/activity categories are intended for generic types of interior spaces. Where a specific area/activity cannot be found in the table, the values for similar areas/activities should be used.

4 Higher or lower illuminance values may be required based on the clinical needs of the residents. For example, a resident with Alzheimer's disease may require lower illuminance values.

5 Variable (dimming or switching).

9. OUTPATIENT FACILITIES

9.1 General

9.1.A. Section Applicability
This section applies to the outpatient unit, which may be a separate freestanding facility within a nonmedical facility or part of a health maintenance organization (HMO) or other health service. This section does not apply to the offices of private-practice physicians in commercial office space and should not be applied to such offices in ancillary outpatient facilities.

The general standards set forth in Sections 9.1 and 9.2 apply to each of the items below. Additions and/or modifications shall be made as described for the specific facility type. (See Section 7 for emergency and outpatient services that are part of the general hospital.)

Specialty facilities such as those for renal dialysis, cancer treatment, mental health, rehabilitation, etc., have needs that are not addressed here. They must satisfy additional conditions to meet respective programs' standards.

Specifically described are:

9.1.A1. Primary Care Outpatient Center (Section 9.3).

9.1.A2. The Small Primary (Neighborhood) Outpatient Facility (Section 9.4).

9.1.A3. The Outpatient Surgical Facility (Section 9.5).

9.1.A4. The Freestanding Emergency Facility (Section 9.6).

9.1.A5. Freestanding Birthing Center (Section 9.7).

9.1.B. Outpatient Facility Classification
Except for the emergency unit, the outpatient facilities described herein are used primarily by patients capable of traveling into, around, and out of the facility unassisted. This includes the handicapped disabled confined to wheelchairs. Occasional facility use by stretcher patients should not be used as a basis for more restrictive institutional occupancy classifications.

Facilities shall comply with the "Ambulatory Health Care Centers" section of NFPA 101, in addition to details herein, where patients incapable of self-preservation or those receiving inhalation anesthesia are treated. The "Business Occupancy" section of NFPA 101 applies to other types of outpatient facilities. Outpatient units that are part of another facility may be subject to the additional requirements of the other occupancy.

References are made to Section 7, General Hospital, for certain service spaces such as the operating rooms of the outpatient surgical unit. Those references are intended only for the specific areas indicated.

9.1.C. Facility Access
Where the outpatient unit is part of another facility, separation and access shall be maintained as described in NFPA 101. Building entrances used to reach the outpatient services shall be at grade level, clearly marked, and located so that patients need not go through other activity areas. (Lobbies of multi-occupancy buildings may be shared.) Design shall preclude unrelated traffic within the unit.

9.1.D. Functional Program Provision
Each project sponsor shall provide a functional program for the facility. (See Section 1.1.F.)

9.1.E. Shared/Purchased Services
When services are shared or purchased, space and equipment should be modified or eliminated to avoid unnecessary duplication.

9.1.F. Location
Community outpatient units shall be conveniently accessible to patients and staff via available public transportation.

9.1.G. Parking
In the absence of a formal parking study, parking for outpatient facilities shall be provided at the rate noted for each type of unit. On-street parking, if available, may satisfy part of this requirement unless described otherwise. If the facility is located in a densely populated area where a large percentage of patients arrive as pedestrians; or if adequate public parking is available nearby; or if the facility is conveniently accessible via public transportation, adjustments to this standard may be made with approval of the appropriate authorities.

9.1.H. Privacy for Patients
Each facility design shall ensure patient audible and visual privacy and dignity during interviews, examinations, treatment, and recovery.

9.2 Common Elements for Outpatient Facilities

The following shall apply to each outpatient facility described herein with additions and/or modifications as noted for each specific type. Special consideration shall be given to needs of children for pediatric services.

9.2.A. Administration and Public Areas

9.2.A1. Entrance. Located at grade level and able to accommodate wheelchairs.

9.2.A2. Public services shall include:

a. Conveniently accessible wheelchair storage.

b. A reception and information counter or desk.

c. Waiting space(s). Where an organized pediatric service is part of the outpatient facility, provisions shall be made for separating pediatric and adult patients.

d. Conveniently accessible public toilets.

e. Conveniently accessible public telephone(s).

f. Conveniently accessible drinking fountain(s).

9.2.A3. Interview space(s) for private interviews related to social service, credit, etc., shall be provided.

9.2.A4. General or individual office(s) for business transactions, records, administrative, and professional staffs shall be provided.

9.2.A5. Clerical space or rooms for typing, clerical work, and filing, separated from public areas for confidentiality, shall be provided.

9.2.A6. Multipurpose room(s) equipped for visual aids shall be provided for conferences, meetings, and health education purposes.

9.2.A7. Special storage for staff personal effects with locking drawers or cabinets (may be individual desks or cabinets) shall be provided. Such storage shall be near individual workstations and staff controlled.

9.2.A8. General storage facilities for supplies and equipment shall be provided as needed for continuing operation.

9.2.B. Clinical Facilities

As needed, the following elements shall be provided for clinical services to satisfy the functional program:

9.2.B1. General-purpose examination room(s). For medical, obstetrical, and similar examinations, rooms shall have a minimum floor area of 80 square feet (7.43 square meters), excluding vestibules, toilets, and closets. Room arrangement should permit at least 2 feet 8 inches (81.28 centimeters) clearance at each side and at the foot of the examination table. A handwashing fixture and a counter or shelf space for writing shall be provided.

9.2.B2. Special-purpose examination rooms. Rooms for special clinics such as eye, ear, nose, and throat examinations, if provided, shall be designed and outfitted to accommodate procedures and equipment used. A handwashing fixture and a counter or shelf space for writing shall be provided.

9.2.B3. Treatment room(s). Rooms for minor surgical and cast procedures (if provided) shall have a minimum floor area of 120 square feet (11.15 square meters), excluding vestibule, toilet, and closets. The minimum room dimension shall be 10 feet (3.05 meters). A handwashing fixture and a counter or shelf for writing shall be provided.

9.2.B4. Observation room(s). Observation rooms for the isolation of suspect or disturbed patients shall have a minimum floor area of 80 square feet (7.43 square meters) and shall be convenient to a nurse or control station. This is to permit close observation of patients and to minimize possibilities of patients' hiding, escape, injury, or suicide. An examination room may be modified to accommodate this function. A toilet room with lavatory should be immediately accessible.

9.2.B5. Nurses station(s). A work counter, communication system, space for supplies, and provisions for charting shall be provided.

9.2.B6. Drug distribution station. This may be a part of the nurses station and shall include a work counter, sink, refrigerator, and locked storage for biologicals and drugs.

9.2.B7. Clean storage. A separate room or closet for storing clean and sterile supplies shall be provided. This storage shall be in addition to that of cabinets and shelves.

9.2.B8. Soiled holding. Provisions shall be made for separate collection, storage, and disposal of soiled materials.

9.2.B9. Sterilizing facilities. A system for sterilizing equipment and supplies shall be provided. Sterilizing procedures may be done on- or off-site, or disposables may be used to satisfy functional needs.

9.2.B10. Wheelchair storage space. Such storage shall be out of the direct line of traffic.

9.2.C. Radiology

Basic diagnostic procedures (these may be part of the outpatient service, off-site, shared, by contract, or by referral) shall be provided, including the following:

9.2.C1. Radiographic room(s). See Section 7.10 for special requirements.

9.2.C2. Film processing facilities.

9.2.C3. Viewing and administrative areas(s).

9.2.C4. Storage facilities for exposed film.

9.2.C5. Toilet rooms with handwashing facilities accessible to fluoroscopy room(s), if fluoroscopic procedures are part of the program.

9.2.C6. Dressing rooms or booths, as required by services provided, with convenient toilet access.

9.2.D. Laboratory

Facilities shall be provided within the outpatient department, or through an effective contract arrangement with a nearby hospital or laboratory service, for hematology, clinical chemistry, urinalysis, cytology, pathology, and bacteriology. If these services are provided on contract, the following laboratory facilities shall also be provided in (or be immediately accessible to) the outpatient facility:

9.2.D1. Laboratory work counter(s), with sink, vacuum, gas, and electric services.

9.2.D2. Lavatory(ies) or counter sink(s) equipped for handwashing.

9.2.D3. Storage cabinet(s) or closet(s).

9.2.D4. Specimen collection facilities with a water closet and lavatory. Blood collection facilities shall have seating space, a work counter, and handwashing facilities.

9.2.E. Housekeeping Room(s)

At least one housekeeping room per floor shall be provided. It shall contain a service sink and storage for housekeeping supplies and equipment.

9.2.F. Staff Facilities

Staff locker rooms and toilets shall be provided.

9.2.G. Engineering Service and Equipment Areas

The following shall be provided (these may be shared with other services provided capacity is appropriate for overall use):

9.2.G1. Equipment room(s) for boilers, mechanical equipment, and electrical equipment.

9.2.G2. Storage room(s) for supplies and equipment.

9.2.G3. Waste processing services:

a. Space and facilities shall be provided for the sanitary storage and disposal of waste.

b. If incinerators and/or trash chutes are used, they shall comply with NFPA 82.

c. Incinerators, if used, shall also conform to the standards prescribed by area air pollution regulations.

9.2.H. Details and Finishes

9.2.H1. Details shall comply with the following standards:

a. Minimum public corridor width shall be 5 feet (1.52 meters). Work corridors less than 6 feet (1.83 meters) long may be 4 feet (1.22 meters) wide.

b. Each building shall have at least two exits that are remote from each other. Other details relating to exits and fire safety shall comply with NFPA 101 and the standards outlined herein.

c. Items such as drinking fountains, telephone booths, vending machines, etc., shall not restrict corridor traffic or reduce the corridor width below the required minimum. Out-of-traffic storage space for portable equipment shall be provided.

d. The minimum door width for patient use shall be 2 feet 10 inches (86.36 centimeters). If the outpatient facility services hospital inpatients, the minimum width of doors to rooms used by hospital inpatients transported in beds shall be 3 feet 8 inches (1.12 meters).

e. Doors, sidelights, borrowed lights, and windows glazed to within 18 inches (45.72 centimeters) of the floor shall be constructed of safety glass, wired glass, or plastic glazing material that resists breakage and creates no dangerous cutting edges when broken. Similar materials shall be used in wall openings of playrooms and exercise rooms unless otherwise required for fire safety. Glazing materials used for shower doors and bath enclosures shall be safety glass or plastic.

f. Threshold and expansion joint covers shall be flush with the floor surface to facilitate use of wheelchairs and carts.

g. Handwashing facilities shall be located and arranged to permit proper use and operation. Particular care shall be taken to provide the required clearance for blade-type handle operation.

h. Provisions for hand drying shall be included at all handwashing facilities except scrub sinks.

i. Radiation protection for X-ray and gamma ray installations shall comply with Section 7.10.

j. The minimum ceiling height shall be 7 feet 10 inches (2.39 meters) with the following exceptions:

i.   Boiler rooms shall have ceiling clearances not less than 2 feet 6 inches (76.20 centimeters) above the main boiler header and connecting piping.

ii. Radiographic and other rooms containing ceiling-mounted equipment shall have ceilings of sufficient height to accommodate the equipment and/or fixtures.

iii. Ceilings in corridors, storage rooms, toilet rooms, and other minor rooms shall not be less than 7 feet 8 inches (2.34 meters).

iv. Tracks, rails, and pipes suspended along the path of normal traffic shall be not less than 6 feet 8 inches (2.03 meters) above the floor.

k. Rooms containing heat-producing equipment (such as boiler or heater rooms) shall be insulated and ventilated to prevent occupied adjacent floor or wall surfaces from exceeding a temperature 10 degrees above the ambient room temperature.

9.2.H2. Finishes shall comply with the following standards:

a. Cubicle curtains and draperies shall be non-combustible or flame-retardant and shall pass both the large- and small-scale tests required by NFPA 701.

b. The flame-spread and smoke-developed ratings of finishes shall comply with Section 7.29 and Table 10. Where possible, the use of materials known to produce large amounts of noxious gases shall be avoided.

c. Floor materials shall be readily cleanable and appropriately wear-resistant. In all areas subject to wet cleaning, floor materials shall not be physically affected by liquid germicidal and cleaning solutions. Floors subject to traffic while wet, including showers and bath areas, shall have a nonslip surface.

d. Wall finishes shall be washable and, in the proximity of plumbing fixtures, shall be smooth and moisture resistant.

e. Wall bases in areas that are frequently subject to wet cleaning shall be monolithic and coved with the floor; tightly sealed to the wall; and constructed without voids.

f. Floor and wall areas penetrated by pipes, ducts, and conduits shall be tightly sealed to minimize entry of rodents and insects. Joints of structural elements shall be similarly sealed.

9.2.I. Design and Construction, Including Fire-Resistive Standards

9.2.I1. Construction and structural elements of free-standing outpatient facilities shall comply with recognized model-building-code requirements for offices and to the standards contained herein. Outpatient facilities that are an integral part of the hospital or that share common areas and functions shall comply with the construction standards for general hospitals. See applicable sections of this document for additional details.

9.2.I2. Interior finish materials shall have flame-spread and smoke-production limitations as described in NFPA 101. Wall finishes less than 4 mil thick applied over a noncombustible material are not subject to flame-spread rating requirements.

9.2.I3. Building insulation materials, unless sealed on all sides and edges, shall have a flame-spread rating of 25 or less and a smoke-developed rating of 150 or less when tested in accordance with NFPA 255.

9.2.J. Provision for Disasters
Seismic-force resistance of new construction for outpatient facilities shall comply with Section 1.4 and shall be given an importance factor of one. Where the outpatient facility is part of an existing building, that facility shall comply with applicable local codes. Special design provisions shall be made for buildings in regions that have sustained loss of life or damage to buildings from hurricanes, tornadoes, floods, or other natural disasters.

▼ **9.2.K. Elevators**

9.2.K1. All buildings with patient or service areas on other than the grade-level main entrance floor shall have electric or hydraulic elevators. Installation and testing of elevators shall comply with ANSI A117.1.

a. Cars shall have a minimum inside floor dimension of not less than 5 feet (1.52 meters).

b. Elevators shall be equipped with an automatic two-way leveling device with an accuracy of + ½ inch (+ 1.27 centimeters).

c. Elevator controls, alarm buttons, and telephones shall be accessible to wheelchair occupants and usable by the blind.

d. Heat-sensitive call buttons shall not be used. Where light beams are used to activate safety stops, these shall be in addition to door-edge stops and shall be deactivated by smoke detectors located at each landing.

9.2.K2. Elevator inspections and tests shall be made. The owner shall be furnished with written certification that the installation meets all applicable safety regulations and codes and the standards set forth in this section.

9.2.L. Mechanical Standards

The following requirements shall apply to outpatient facilities that are freestanding; or within a nonmedical facility; or part of a health maintenance organization or other health service; or physically attached to a general hospital but independent of hospital areas, services, or equipment.

Where general hospital areas, services, and/or equipment are shared with the outpatient facility, the mechanical standards of Section 7.31 shall apply only to the specific areas, services, and/or equipment being shared (i.e., operating room, recovery room, etc.).

9.2.L1. General mechanical systems standards are as follows:

a. The mechanical system should be subject to general review for overall efficiency and life-cycle cost. Details for cost-effective implementation of design features are interrelated and too numerous (as well as too basic) to list individually. Recognized engineering procedures shall be followed for the most economical and effective results. A well-designed system can generally achieve energy efficiency at minimal additional cost and simultaneously provide for improved patient comfort. Different geographic areas may have climatic variations and use conditions that favor one system over another in terms of overall cost and efficiency. For instance, adiabatic cooling and dead-load controls may be common designs for certain western states but relatively unknown elsewhere. In no case shall patient care or safety be sacrificed for conservation.

b. Remodeling and work in existing facilities may present special problems. As practicality and funding permit, existing insulation, weather stripping, etc., shall be brought up to standard for maximum economy and efficiency. Consideration shall be given to additional work that may be needed to achieve this.

c. Facility design considerations shall include site, building mass, orientation, configuration, fenestration, and other features relative to passive and active energy systems.

Table 10

Flame-Spread and Smoke-Production Limitations on Interior Finishes

	Flame-spread rating	Smoke-production rating
Walls and ceiling		
Exitways, storage rooms, and areas of unusual fire hazard	25 or less (ASTM E84)	450 or less* (NFPA 258)
All other areas (ASTM E84)	75 or less (NFPA 258)	450 or less
Floors**		
Corridors and means of egress	Minimum of .45 watts/cm² (NFPA 253, Floor Radiant Panel Test)	

* Average of flaming and nonflaming values.

**See Section 1.3 for requirements relative to carpeting areas that may be subject to use by handicapped individuals. These areas include offices, waiting spaces, etc., as well as corridors that might be used by handicapped employees, visitors, or staff.

d. Insofar as practical, the facility shall include provisions for recovery of waste cooling and heating energy (ventilation, exhaust, water and steam discharge, cooling towers, incinerators, etc.).

e. Facility design shall include consideration of recognized procedures such as variable-air-volume systems, load shedding, programmed controls for unoccupied periods (nights and weekends, etc.), and use of natural ventilation, site and climatic conditions permitting. Systems with excessive operational and/or maintenance costs that negate long-range energy savings should be avoided.

f. Controls for air-handling systems shall be designed with an economizer cycle to use outside air for cooling and/or heating. (Use of mechanically circulated outside air does not reduce need for filtration.) It may be practical in many areas to reduce or shut down mechanical ventilation during appropriate climatic and patient-care conditions and to use open windows for ventilation.

g. Ventilation standards permit maximum use of simplified systems including those for variable-air-volume (VAV) supply. However, care must be taken in design to avoid possibility of large temperature differentials, high-velocity supply, excessive noise, and air stagnation, etc. Air supply and exhaust in rooms for which no minimum air change rate is noted may vary down to zero in response to room load. Temperature control shall also comply with these standards. To maintain asepsis control, airflow supply and exhaust should generally be controlled to insure movement of air from "clean" to "less clean" areas.

h. Prior to acceptance of the facility, all mechanical systems shall be tested, balanced, and operated to demonstrate to the design engineer or to his or her representative that the installation and performance of these systems conform to design intent. Test results shall be documented for maintenance files.

i. Upon completion of the equipment installation contract, the owner shall be furnished with a complete set of manufacturers' operating, maintenance, and preventive maintenance instructions, a parts lists, and complete procurement information including equipment numbers and descriptions. Operating staff persons shall also be provided with instructions for properly operating systems and equipment. Required information shall include energy ratings needed for future conservation calculations.

▼ **9.2.L2.** Thermal and acoustical insulation shall meet the following standards:

a. Insulation within the building shall be provided to conserve energy, protect personnel, prevent vapor condensation, and reduce noise and vibration.

b. Insulation on cold surfaces shall include an exterior vapor barrier. (Material that will not absorb or transmit moisture need not have a separate vapor barrier.)

▲

c. Insulation, including finishes and adhesives on the exterior surfaces of ducts and equipment, shall have a flame-spread rating of 25 or less and a smoke-developed rating of 50 or less as determined by an independent testing laboratory in accordance with NFPA 255. The smoke-development rating for pipe insulation shall not exceed 150. This includes mechanical refrigeration and distribution equipment and hot water distribution equipment such as valves, pumps, chillers, etc.

▼ d. If duct linings are used, they shall meet the erosion test method described in ASTM C1071. These linings (including coatings, adhesives, and exterior surface insulation of pipes and ducts in spaces used as air supply plenums) shall have a flame-spread rating of 25 or less and a smoke-developed rating of 50 or less, as determined by an independent testing laboratory in accordance with NFPA 255. Duct lining may not be installed
▲ downstream of humidifiers.

e. Duct lining exposed to air movement shall not be used in ducts serving operating rooms, delivery rooms, LDR rooms, and intensive care units. Where its use cannot be avoided, terminal filters of at least 90 percent efficiency shall be installed downstream of all lining material. This requirement shall not apply to mixing boxes and acoustical traps that have special coverings over such linings.

f. Asbestos insulation shall not be used in health facilities.

g. Existing accessible insulation within areas of facilities to be modernized shall be inspected, repaired, and/or replaced, as appropriate.

9.2.L3. Mechanical standards for steam and hot water systems (where used) are as follows:

a. Boilers shall have the capacity, based upon the net ratings published by the Hydronics Institute or another acceptable national standard, to supply the normal heating, hot water, and steam requirements of all systems and equipment.

b. Boiler accessories including feed pumps/heating circulating pumps, condensate return pumps, fuel oil pumps, and waste heat boilers shall be connected and installed to provide both normal and standby service.

c. Supply and return mains and risers for cooling, heating, and steam systems shall be equipped with valves to isolate the various sections of each system. Each piece of the equipment shall have valves at the supply and return ends. However, vacuum condensate returns need not be valved at each piece of equipment.

9.2.L4. Air conditioning, heating, and ventilating systems shall comply with the following standards:

a. The ventilation rates shown in Table 2 shall be used only as model standards; they do not preclude the use of higher, more appropriate rates. All rooms and areas in the facility shall have provisions for ventilation. Though natural window ventilation for noncritical areas may be employed, weather permitting, mechanical ventilation should be considered for use in interior areas and during periods of temperature extremes. Fans serving exhaust systems shall be located at the discharge end and shall be readily serviceable. Exhaust systems may be combined to enhance the efficiency of recovery devices required for energy conservation.

i. Facility design should utilize energy conserving mechanisms including recovery devices, variable air volume, load shedding, and systems to shut down or reduce ventilation of unoccupied areas, insofar as patient care is not compromised. When appropriate, mechanical ventilation should employ an economizer cycle that uses outside air to reduce heating- and cooling-system loads. Filtering requirements shall be met when outside air is used as part of the mechanical ventilation system. Innovative design that provides for additional energy conservation while meeting the intent of these standards for acceptable patient care should be considered (see Appendix B).

ii. Fresh air intakes shall be located at least 25 feet (7.62 meters) from exhaust outlets of ventilating systems, combustion equipment stacks, medical-surgical vacuum systems, plumbing vents, or areas that may collect vehicular exhaust or other noxious fumes. (Prevailing winds and/or proximity to other structures may require greater clearances.) Plumbing and vacuum vents that terminate at a level above the top of the air intake may be located as close as 10 feet (3.05 meters). The bottom of outdoor air intakes serving central systems shall be as high as practical, but at least 6 feet (1.83 meters) above ground level, or, if installed above the roof, 3 feet (91.44 centimeters) above the roof level. Exhaust outlets from areas that may be contaminated shall be above roof level and arranged to minimize recirculation of exhaust air into the building.

iii. The ventilation systems shall be designed and balanced to provide directional flow as shown in Table 2. (See also note 8 of Table 2 for reductions and shutdown of ventilation systems during room vacancy.)

iv. Operating room air supply shall be from ceiling outlets near the center of the work area for effective air movement control. Return air shall be from the floor level. Each operating room shall have at least two return air inlets located as remotely from each other as practical. (Design should consider turbulence and other factors of air movement to minimize fall of particulates onto sterile surfaces.)

v. Each space routinely used for administering inhalation anesthesia shall be equipped with a scavenging system to vent waste gases. If a vacuum system is used, the gas-collecting system shall be arranged so that it does not disturb patients' respiratory systems. Gases from the scavenging system shall be exhausted directly to the outside. The anesthesia gas scavenging exhausts directly to the outside and is not part of the recirculation system. Separate scavenging systems are not required for areas where gases are used only occasionally, such as the emergency room, and offices for routine dental work, etc. Acceptable concentration of anesthetizing agents are unknown at this time. The absence of specific data makes it difficult to set specific standards. However, any scavenging system should be designed to remove as much of the gas as possible from the room environment. While not within the scope of this document, it is assumed that anesthetizing equipment will be selected and maintained to minimize leakage and contamination of room air.

vi. The bottoms of ventilation (supply/return) openings shall be at least 3 inches (7.62 centimeters) above the floor.

vii. All central ventilation or air conditioning systems shall be equipped with filters having efficiencies equal to, or greater than, those specified in Table 11. Where two filter beds are used, filter bed no. 1 shall be located upstream of the air conditioning equipment and filter bed no. 2 shall be downstream of any fan or blower. Where only one filter bed is required, it shall be located upstream of the air conditioning equipment, unless an additional prefilter is used. In this case, the prefilter shall be upstream of the equipment and the main filter may be located further downstream. Filter efficiencies, tested in accordance with ASHRAE 52-76, shall be average, except as noted otherwise. Filter frames shall be durable and proportioned to provide an airtight fit with the enclosing ductwork. All joints between filter segments and enclosing ductwork shall have gaskets or seals to provide a positive seal against air leakage. A manometer shall be installed across each filter bed having a required efficiency of 75 percent or more, including hoods requiring HEPA filters. Reservoir-type sprays shall not be used.

viii. Air-handling duct systems shall meet the requirements of NFPA 90A and those contained herein.

Table 11

Filter Efficiencies for Central Ventilation and Air Conditioning Systems in Outpatient Facilities

Area designation	No. filter beds	Filter bed no. 1	Filter bed no. 2
All areas for patient care, treatment, and/or diagnosis, and those areas providing direct service or clean supplies such as sterile and clean processing, etc.	2	25	90
Laboratories	1	80	—
Administrative, bulk storage, soiled holding areas, food preparation areas, and laundries	1	25	—

Note: Additional roughing or prefilters should be considered to reduce maintenance required for main filters. Ratings shall be based on ASHRAE 52-76.

ix. Ducts that penetrate construction intended for X-ray or other ray protection shall not impair the effectiveness of the protection.

x. Fire and smoke dampers shall be constructed, located, and installed in accordance with the requirements of NFPA 101 and 90A. Fans, dampers, and detectors shall be interconnected so that damper activation will not damage the ducts. Maintenance access shall be provided at all dampers. All damper locations shall be shown on drawings. Dampers should be activated by fire or smoke sensors, not by fan cutoff alone. Switching systems for restarting fans may be installed for fire department use in venting smoke after a fire has been controlled. However, provisions should be made to avoid possible damage to the system due to closed dampers. When smoke partitions are required, heating, ventilating, and air conditioning zones shall be coordinated with compartmentation insofar as practical to minimize need to penetrate fire smoke partitions.

xi. If air change standards in Table 2 do not provide sufficient air for use by hoods and safety cabinets, makeup air shall be provided to maintain the required airflow direction and to avoid dependence upon infiltration from outdoor or contaminated areas.

xii. Laboratory hoods shall have an average face-velocity of at least 75 feet per minute (0.38 meters per second). They shall be connected to an outside-vented exhaust system separate from the building exhaust system and have an exhaust fan located at the discharge end. In addition, they shall have an exhaust duct system made of noncombustible corrosion-resistant material designed to accommodate the planned usage of the hood.

xiii. Laboratory hoods used to process infectious or radioactive materials shall meet special standards. In new construction and major renovation work, each hood used to process infectious or radioactive materials shall have a minimum face-velocity of 150 feet per minute (0.76 meters per second) with suitable static-pressure-operated-dampers and alarms to alert staff of fan shutdown. Each shall also have filters with a 99.97 percent efficiency (based on the DOP, dioctyl-phthalate test method) in the exhaust stream, and be designed and equipped to permit the safe removal, disposal, and replacement of contaminated filters. Filters shall be as close to the hood as practical to minimize duct contamination. Hoods that process radioactive materials shall meet requirements of the Nuclear Regulatory Commission. (**Note:** Radioactive isotopes used for injections, etc., without probability of airborne particulates or gases, might be processed in a clean workbench-type hood in keeping with standards acceptable to the Nuclear Regulatory Commission.) Ducts serving hoods for radioactive material shall be constructed of acid-resistant stainless steel overall and have a minimum number of joints. Duct systems serving hoods in which strong oxidizing agents (e.g., perchloric acid) are used shall be constructed of acid-resistant stainless steel for at least 10 feet (3.05 meters) from the hood and shall be equipped with washdown facilities. Provisions shall be made for safe removal of filters during washdown operations.

xiv. The ventilation system for anesthesia storage rooms shall conform to the requirements of NFPA 99.

xv. Where ethylene oxide is used for sterilization, provisions shall be made for complete exhaust of gases to the exterior. Provisions shall be made to insure that when the sterilizer door is open, gases are pulled away from the operator. Provisions shall also be made for appropriate aeration of supplies. Aeration cabinets shall be vented to the outside. Where aeration cabinets are not used in ethylene oxide processing, an isolated area for mechanically venting gases to the outside shall be provided.

xvi. Boiler rooms shall be provided with sufficient outdoor airflow to maintain equipment combustion rates and to limit workstation temperatures.

xvii. Gravity exhaust may be used, conditions permitting, for nonpatient areas such as boiler rooms, central storage, etc.

xviii. The energy-saving potential of variable-air-volume systems is recognized, and the standards herein are intended to maximize appropriate use of such systems. Any ventilation system used for occupied areas must include provisions to avoid air stagnation in interior spaces where thermostat demands are met by temperatures of surrounding areas.

9.2.M. Plumbing and Other Piping Systems

All plumbing systems shall be designed and installed in accordance with the *National Standard Plumbing Code*, chapter 14, "Medical Care Facility Plumbing Equipment."

9.2.M1. The following standards shall apply to plumbing fixtures:

a. The material used for plumbing fixtures shall be nonabsorptive and acid-resistant.

b. Handwashing facilities for staff in patient care areas shall be trimmed with valves that can be operated without hands (single-lever devices may be used, subject to above). Where blade handles are used, they shall not exceed 4½ inches (11.43 centimeters) in length, except that handles on clinical sinks shall be not less than 6 inches (15.24 centimeters) long.

9.2.M2. The following standards shall apply to water systems:

a. Systems shall be designed to supply water at sufficient pressure to operate all fixtures and equipment during maximum demand.

b. Each water service main, branch main, riser, and branch to a group of fixtures shall have valves. Stop valves shall be provided at each fixture.

c. Backflow preventers (vacuum breakers) shall be installed on fixtures to which hoses or tubing can be attached.

9.2.M3. The following standards shall apply to drainage systems: Building sewers shall discharge into a community sewage system. Where such a system is not available, sewage treatment must conform to applicable local and state regulations.

9.2.M4. All piping in the HVAC and service-water systems shall be color coded or otherwise marked for easy identification.

▼ **9.2.M5.** In any outpatient facility where general anesthesia is used, piped-in oxygen, vacuum, and medical air shall be provided in accordance with ▲ NFPA-99 and Table 5.

9.2.N. Electrical Standards

9.2.N1. All material and equipment, including conductors, controls, and signaling devices, shall be installed to provide a complete electrical system with the necessary characteristics and capacity to supply the electrical systems as indicated on plans and in the functional program. All materials shall be listed as complying with available standards of Underwriters' Laboratories, Inc., or other similar established standards. All electrical installations and systems shall be tested to show that the equipment operates in accordance with design intent. Installation shall be in accordance with applicable sections of NFPA 70.

9.2.N2. Circuit breakers or fused switches that provide electrical disconnection and overcurrent protection for switchboard and panelboard conductors shall be enclosed or guarded to provide a dead-front assembly. The main switchboard shall be readily accessible for use and maintenance, set apart from traffic lanes, and located in a dry, ventilated space, free of corrosive fumes or gases. Overload protective devices shall operate properly in ambient temperature conditions.

9.2.N3. Panelboards serving lighting and appliance circuits shall be on the same floor and in the same facility area as the circuits they serve.

9.2.N4. The following standards for lighting shall apply:

a. All spaces occupied by people, machinery, or equipment within buildings, approaches to buildings, and parking lots shall have lighting.

b. A portable or fixed examination light shall be provided for examination, treatment, and trauma rooms.

9.2.N5. Duplex grounded-type receptacles (convenience outlets) shall be installed in all areas in sufficient quantities for tasks to be performed as needed. Each examination and work table shall have access to a minimum of two duplex receptacles.

9.2.N6. Automatic emergency lighting shall be provided for safe egress from the building in the event of power failure in accordance with NFPA 99.

▼ **9.2.N7.** A manually operated, electrically supervised fire alarm system shall be installed in each facility. The fire alarm system shall be as described in
▲ NFPA 101.

9.3 Primary Care Outpatient Centers

9.3.A. General
The primary care center provides comprehensive community outpatient medical services. The number and type of diagnostic, clinical, and administrative areas shall be sufficient to support the services and estimated patient load described in the program. All standards set forth in Sections 9.1 and 9.2 shall be met for primary care outpatient centers, with additions and modifications described herein. (See Section 9.4 for smaller care centers.)

9.3.B. Parking
Parking spaces for patients and family shall be provided at the rate of not less than two parking spaces for each examination and each treatment room. In addition, one space for each of the maximum number of staff persons on duty at any one shift will be provided. Adjustments, as described in Section 9.1.G, should be made where public parking, public transportation, etc., reduce the need for on-site parking.

9.3.C. Administrative Services
Each outpatient facility shall make provisions to support administrative activities, filing, and clerical work as appropriate. (See also Section 9.2.A.) Service areas shall include:

9.3.C1. Office(s), separate and enclosed, with provisions for privacy.

9.3.C2. Clerical space or rooms for typing and clerical work separated from public areas to insure confidentiality.

9.3.C3. Filing cabinets and storage for the safe and secure storage of patient records with provisions for ready retrieval.

9.3.C4. Office supply storage (closets or cabinets) within or convenient to administrative services.

9.3.C5. A staff toilet and lounge in addition to and separate from public and patient facilities.

9.3.C6. Multiuse rooms for conferences, meetings, and health education. One room may be primarily for staff use but also available for public access as needed. In smaller facilities the room may also serve for consultation, etc.

9.3.D. Public Areas
Public areas shall be situated for convenient access and designed to promote prompt accommodation of patient needs, with consideration for personal dignity.

9.3.D1. Entrances shall be well marked and at grade level. Where entrance lobby and/or elevators are shared with other tenants, travel to the outpatient unit shall be direct and accessible to the handicapped. Except for passage through common doors, lobbies, or elevator stations, patients shall not be required to go through other occupied areas or outpatient service areas. Entrance shall be convenient to parking and available via public transportation.

9.3.D2. A reception and information counter or desk shall be located to provide visual control of the entrance to the outpatient unit, and shall be immediately apparent from that entrance.

9.3.D3. The waiting area for patients and escorts shall be under staff control. The seating area shall contain not less than two spaces for each examination and/or treatment room. Where the outpatient unit has a formal pediatrics service, a separate, controlled area for pediatric patients shall be provided. Wheelchairs within the waiting area will be accommodated.

9.3.D4. Toilet(s) for public use shall be immediately accessible from the waiting area. In smaller units the toilet may be unisex and also serve for specimen collection.

9.3.D5. Drinking fountains shall be available for waiting patients. In shared facilities, drinking fountains may be outside the outpatient area if convenient for use.

9.3.D6. A control counter (may be part of the reception, information, and waiting room control) shall have access to patient files and records for scheduling of services.

9.3.E. Diagnostic
Provisions shall be made for X-ray and laboratory procedures as described in Sections 9.2.C and D. Services may be shared or provided by contract off-site. Each outpatient unit shall have appropriate facilities for storage and refrigeration of blood, urine, and other specimens.

9.3.F. Clinical Facilities

Examination rooms and services as described in Section 9.2.B shall be provided. In addition, offices and consultation rooms shall be provided as required for practitioner use.

9.4 Small Primary (Neighborhood) Outpatient Facility

9.4.A. General

Facilities covered under this section are often contained within existing commercial or residential buildings as "storefront" units, but they may also be a small, free-standing, new, or converted structure. The size of these units limits occupancy, thereby minimizing hazards and allowing for less stringent standards. Needed community services can therefore be provided at an affordable cost. The term *small structure* shall be defined as space and equipment serving four or fewer workers at any one time. Meeting all provisions of Section 9.2 for general outpatient facilities is desirable, but limited size and resources may preclude satisfying any but the basic minimums described. This section does not apply to outpatient facilities that are within a hospital, nor is it intended for the larger, more sophisticated units.

9.4.B. Location

The small neighborhood center is expected to be especially responsive to communities with limited income. It is essential that it be located for maximum accessibility and convenience. In densely populated areas, many of the patients might walk to services. Where a substantial number of patients rely on public transportation, facility location shall permit convenient access requiring a minimum of transfers.

9.4.C. Parking

Not less than one convenient parking space for each staff member on duty at any one time and not less than four spaces for patients shall be provided. Parking requirements may be satisfied with street parking, or by a nearby public parking lot or garage. Where the facility is within a shopping center or similar area, customer spaces may meet parking needs.

9.4.D. Administration and Public Areas

9.4.D1. Public areas shall include:

a. A reception and information center or desk.

b. Waiting space, including provisions for wheelchairs.

c. Patient toilet facilities.

9.4.D2. An office area for business transactions, records, and other administrative functions, separate from public and patient areas, shall be provided.

9.4.D3. General storage facilities for office supplies, equipment, sterile supplies, and pharmaceutical supplies shall be provided.

9.4.D4. Locked storage (cabinets or secure drawers) convenient to workstations shall be provided for staff valuables.

9.4.E. Clinical Facilities

9.4.E1. At least one examination room shall be available for each provider who may be on duty at any one time. Rooms may serve both as examination and treatment spaces (see Section 9.2.B1).

9.4.E2. A clean work area with a counter, a sink equipped for handwashing, and storage for clean supplies shall be provided. This may be a separate room or an isolated area.

9.4.E3. A soiled holding room shall be provided (see Section 9.2.B8).

9.4.E4. Sterile equipment and supplies shall be provided to meet functional requirements. Sterile supplies may be prepackaged disposables or processed off-site.

9.4.E5. Locked storage for biologicals and drugs shall be provided.

9.4.E6. A toilet room containing a lavatory for handwashing shall be accessible from all examination and treatment rooms. Where a facility contains no more than three examination and/or treatment rooms, the patient toilet may also serve waiting areas.

9.4.F. Diagnostic Facilities

9.4.F1. The functional program shall describe where and how diagnostic services will be made available to the outpatient if these are not offered within the facility. When provided within the facility, these services shall meet the standards of Section 9.2.

9.4.F2. Laboratory services and/or facilities shall meet the following standards:

a. Urine collection rooms shall be equipped with a water closet and lavatory. Blood collection facilities shall have space for a chair and work counter. (The toilet room provided within the examination and treatment room may be used for specimen collection.)

b. Services shall be available within the facility or through a formal agreement or contract with a hospital or other laboratory for hematology, clinical chemistry, urinalysis, cytology, pathology, and bacteriology.

9.4.G. Details and Finishes

See Section 9.2.H.

9.4.H. Design and Construction

9.4.H1. Every building and every portion thereof shall be designed and constructed to sustain all dead and live loads in accordance with accepted engineering practices and standards. If existing buildings are converted for use, consideration shall be given to the structural requirements for concentrated floor loadings, including X-ray equipment, storage files, and similar heavy equipment that may be added.

9.4.H2. Construction and finishes may be of any type permitted for business occupancies as described in NFPA 101 and as specified herein.

9.4.I. Mechanical Standards

The following shall apply for the small outpatient facility of this section in lieu of Sections 9.2.L and 9.2.M:

9.4.I1. Prior to completion and acceptance of the facility, all mechanical systems shall be tested and operated to demonstrate to the owner that the installation and performance of these systems conform to the functional and operational design intent.

9.4.I2. Manuals shall be provided for all new equipment. These shall include manufacturers' operating and maintenance instructions and a complete parts list.

9.4.I3. Heating and ventilation systems shall meet the following standards:

a. A minimum indoor winter-design-capacity temperature of 75°F (24°C) shall be set for all patient areas. Controls shall be provided for adjusting temperature as appropriate for patient activities and comfort.

b. All occupied areas shall be ventilated by natural or mechanical means.

c. Air-handling duct systems shall meet the requirements of NFPA 90A.

9.4.I4. Plumbing and other piping systems shall meet the following standards:

a. Systems shall comply with applicable codes, be free of leaks, and be designed to supply water at sufficient pressure to operate all fixtures and equipment during maximum demand.

b. Backflow preventer (vacuum breakers) shall be installed on all water supply outlets to which hoses or tubing can be attached.

c. Water temperature at lavatories shall not exceed 110°F (43°C).

d. All piping registering temperatures above 110°F (43°C) shall be covered with thermal insulation.

9.4.J. Electrical Standards

The following shall apply to the small outpatient facility of this section in lieu of Section 9.2.N:

9.4.J1. Prior to completion and acceptance of the facility, all electrical systems shall be tested and operated to demonstrate that installation and performance conform to applicable codes and functional needs.

9.4.J2. Lighting shall be provided in all facility spaces occupied by people, machinery, and/or equipment, and in outside entryways. An examination light shall be provided for each examination and treatment room.

9.4.J3. Sufficient duplex grounded-type receptacles shall be available for necessary task performance. Each examination and work table area shall be served by at least one duplex receptacle.

9.4.J4. X-ray equipment installations, when provided, shall conform to NFPA 70.

9.4.J5. Automatic emergency lighting shall be provided in every facility that has a total floor area of more than 1,000 square feet (92.9 square meters), and in every facility requiring stairway exit.

9.5 Outpatient Surgical Facility

9.5.A. General

Outpatient surgery is performed without anticipation of overnight patient care. The functional program shall describe in detail staffing, patient types, hours of operation, function and space relationships, transfer provisions, and availability of off-site services.

If the outpatient surgical facility is part of an acute-care hospital or other medical facility, service may be shared to minimize duplication as appropriate. Where outpatient surgical services are provided within the same area or suite as inpatient surgery, additional space shall be provided as needed. If inpatient and outpatient procedures are performed in the same room(s), the functional program shall describe in detail scheduling and techniques used to separate inpatients and outpatients.

▼ Visual and audible privacy should be provided by design and include the registration, preparation, examination, treatment, and recovery areas.

9.5.B. Size

The extent (number and types) of the diagnostic, clinical, and administrative facilities to be provided will be determined by the services contemplated and the estimated patient load as described in the narrative program. Provisions shall be made for patient examination, interview, preparation testing, and obtaining vital signs ▲ of patient for outpatient surgeries.

9.5.C. Parking

Four spaces for each room routinely used for surgical procedures plus one space for each staff member shall be provided. Additional parking spaces convenient to the entrance for pickup of patients after recovery shall be provided.

9.5.D. Administration and Public Areas

The following shall be provided:

9.5.D1. A covered entrance for pickup of patients after surgery.

▼ **9.5.D2.** A lobby area including a waiting area, conveniently accessible wheelchair storage, a reception/information desk, accessible public toilets, public ▲ telephone(s), drinking fountain(s).

9.5.D3. Interview space(s) for private interviews relating to admission, credit, and demographic information gathering.

9.5.D4. General and individual office(s) for business transactions, records, and administrative and professional staff. These shall be separate from public and patient areas with provisions for confidentiality of records. Enclosed office spaces for administration and consultation shall be provided.

9.5.D5. Multipurpose or consultation room(s).

9.5.D6. A medical records room equipped for dictating, recording, and retrieval.

9.5.D7. Special storage, including locking drawers and/or cabinets, for staff personal effects.

9.5.D8. General storage facilities.

9.5.E. Sterilizing Facilities

A system for sterilizing equipment and supplies shall be provided. This may be off-site. When processing equipment is provided on-site, the following shall be provided:

▼ **9.5.E1.** Soiled Workroom

This room shall be physically separated from all other areas of the department. Workspace should be provided to handle the cleaning and terminal sterilization/disinfection of all medical/surgical instruments and equipment. The soiled workroom shall contain worktables, sinks, flush-type devices, and washer/sterilizer decontaminators or other decontamination equipment. Pass-through doors and washer/sterilizer decontaminators should deliver into clean processing areas/workrooms.

9.5.E2. Clean Assembly/Workroom

This workroom shall contain handwashing facilities, workspace, and equipment for terminal sterilizing of medical and surgical equipment and supplies. Clean and soiled work areas should be physically separated. Access to sterilization room should be restricted. This room should contain high-speed autoclaves and ETO sterilizer and ETO aerators. ETO sterilization may be done off-site, provided that adequate sterile supplies are on hand to meet the maximum demand of one day's case load.

This room is exclusively for the inspection, assembly, and packaging of medical/surgical supplies and equipment for sterilization. Area should contain worktables, counters, ultrasonic storage facilities for backup supplies and instrumentation, and a drying cabinet or equipment. The area should be spacious enough to hold sterilizer cars for loading or prepared supplies for sterilization.

9.5.E3. Clean/Sterile Supplies

Storage for packs, etc., shall include provisions for ▲ ventilation, humidity, and temperature control.

9.5.F. Clinical Facilities

▼ Provisions should be made to separate pediatric from adult patients. This should include pre- and post-operative care areas and should allow for parental presence.

9.5.F1. At least one room shall be provided for examination and testing of patients prior to surgery, assuring both visual and audible privacy. This may be an examination room or treatment room as described in Sections 9.2.B1 and 3.

9.5.F2. Each operating room shall have a minimum clear area of 360 square feet (33.45 square meters), exclusive of cabinets and shelves, but may be larger to accommodate the functional plan which requires additional staff and/or equipment. Rooms that will be dedicated to laser procedure shall have a minimum clear area of 400 square feet (37.16 square meters), exclusive of cabinets and shelves. An emergency communication system connected with the surgical suite control station shall be provided. There shall be at least one X-ray film illuminator in each room. If the outpatient surgery service is to be integrated with hospital inpatient surgery service, at least one room shall be specifically designated for outpatient surgery. When the same operating rooms are used for inpatients, the functional program shall ▲ describe how scheduling conflicts will be avoided.

9.5.F3. Room(s) for post-anesthesia recovery of out-patient surgical patients shall be provided. At least 3 feet (0.91 meter) shall be provided at each side and at the foot of each bed as needed for work and/or circulation. If pediatric surgery is part of the program, separation from the adult section and space for parents shall be provided. Soundproofing of the area and the ability to visualize the patient from the nursing station should be considered. Bedpans and bedpan-cleaning services shall be supplied in this area.

▼ **9.5.F4.** A designated supervised recovery lounge shall be provided for patients who do not require post-anesthesia recovery but need additional time for their vital signs to stabilize before safely leaving the facility. This lounge shall contain a control station, space for family members, and provisions for privacy. It shall have convenient patient access to toilets large enough to accommodate a patient and an assistant. Handwashing and nourishment facilities must
▲ be included.

9.5.F5. The following services shall be provided in surgical service areas:

a. A control station located to permit visual surveillance of all traffic entering the operating suite.

▼ b. A drug distribution station. Provisions shall be made for storage and preparation of medications administered to patients. A refrigerator for pharmaceuticals and a double locked storage for controlled substances shall be provided. Convenient access to handwashing facilities shall be provided.

c. Scrub facilities. Station(s) shall be provided near the entrance to each operating room and may service two operating rooms if needed. Scrub facilities shall be arranged to minimize incidental
▲ splatter on nearby personnel or supply carts.

d. Soiled workroom. The soiled workroom shall contain a clinical sink or equivalent flushing-type fixture, a work counter, a sink for handwashing, and waste receptacle(s).

▼ e. Fluid waste disposal facilities. These shall be convenient to the general operating rooms. A clinical sink or equivalent equipment in a soiled workroom shall meet this standard.

f. Anesthesia storage facilities shall be in accordance with the standards detailed in Section
▲ 7.7.C9 for general hospitals.

g. Anesthesia workroom for cleaning, testing, and storing anesthesia equipment. It shall contain a work counter and sink.

h. Medical gas supply and storage with space for reserve nitrous oxide and oxygen cylinders.

i. Equipment storage room(s) for equipment and supplies used in the surgical suite.

j. Staff clothing change areas. Appropriate change areas shall be provided for staff working within the surgical suite. The areas shall contain lockers, showers, toilets, lavatories for handwashing, and space for donning scrub attire.

k. Outpatient surgery change areas. A separate area shall be provided for outpatients to change from street clothing into hospital gowns and to prepare for surgery. This area shall include waiting room(s), lockers, toilets, clothing change or gowning area(s), and space for administering medications. Provisions shall be made for securing patients' personal effects.

l. Stretcher storage area. This area shall be convenient for use and out of the direct line of traffic.

m. Lounge and toilet facilities for surgical staff. These shall be provided in facilities having three or more operating rooms. A toilet room will be provided near the recovery area.

n. Housekeeping room. Space containing a floor receptor or service sink and storage space for housekeeping supplies and equipment shall be provided exclusively for the surgical suite.

o. Space for temporary storage of wheelchairs.

p. Provisions for convenient access to and use of emergency crash carts at both the surgical and recovery areas.

▼ q. For a freestanding surgical unit refer to Sections 7.7, Surgical Suites; 9.2, Common Elements for Outpatient Facilities; 7.16 through
▲ 7.25; and 7.27, Waste Processing Services.

9.5.G. Diagnostic Facilities

Diagnostic services shall be provided on- or off-site for preadmission tests as required by the functional program.

9.5.H. Details and Finishes

All details and finishes shall meet the standards in Section 9.2 and below.

9.5.H1. Details shall conform to the following guidelines:

a. Minimum public corridor width shall be 6 feet (1.83 meters), except that corridors in the operating room section, where patients are transported on stretchers or beds, shall be 8 feet (2.44 meters) wide.

b. The separate facility or section shall comply with the "New Ambulatory Health Care Centers" section of NFPA 101 and as described herein. Where the outpatient surgical unit is part of another facility that does not comply with, or exceeds, the fire safety requirements of NFPA 101, there shall be not less than one-hour separation between the outpatient surgical unit and other sections. The outpatient surgical facility shall have not less than two exits to the exterior. Exits, finishes, separation for hazardous areas, and smoke separation shall conform to NFPA 101.

c. Toilet rooms in surgery and recovery areas for patient use shall be equipped with doors and hardware that permit access from the outside in emergencies. When such rooms have only one opening or are small, the doors shall open outward or be otherwise designed to open without pressing against a patient who may have collapsed within the room.

d. Flammable anesthetics shall not be used in outpatient surgical facilities.

9.5.H2. Finishes shall conform to the following guidelines:

a. All ceilings and walls shall be cleanable. Those in sensitive areas such as surgical rooms shall be readily washable and free of crevices that can retain dirt particles. These sensitive areas shall have a finished ceiling that covers all overhead ductwork and piping. Finished ceilings may be omitted in mechanical and equipment spaces, shops, general storage areas, and similar spaces, unless required for fire-resistive purposes (see NFPA 99 and NFPA 70).

9.5.I. Plumbing
See Section 9.2.M.

9.5.J. Electrical
See Section 9.2.N.

9.5.K. Fire Alarm System
A manually operated, electrically supervised fire alarm system shall be installed in each facility as described in NFPA 101.

9.5.L. Mechanical
Heating, ventilation, and air conditioning should be described for similar areas in Section 9.2.L and Table 2, except that the recovery lounge need not be considered a sensitive area and outpatient operating rooms may meet the standards for emergency trauma rooms. See Table 11 for filter efficiency standards.

9.6 Freestanding Emergency Facility

9.6.A. General
This section applies to the emergency facility that is separate from the acute-care hospital and that therefore requires special transportation planning to accommodate transfer of patients and essential services. The separate emergency facility provides expeditious emergency care where travel time to appropriate hospital units may be excessive. It may include provisions for temporary observation of patients until release or transfer.

Where hours of operation are limited, provisions shall be made in directional signs, notices, and designations to minimize potential for mistakes and loss of time by emergency patients seeking care during nonoperating hours.

Facility size, type, and design shall satisfy the functional program. In addition to standards in Sections 9.1 and 9.2, the following guidelines shall be met:

9.6.B. Location
The emergency facility shall be conveniently accessible to the population served and shall provide patient transfer to appropriate hospitals. In selecting location, consideration shall be given to factors affecting source and quantity of patient load, including highway systems, industrial plants, and recreational areas. Though most emergency patients will arrive by private cars, consideration should also be given to availability of public transportation.

9.6.C. Parking
Not less than one parking space for each staff member on duty at any one time and not less than two spaces for each examination and each treatment room shall be provided. Additional spaces shall be provided for emergency vehicles. Street, public, and shared lot spaces, if included as part of this standard, shall be exclusively for the use of the emergency facility. All required parking spaces shall be convenient to the emergency entrance.

9.6.D. Administrative and Public Areas
Administrative and public areas shall conform to the standards in Section 9.2.A with the following additions.

9.6.D1. Entrances shall be covered to permit protected transfer of patients from ambulance and/or automobiles. If a platform is provided for ambulance use, a ramp for wheelchairs and stretchers shall be provided in addition to steps. Door(s) to emergency services shall be not less than 4 feet (1.22 meters) wide to allow the passage of a stretcher and assistants. The emergency entrance shall have vision panels to minimize conflict between incoming and outgoing traffic and to allow for observation of the unloading area from the control station.

9.6.D2. Lobby and waiting areas shall satisfy the following requirements:

a. Convenient access to wheelchairs and stretchers shall be provided at the emergency entrance.

b. Reception and information function may be combined or separate. These shall provide direct visual control of the emergency entrance, and access to the treatment area and the lobby. Control stations will normally include triage function and shall be in direct communication with medical staff. Emergency entrance control functions shall include observation of arriving vehicles.

c. The emergency waiting area shall include provisions for wheelchairs and be separate from the area provided for scheduled outpatient service.

9.6.D3. Initial interviews may be conducted at the triage reception/control area. Facilities for conducting interviews on means of reimbursement, social services, and personal data shall include provisions for acoustical privacy. These facilities may be separate from the reception area but must be convenient to the emergency service waiting area.

9.6.D4. For standards concerning general and individual offices, see Section 9.2.A4.

9.6.D5. For standards concerning clerical space, see Section 9.2.A5.

9.6.D6. Multipurpose room(s) shall be provided for staff conferences. This room may also serve for consultation.

9.6.D7. For standards concerning special storage, see Section 9.2.A7.

9.6.D8. For standards concerning general storage, see Section 9.2.A8.

9.6.E. Clinical Facilities
See Section 9.2.B and, in addition, provide:

9.6.E1. A trauma/cardiac room for complex procedures as described in Section 9.5.F2 for the outpatient surgery unit. The trauma/cardiac room may be set up to accommodate more than one patient. Where the emergency trauma/cardiac room is set up for multipatient use, there shall be not less than 180 square feet (16.72 square meters) per patient area, and there shall be utilities and services for each patient. Provisions shall be included for patient privacy.

9.6.E2. In addition to wheelchair storage, a holding area for stretchers within the clinical area, away from traffic and under staff control.

▼ **9.6.E3.** A poison control service with immediately accessible antidotes and a file of common poisons. Communication links with regional and/or national poison centers and regional EMS centers shall be provided. This service may be part of the nurses control and workstation. ▲

9.6.E4. A nurses work and control station. This shall accommodate charting, files, and staff consultation activities. It shall be located to permit visual control of clinical area and its access. Communication links with the examination/treatment area, trauma/cardiac room, reception control, laboratory, radiology, and on-call staff shall be provided.

9.6.E5. A CPR emergency cart, away from traffic but immediately available to all areas including entrance and receiving areas.

9.6.E6. Scrub stations at each trauma/cardiac room. Water and soap controls shall not require use of hands.

9.6.E7. At least two examination rooms and one trauma/cardiac room (treatment room may also be utilized for examination).

9.6.F. Radiology
Standards stipulated in Section 9.2.C shall be met during all hours of operation. Radiographic equipment shall be adequate for any part of the body including, but not limited to, fractures. Separate dressing rooms are not required for unit(s) used only for emergency procedures.

9.6.G. Laboratory
See Section 9.2.D for applicable standards. In addition, immediate access to blood for transfusions and provisions for cross-match capabilities shall be provided.

9.6.H. Employee Facilities
See Section 9.2.F for applicable standards. In addition, facilities for on-call medical staff shall be provided.

9.6.I. Observation
▼ Facilities shall be provided for holding emergency patients until they can be discharged or transferred to an appropriate hospital. Size, type, and equipment shall be as required for anticipated patient load and lengths of stay. One or more examination/treatment rooms may be utilized for this purpose. Each observation bed shall permit: ▲

9.6.I1. Direct visual observation of each patient from the nurses station, except where examination/treatment rooms are used for patient holding. View from the duty station may be limited to the door.

9.6.I2. Patient privacy.

9.6.I3. Access to patient toilets.

9.6.I4. Secure storage of patients' valuables and clothing.

9.6.I5. Dispensing of medication.

9.6.I6. Bedpan storage and cleaning.

9.6.I7. Provision of nourishment (see Section 7.2.B15). In addition, meal provisions shall be made for patients held for more than four hours during daylight.

9.6.J. Mechanical
See Section 9.2.L for applicable mechanical standards.

9.6.K. Plumbing
See Section 9.2.M for applicable plumbing standards.

9.6.L. Electrical
See Section 9.2.N for applicable electrical standards.

*9.7 Freestanding Birth Center

▼ The freestanding birth center is "any health facility, place, or institution which is not a hospital and where births are planned to occur away from the mother's usual place of residence" (American Public Health Association, 1982).

All standards set forth in Sections 9.1 and 9.2 shall be met for new construction of birth centers, with modifications described herein. Birth rooms shall have available oxygen, vacuum, and medical air per Table 5, LDRP rooms.

9.7.A. Parking
Parking spaces for the client and family shall be provided at a rate of not less than two for each birth room. In addition, one space for each of the maximum number of staff persons on duty at any given time will be provided. Adjustments, as described in Section 9.1.G, should be made where public parking, public transportation, etc., reduce the need for on-site parking.

9.7.B. Administrative and Public Areas

9.7.B1. Entrance: The entrance to the birth center shall be at ground level.

9.7.B2. Provisions for the handicapped: See Section 1.3.

9.7.B3. Public areas shall include:

a. A reception area with facility to accommodate outdoor wear.

b. A family room with a designated play area for children.

c. Child-proof electrical outlets.

d. A nourishment area for families to store and serve light refreshment of their dietary and cultural preferences shall include a sink and counter space, range, oven or microwave, refrigerator, cooking utensils, disposable tableware or dishwasher, storage space, and seating area.

e. Convenient access to toilet and handwashing facilities.

f. Convenient access to telephone service.

g. Convenient access to drinking fountain or potable drinking water with disposable cup dispenser.

9.7.B4. Staff area: A secure storage space for personal effects, toilet, shower, change and lounge area sufficient to accommodate staff needs shall be provided.

9.7.B5. Records: Space for performing administrative functions, charting, and secure record storage shall be provided.

9.7.B6. Drugs and biologicals: An area for locked storage for drugs and refrigeration for biologicals (separate from the nourishment area refrigerator) shall be provided.

9.7.B7. Clean storage: A separate area for storing clean and sterile supplies shall be provided.

9.7.B8. Soiled holding: Provisions shall be made for separate collection, storage, and disposal of soiled materials. Fluid waste may be disposed of in the toilet adjacent to the birth room.

9.7.B9. Sterilizing facilities: Sterile supplies may be prepackaged disposables or processed off-site. If instruments and supplies are sterilized on-site, an area for accommodation of sterilizing equipment appropriate to the volume of the birth center shall be provided.

9.7.B10. Laundry: May be done on- or off-site. If on-site, an area for laundry equipment with counter and storage space shelving shall be provided. Depending on size and occupancy of center, ordinary household laundry equipment may be provided. (Soiled laundry shall be held in the soiled holding area until deposited in the washer.)

9.7.C. Clinical Facilities
As needed, the following elements shall be provided for clinical services to satisfy the functional program.

9.7.C1. Birth rooms: A minimum of two birth rooms with storage space sufficient to accommodate belongings of occupants, bedding, equipment, and supplies needed for a family-centered childbirth shall be provided.

a. Birth rooms shall be adequate in size to accommodate one patient, her family, and attending staff. A minimum floor area of 160 square feet (14.86 square meters) for new construction will be provided with a minimum dimension of 11 feet (3.25 meters). For renovation, a minimum floor area of 120 square feet (11.15 square meters) excluding vestibule, toilet, and closets will be provided with a minimum dimension of 10 feet (3.05 meters).

b. An area for equipment and supplies for routine and remedial newborn care, separate from the equipment supplies for maternal care, shall be provided in each birth room in built-in cabinets, closets, or furniture.

c. Medicant, syringes, specimen containers, and instrument packs shall be contained in storage areas not accessible to children.

d. The plan for the birth room shall be such that it will permit the need for emergency transfer by stretcher unimpeded.

9.7.C2. Toilet and bathing facilities: toilet, sink, and bath/shower facilities with appropriately placed grab bars shall be adjacent to each birth room. Bath/shower facilities shall be shared by not more than two birth rooms.

9.7.C3. Scrub areas: Handwashing fixtures with hands-free faucets shall be located conveniently accessible to the birth rooms.

9.7.C4. Emergency equipment: An area for maternal and newborn emergency equipment and supplies (carts or trays) shall be designated out of the direct line of traffic and conveniently accessible to the birth rooms.

9.7.C5. Communication: Each birth room shall be equipped with a system for communicating to other parts of the center and to an outside telephone line.

9.8 Freestanding Outpatient Diagnostic and Treatment Facility

*9.8.A. General
This section applies to the outpatient diagnostic and treatment facility that is separate from the acute-care hospital. This facility is a new and emerging form of outpatient center which is capable of providing a wide array of outpatient diagnostic services and minimally invasive procedures.

The general standards for outpatient facilities set forth in Sections 9.1 and 9.2 shall be met for the freestanding outpatient diagnostic and treatment facility with two modifications.

9.8.A1. For those facilities performing diagnostic imaging and minimally invasive interventional procedures, all provisions of Section 7.10, General Hospital—Imaging Suite, shall also apply, except that adjacencies to emergency, surgery, cystoscopy, and outpatient clinics are not required.

9.8.A2. For those facilities performing nuclear medicine procedures, all provisions of Section 7.11, Nuclear Medicine, shall also apply, except that support services such as radiology, pathology, emergency room, and outpatient clinics are not required.

9.9 Endoscopy Suite

The endoscopy suite may be divided into three major functional areas: the procedure room(s), instrument processing room(s), and patient holding/preparation and recovery room or area.

9.9.A. Procedure Room(s)

9.9.A1. Each procedure room shall have a minimum clear area of 200 square feet (15 square meters) exclusive of fixed cabinets and built-in shelves.

9.9.A2. A freestanding handwashing fixture with hands-free controls shall be available in the suite.

9.9.A3. Station outlets for oxygen, vacuum (suction), and medical air. See Table 5, Section 7.7.A4.

9.9.A4. Floor covering shall be monolithic and joint free.

9.9.A5. A system for emergency communication shall be provided.

9.9.B. Instrument Processing Room(s)

9.9.B1. Dedicated processing room(s) for cleaning and disinfecting instrumentation must be provided. In an optimal situation, cleaning room(s) should be located between two procedure rooms. However, one processing room may serve multiple procedure rooms. Size of the cleaning room(s) is dictated by the amount of equipment to be processed.

Cleaning rooms should allow for flow of instrumentation from the contaminated area to the clean area and, finally, to storage. The clean equipment rooms, including storage, should protect the equipment from contamination.

9.9.B2. The decontamination room should be equipped with the following:

a. Two utility sinks remote from each other.

b. One freestanding handwashing fixture.

c. Work counter space(s).

d. Space and plumbing fixtures for automatic endoscope cleaners, sonic processor, and flash sterilizers (where required).

e. Ventilation system. Negative pressure shall be maintained and a minimum of 10 air changes per hour shall be maintained. A hood is recommended over the work counter. All air should be exhausted to the outside to avoid recirculation within the facility.

f. Outlets for vacuum and compressed air.

g. Floor covering—monolithic and joint free.

9.9.B3. Patient Holding/Prep/Recovery Area

The following elements should be provided in this area:

a. Each patient cubicle should be equipped with oxygen and suction outlets.

b. Cubicle curtains for patient privacy.

c. Medication preparation and storage with handwashing facilities.

d. Toilet facilities (may be accessible from patient holding or directly from procedure room(s) or both).

e. Change areas and storage for patients' personal effects.

f. Nurses reception and charting area with visualization of patients.

g. Clean utility room or area.

▲ h. Janitor/housekeeping closet.

10. REHABILITATION FACILITIES

10.1 General Considerations

▼ Rehabilitation facilities may be organized under hospitals (organized departments of rehabilitation), outpatient clinics, rehabilitation centers, and other facilities designed to serve either single- or multiple-disability categories including but not limited to: cerebrovascular, head trauma, spinal cord injury, amputees, complicated fractures, arthritis, neurological degeneration, genetic, and cardiac.

In general, rehabilitation facilities will have larger space requirements than general hospitals, have longer lengths of stay, and have less institutional and more res-
▲ idential environments.

10.1.A. Functional Units and Service Areas
Functional units and service areas shall include:

10.1.A1. Required units. Each rehabilitation facility shall contain a medical evaluation unit and one or more of the following units:

a. Psychological services unit.

b. Social services unit.

c. Vocational services.

10.1.A2. Required service areas. Each rehabilitation facility shall provide the following service areas, if they are not otherwise conveniently accessible to the facility and appropriate to program functions:

a. Patient dining, recreation, and day spaces.

b. Dietary unit.

c. Personal care facilities.

d. Unit for teaching activities of daily living.

e. Administration department.

▼ f. Convenience store (i.e., expanded gift shop) with toiletries and other items accessible to
▲ patients during extended lengths of stay.

g. Engineering service and equipment areas.

h. Linen service.

i. Housekeeping rooms.

j. Employees' facilities.

k. Nursing unit.

10.1.A3. Optional units. The following special services areas, if required by the functional program, shall be provided as outlined in these sections. The sizes of the various departments will depend upon the requirements of the service to be provided:

a. Sterilizing facilities.

b. Physical therapy unit.

c. Occupational therapy unit.

d. Prosthetics and orthotics unit.

e. Speech and hearing unit.

f. Dental unit.

g. Radiology unit.

h. Pharmacy unit.

i. Laboratory facilities.

j. Home health service.

k. Outpatient services.

l. Therapeutic pool.

10.2 Evaluation Unit

10.2.A. Office(s) for Personnel

10.2.B. Examination Room(s)
▼ Examination rooms shall have a minimum floor area of 140 square feet (13.01 square meters), excluding such spaces as the vestibule, toilet, closet, and work counter (whether fixed or movable). The minimum room dimension shall be 10 feet (3.05 meters). The room shall contain a lavatory or sink equipped for handwashing, a work counter, and storage facilities, and a desk,
▲ counter, or shelf space for writing.

10.2.C. Evaluation Room(s)
Evaluation room areas shall be arranged to permit appropriate evaluation of patient needs and progress and to determine specific programs of rehabilitation. Rooms shall include a desk and work area for the evaluators; writing and workspace for patients; and storage for supplies. Where the facility is small and workload light, evaluation may be done in the examination room(s).

10.2.D. Laboratory Facilities
Facilities shall be provided within the rehabilitation department or through contract arrangement with a nearby hospital or laboratory service for hematology, clinical chemistry, urinalysis, cytology, pathology, and bacteriology. If these facilities are provided through contract, the following minimum laboratory services shall be provided in the rehabilitation facility:

10.2.D1. Laboratory work counter(s) with a sink, and gas and electric service.

10.2.D2. Handwashing facilities.

10.2.D3. Storage cabinet(s) or closet(s).

10.2.D4. Specimen collection facilities. Urine collection rooms shall be equipped with a water closet and lavatory. Blood collection facilities shall have space for a chair and work counter.

10.2.E. Imaging Facilities
If required by the functional program, electromyographic, CAT scan, MRI and nuclear medicine rooms, and equipment shall be provided.

10.3 Psychological Services Unit

This shall include office(s) and workspace for testing, evaluation, and counseling.

10.4 Social Services Unit

This shall include office space(s) for private interviewing and counseling.

10.5 Vocational Services Unit

Office(s) and workspace for vocational training, counseling, and placement shall be provided.

10.6 Dining, Recreation, and Day Spaces

The following standards shall be met for patient dining, recreation, and day spaces (areas may be in separate or adjoining spaces):

▼ **10.6.A. Inpatients and Residents**
A total of 55 square feet (5.11 square meters) per bed.

10.6.B. Outpatients
If dining is part of the day care program, a total of 55 square feet (5.11 square meters) per person shall be provided. If dining is not part of the program, at least 35 square feet (3.25 square meters) per person shall be pro-
▲ vided for recreation and day spaces.

10.6.C. Storage
Storage spaces shall be provided for recreational equipment and supplies.

10.7 Dietary Department

10.7.A. General
Construction, equipment, and installation of food service facilities shall meet the requirements of the functional program. Services may consist of an on-site conventional food preparation system, a convenience food
▼ service system, or an appropriate combination thereof. On-site facilities should be provided for emergency food preparation and refrigeration.

The following facilities shall be provided as required to implement the food service selected:

10.7.A1. A control station for receiving food
▲ supplies.

10.7.A2. Food preparation facilities. Conventional food preparation systems require space and equipment for preparing, cooking, and baking. Convenience food service systems such as frozen prepared meals, bulk packaged entrees, individually packaged portions, and contractual commissary services require space and equipment for thawing, portioning, cooking, and/or baking.

10.7.A3. Handwashing facility(ies) located in the food preparation area.

▼ **10.7.A4.** Patients' meal service facilities for tray assembly and distribution.

10.7.A5. Separate dining space shall be provided
▲ for staff.

10.7.A6. Warewashing space. This shall be located in a room or an alcove separate from the food preparation and serving area. Commercial dishwashing equipment shall be provided. Space shall also be provided for receiving, scraping, sorting, and stacking soiled tableware and for transferring clean tableware to the using areas. A lavatory shall be conveniently available.

10.7.A7. Potwashing facilities.

10.7.A8. Storage areas for cans, carts, and mobile tray conveyors.

10.7.A9. Waste storage facilities. These shall be located in a separate room easily accessible to the outside for direct waste pickup or disposal.

10.7.A10. Office(s) or desk spaces for dietitian(s) or the dietary service manager.

10.7.A11. Toilets for dietary staff. Handwashing facilities shall be immediately available.

10.7.A12. Housekeeping room. This shall be located within the dietary department and shall contain a floor receptor or service sink and storage space for housekeeping equipment and supplies.

10.7.A13. Self-dispensing icemaking facilities. This may be in an area or room separate from the food preparation area but must be easily cleanable and convenient to dietary facilities.

10.8 Personal Care Unit for Inpatients

A separate room with appropriate fixtures and utilities shall be provided for patient grooming.

10.9 Activities for Daily Living Unit

▼ A unit for teaching daily living activities shall be provided. It shall include a bedroom, bath, kitchen, and space for training stairs. Equipment shall be functional. The bathroom must be in addition to other toilet and bathing requirements. The facilities should be similar to a residential environment so that the patient may learn
▲ to use them at home.

10.10 Administration and Public Areas

10.10.A. Entrance
A grade-level entrance, sheltered from the weather and able to accommodate wheelchairs, shall be provided.

10.10.B. Lobby
The lobby shall include:

10.10.B1. Wheelchair storage space(s).

10.10.B2. A reception and information counter or desk.

10.10.B3. Waiting space(s).

10.10.B4. Public toilet facilities.

10.10.B5. Public telephone(s).

10.10.B6. Drinking fountain(s).

10.10.B7. Convenience store (as described in Section 10.1.B2).

10.10.C. Interview Space(s)
Space for private interviews relating to social service, credit, and admissions shall be provided if not provided under Section 10.1.A1.

10.10.D. General or Individual Office(s)
General or individual offices for business transactions, records, and administrative and professional staffs shall be provided if not provided under Section 10.1.A2.

10.10.E. Multipurpose Room(s)
Multipurpose room(s) for conferences, meetings, health education, and library services shall be provided.

▼ **10.10.F. Patient Storage**
Due to length of stay being longer than typical acute care patients, rehab patients may require more space for
▲ storage of personal effects.

10.10.G. General Storage
Separate space for office supplies, sterile supplies, pharmaceutical supplies, splints and other orthopedic supplies, and housekeeping supplies and equipment shall be provided.

10.11 Engineering Service and Equipment Areas

10.11.A. Equipment Rooms
Rooms for boilers, mechanical equipment, and electrical equipment shall be provided.

10.11.B. Storage Room(s)
Storage rooms for building maintenance supplies and yard equipment shall be provided.

10.11.C. Waste Processing Services

10.11.C1. Space and facilities shall be provided for the sanitary storage and disposal of waste.

10.11.C2. If provided, design and construction of incinerators and trash chutes shall be in accordance with NFPA 82 and shall also conform to the requirements prescribed by environment regulations.

10.12 Linen Services

10.12.A. On-site Processing
If linen is to be processed on the site, the following shall be provided:

10.12.A1. Laundry processing room with commercial equipment that can process seven days' laundry within a regularly scheduled workweek. Handwashing facilities shall be provided.

10.12.A2. Soiled linen receiving, holding, and sorting room with handwashing and cart-washing facilities.

10.12.A3. Storage for laundry supplies.

10.12.A4. Clean linen storage, issuing, and holding room or area.

10.12.A5. Housekeeping room containing a floor receptor or service sink and storage space for housekeeping equipment and supplies.

10.12.B. Off-site Processing
If linen is processed off the rehabilitation facility site, the following shall be provided:

10.12.B1. Soiled linen holding room.

10.12.B2. Clean linen receiving, holding, inspection, and storage room(s).

10.13 Housekeeping Room(s)

In addition to the housekeeping rooms called for in certain departments, housekeeping rooms shall be provided throughout the facility as required to maintain a clean and sanitary environment. Each shall contain a floor receptor or service sink and storage space for housekeeping supplies and equipment.

10.14 Employee Facilities

In addition to the employee facilities such as locker rooms, lounges, toilets, or showers called for in certain departments, a sufficient number of such facilities to accommodate the needs of all personnel and volunteers shall be provided.

10.15 Nursing Unit (for Inpatients)

Where inpatients are a part of the facility, each nursing unit shall provide the following:

10.15.A. Patient Rooms
Each patient room shall meet the following requirements:

10.15.A1. Maximum room occupancy shall be four patients. Larger units may be provided if justified by the functional program. At least two single-bed rooms with private toilet rooms shall be provided for each nursing unit.

▼ **10.15.A2.** Minimum room areas exclusive of toilet rooms, closets, lockers, wardrobes, alcoves, or vestibules shall be 140 square feet (13.01 square meters) in single-bed rooms and 125 square feet (11.61 square meters) per bed in multi-bed rooms. In multi-bed rooms, a clearance of 3 feet 8 inches (1.12 meters) shall be maintained at the foot of each
▲ bed to permit the passage of equipment and beds.

10.15.A3. Each patient sleeping room shall have a window in accordance with Section 7.28.A11.

10.15.A4. A nurses' calling system shall be provided.

10.15.A5. Handwashing facilities shall be provided in each patient room. The handwashing fixture may be omitted from the bedroom where a water closet and handwashing fixture are provided in a toilet room designed to serve one single-bed room, or one two-bed room.

▼ **10.15.A6.** Each patient shall have access to a toilet room without having to enter the general corridor area. One toilet room shall serve no more than four beds and no more than two patient rooms. The toilet room shall contain a water closet and a handwashing fixture. The handwashing fixture may be omitted from a toilet room that serves single-bed and two-bed rooms if each such patient's room contains a handwashing fixture. Each toilet room shall be of sufficient size to ensure that wheelchair users will
▲ have access.

10.15.A7. Each patient shall have a wardrobe, closet, or locker with minimum clear dimensions of 1 foot 10 inches (55.88 centimeters) by 1 foot 8 inches (50.80 centimeters). A clothes rod and adjustable shelf shall be provided.

10.15.A8. Visual privacy shall be provided for each patient in multibed rooms.

10.15.B. Service Areas

The service areas noted below shall be in or readily available to each nursing unit. The size and disposition of each service area will depend upon the number and types of disabilities for which care will be provided. Although identifiable spaces are required for each indicated function, consideration will be given to alternative designs that accommodate some functions without designating specific areas or rooms. Such proposals shall be submitted for prior approval. Each service area may be arranged and located to serve more than one nursing unit, but at least one such service area shall be provided on each nursing floor. The following service areas shall be provided:

10.15.B1. Administrative center or nurse station.

10.15.B2. Nurses' office.

10.15.B3. Storage for administrative supplies.

10.15.B4. Handwashing facilities located near the nurse station and the drug distribution station. One lavatory may serve both areas.

10.15.B5. Charting facilities for nurses and doctors.

10.15.B6. Lounge and toilet room(s) for staff.

10.15.B7. Individual closets or compartments for safekeeping personal effects of nursing personnel, located convenient to the duty station or in a central location.

10.15.B8. Room for examination and treatment of patients. This room may be omitted if all patient rooms are single-bed rooms. It shall have a minimum floor area of 120 square feet (11.15 square meters), excluding space for vestibules, toilet, closets, and work counters (whether fixed or movable).

The minimum room dimension shall be 10 feet (3.05 meters). The room shall contain a lavatory or sink equipped for handwashing, work counter, storage facilities, and a desk, counter, or shelf space for writing. The examination room in the evaluation unit may be used if it is conveniently located.

10.15.B9. Clean workroom or clean holding room.

10.15.B10. Soiled workroom or soiled holding room.

10.15.B11. Medication station. Provisions shall be made for convenient and prompt 24-hour distribution of medicine to patients. Distribution may be from a medicine preparation room, a self-contained medicine dispensing unit, or through another approved system. If used, a medicine preparation room shall be under the nursing staff's visual control and contain a work counter, refrigerator, and locked storage for biologicals and drugs. A medicine dispensing unit may be located at a nurse station, in the clean workroom, or in an alcove or other space under direct control of nursing or pharmacy staff.

10.15.B12. Clean linen storage. A separate closet or an area within the clean workroom shall be provided for this purpose. If a closed-cart system is used, storage may be in an alcove.

▼ **10.15.B13.** Nourishment station. This shall be accessible to patients and contain a sink for handwashing, equipment for serving nourishment between scheduled meals, a refrigerator, storage cabinets, and ice-maker-dispenser units to provide for patient service
▲ and treatment.

10.15.B14. Equipment storage room. This shall be for equipment such as IV stands, inhalators, air mattresses, and walkers.

10.15.B15. Parking for stretchers and wheelchairs. This shall be located out of the path of normal traffic.

▼ **10.15.B16.** Multipurpose dayroom. Due to patients' length of stay, a dayroom shall be provided for
▲ patients to socialize on the unit.

10.15.C. Patient Bathing Facilities

Bathtubs or showers shall be provided at a ratio of one bathing facility for each eight beds not otherwise served by bathing facilities within patient rooms. At least one island-type bathtub shall be provided in each nursing unit. Each tub or shower shall be in an individual room or privacy enclosure that provides space for the private use of bathing fixtures, for drying and dressing, and for a wheelchair and an assistant. Showers in central bathing facilities shall be at least 4 feet (1.22 meters) square, curb-free, and designed for use by a wheelchair patient.

10.15.D. Patient Toilet Facilities

10.15.D1. The minimum dimensions of a room containing only a water closet shall be 3 feet (0.91 meter) by 6 feet (1.83 meters); additional space shall be provided if a lavatory is located within the same room. Water closets must be usable by wheelchair patients.

10.15.D2. At least one room on each floor containing a nursing unit(s) shall be provided for toilet training. It shall be accessible from the nursing corridor. A minimum clearance of 3 feet (0.91 meter) shall be provided at the front and at each side of the water closet. This room shall also contain a lavatory.

10.15.D3. A toilet room that does not require travel through the general corridor shall be accessible to each central bathing area.

10.15.D4. Doors to toilet rooms shall have a minimum width of 2 feet 10 inches (86.36 centimeters) to admit a wheelchair. The doors shall permit access from the outside in case of an emergency.

10.15.D5. A handwashing facility shall be provided for each water closet in each multifixture toilet room.

10.16 Sterilizing Facilities

Where required by the functional program, a system for sterilizing equipment and supplies shall be provided.

10.17 Physical Therapy Unit

The following elements shall be provided:

10.17.A. Office Space

10.17.B. Waiting Space

10.17.C. Treatment Area(s)
For thermotherapy, diathermy, ultrasonics, hydrotherapy, etc., cubicle curtains around each individual treatment area shall be provided. Handwashing facility(ies) shall also be provided. One lavatory or sink may serve more than one cubicle. Facilities for collection of wet and soiled linen and other material shall be provided.

10.17.D. An Exercise Area

10.17.E. Storage for Clean Linen, Supplies, and Equipment

▼ **10.17.F.**
Patients' dressing areas, showers, lockers, and toilet rooms shall be provided as required by the functional
▲ program.

10.17.G. Wheelchair and Stretcher Storage
(Items A, B, E, F, and G may be planned and arranged for shared use by occupational therapy patients and staff if the functional program reflects this sharing concept.)

10.18 Occupational Therapy Unit

The following elements shall be provided:

10.18.A. Office Space

10.18.B. Waiting Space

10.18.C. Activity Areas
Provisions shall be made for a sink or lavatory and for the collection of waste products prior to disposal.

10.18.D. Storage for Supplies and Equipment

10.18.E.
Patients' dressing areas, showers, lockers, and toilet rooms shall be provided as required by the functional program.

(Items A, B, D, and E may be planned and arranged for shared use by physical therapy patients and staff if the functional program reflects this sharing concept.)

10.19 Prosthetics and Orthotics Unit

The following elements shall be provided:

10.19.A. Workspace for Technician(s)

10.19.B. Space for Evaluation and Fitting
This shall include provision for privacy.

10.19.C. Space for Equipment, Supplies, and Storage

10.20 Speech and Hearing Unit

This shall include:

10.20.A. Office(s) for Therapists

10.20.B. Space for Evaluation and Treatment

10.20.C. Space for Equipment and Storage

10.21 Dental Unit

The following elements shall be provided:

10.21.A. Operatory
This shall contain a handwashing fixture.

10.21.B. Laboratory and Film Processing Facilities

10.22 Imaging Suite

▼ This unit shall contain the following elements:

10.22.A.
Imaging room(s) shall be provided as required by the
functional program. (See Section 7.10 for special
▲ requirements.)

10.23 Pharmacy Unit

The size and type of services to be provided in the pharmacy will depend upon the drug distribution system
chosen and whether the facility proposes to provide,
purchase, or share pharmacy services. This shall be
explained in the narrative program. Provisions shall be
made for the following functional areas:

**10.23.A. A Dispensing Area with a Handwashing
Facility**

10.23.B. An Editing or Order Review Area

10.23.C. An Area for Compounding

10.23.D. Administrative Areas

10.23.E. Storage Areas

10.23.F. A Drug Information Area

10.23.G. A Packaging Area

10.23.H. A Quality-Control Area

10.24 Details and Finishes

Patients in a rehabilitation facility will be disabled to
differing degrees. Therefore, high standards of safety
for the occupants shall be provided to minimize acci-
dents. All details and finishes for renovation projects as
well as for new construction shall comply with the following requirements insofar as they affect patient
services:

10.24.A. Details

   10.24.A1. Compartmentation, exits, automatic extinguishing systems, and other details relating to fire
   prevention and fire protection in inpatient rehabilitation facilities shall comply with requirements listed
   in NFPA 101. In freestanding outpatient rehabilitation facilities, details relating to exits and fire safety
   shall comply with the appropriate business occupancy chapter of NFPA 101 and the requirements outlined herein.

   10.24.A2. Items such as drinking fountains, telephone booths, vending machines, and portable
   equipment shall not restrict corridor traffic or reduce
   the corridor width below the required minimum.

10.24.A3. Rooms containing bathtubs, sitz baths,
showers, and water closets subject to patient use
shall be equipped with doors and hardware that will
permit access from the outside in an emergency.
When such rooms have only one opening or are
small, the doors shall open outward or be otherwise
designed to open without pressing against a patient
who may have collapsed within the room.

10.24.A4. Minimum width of all doors to rooms
needing access for beds shall be 3 feet 8 inches (1.12
meters). Doors to rooms requiring access for stretchers and doors to patient toilet rooms and other rooms
needing access for wheelchairs shall have a minimum width of 2 feet 10 inches (86.36 centimeters).
Where the functional program states that the sleeping facility will be for residential use (and therefore
not subject to in-bed patient transport), patient room
doors may be 3 feet (0.91 meter) wide, if approved
by the local authority having jurisdiction.

10.24.A5. Doors between corridors and rooms or
those leading into spaces subject to occupancy,
except elevator doors, shall be swing-type. Openings
to showers, baths, patient toilets, and other small,
wet-type areas not subject to fire hazard are exempt
from this requirement.

10.24.A6. Doors, except those to spaces such as
small closets not subject to occupancy, shall not
swing into corridors in a manner that obstructs traffic flow or reduces the required corridor width.

10.24.A7. Windows shall be designed to prevent
accidental falls when open, or shall be provided with
security screens where deemed necessary by the
functional program.

10.24.A8. Windows and outer doors that may be frequently left open shall be provided with insect
screens.

10.24.A9. Patient rooms intended for 24-hour occupancy shall have windows that operate without the
use of tools and shall have sills not more than 3 feet
(0.9 meter) above the floor.

10.24.A10. Doors, sidelights, borrowed lights, and
windows glazed to within 18 inches (45.72 centimeters) of the floor shall be constructed of safety glass,
wired glass, or plastic glazing material that resists
breaking or creates no dangerous cutting edges when
broken. Similar materials shall be used in wall openings of playrooms and exercise rooms. Safety glass
or plastic glazing material shall be used for shower
doors and bath enclosures.

10.24.A11. Linen and refuse chutes shall comply with NFPA 101.

10.24.A12. Thresholds and expansion joint covers shall be flush with the floor surface to facilitate use of wheelchairs and carts in new facilities.

10.24.A13. Grab bars shall be provided at all patient toilets, bathtubs, showers, and sitz baths. The bars shall have 1½ inches (3.81 centimeters) clearance to walls and shall be sufficiently anchored to sustain a concentrated load of 250 pounds (113.4 kilograms). Special consideration shall be given to shower curtain rods which may be momentarily used for support.

10.24.A14. Recessed soap dishes shall be provided in showers and bathrooms.

10.24.A15. Handrails shall be provided on both sides of corridors used by patients. A clear distance of 1½ inches (3.81 centimeters) shall be provided between the handrail and the wall, and the top of the rail shall be about 32 inches (81.28 centimeters) above the floor, except for special care areas such as those serving children.

10.24.A16. Ends of handrails and grab bars shall be constructed to prevent snagging the clothes of patients.

10.24.A17. Location and arrangement of handwashing facilities shall permit proper use and operation. Particular care should be given to clearance required for blade-type operating handles. Lavatories intended for use by handicapped patients shall be installed to permit wheelchairs to slide under them.

10.24.A18. Mirrors shall be arranged for convenient use by wheelchair patients as well as by patients in a standing position.

10.24.A19. Provisions for hand drying shall be included at all handwashing facilities.

10.24.A20. Lavatories and handwashing facilities shall be securely anchored to withstand an applied vertical load of not less than 250 pounds (113.4 kilograms) on the front of the fixture.

10.24.A21. Radiation protection requirements of X-ray and gamma ray installations shall conform to necessary state and local laws. Provisions shall be made for testing the completed installation before use. All defects must be corrected before acceptance.

10.24.A22. The minimum ceiling height shall be 7 feet 10 inches (2.39 meters) with the following exceptions:

a. Boiler rooms shall have a ceiling clearance not less than 2 feet 6 inches (76.20 centimeters) above the main boiler header and connecting piping.

b. Ceilings of radiographic and other rooms containing ceiling-mounted equipment, including those with ceiling-mounted surgical light fixtures, shall have sufficient height to accommodate the equipment and/or fixtures.

c. Ceilings in corridors, storage rooms, toilet rooms, and other minor rooms may be not less than 7 feet 8 inches (2.34 meters).

d. Suspended tracks, rails, and pipes located in the path of normal traffic shall be not less than 6 feet 8 inches (2.03 meters) above the floor.

10.24.A23. Recreation rooms, exercise rooms, and similar spaces where impact noises may be generated shall not be located directly over patient bed areas unless special provisions are made to minimize such noise.

10.24.A24. Rooms containing heat-producing equipment (such as boiler or heater rooms and laundries) shall be insulated and ventilated to prevent any floor surface above from exceeding a temperature 10°F (6°C) above the ambient room temperature.

10.24.A25. Noise reduction criteria shown in Table 1 shall apply to partition, floor, and ceiling construction in patient areas.

10.24.B. Finishes

10.24.B1. Cubicle curtains and draperies shall be noncombustible or rendered flame retardant and shall pass both the large and small scale tests in NFPA 701.

▼ **10.24.B2.** Floor materials shall be readily cleanable and appropriately wear-resistant for the location. Floor surfaces in patient areas shall be smooth, without irregular surfaces to prevent tripping by patients using orthotic devices. Floors in food preparation or assembly areas shall be water-resistant. Joints in tile and similar material in such areas shall also be resistant to food acids. In all areas frequently subject to wet cleaning methods, floor materials shall not be physically affected by germicidal and cleaning solutions. Floors subject to traffic while wet, such as shower and bath areas, kitchens, and similar work ▲ areas, shall have a nonslip surface.

10.24.B3. Wall bases in kitchens, soiled workrooms and other areas that are frequently subject to wet cleaning methods shall be monolithic and coved with the floor, tightly sealed within the wall, and constructed without voids that can harbor insects.

10.24.B4. Wall finishes shall be washable and, in the proximity of plumbing fixtures, shall be smooth and moisture-resistant. Finish, trim, and floor and wall construction in dietary and food preparation areas shall be free from spaces that can harbor pests.

10.24.B5. Floor and wall areas penetrated by pipes, ducts, and conduits shall be tightly sealed to minimize entry of pests. Joints of structural elements shall be similarly sealed.

10.24.B6. Ceilings throughout shall be readily cleanable. All overhead piping and ductwork in the dietary and food preparation area shall be concealed behind a finished ceiling. Finished ceilings may be omitted in mechanical and equipment spaces, shops, general storage areas, and similar spaces, unless required for fire-resistive purposes.

10.24.B7. Acoustical ceilings shall be provided for corridors in patient areas, nurse stations, day rooms, recreational rooms, dining areas, and waiting areas.

10.25 Design and Construction, Including Fire-Resistive Standards

10.25.A. Design
Except as noted below, construction of freestanding outpatient rehabilitation facilities shall adhere to recognized national model building codes and/or to NFPA 101 and the minimum requirements contained herein. Rehabilitation facilities that accommodate inpatients shall comply with the construction requirements for general hospitals as indicated in Section 7.

10.25.B. Interior Finishes
Interior finish materials for inpatient facilities shall comply with the flame-spread limitations and the smoke-production limitations set forth in NFPA 101.

10.25.C. Insulation Materials
Building insulation materials, unless sealed on all sides and edges, shall have a flame-spread rating of 25 or less and a smoke-developed rating of 150 or less when tested in accordance with NFPA 255-1984.

10.25.D. Provisions for Natural Disasters
For design and construction standards relating to hurricanes, tornadoes, and floods, see Section 7.29.F.

10.26 Elevators

10.26.A. General
All buildings having patient facilities (such as bedrooms, dining rooms, or recreation areas) or critical services (such as diagnostic or therapy) located on other than the main entrance floor shall have electric or hydraulic elevators. Installation and testing of elevators shall comply with ANSI A17.1, ANSI A117.1, or UFAS.

10.26.A1. The number of elevators required shall be determined from a study of the facility plan and of the estimated vertical transportation requirements.

10.26.A2. Cars of hospital-type elevators shall have inside dimensions that will accommodate a patient bed and attendants. They shall be at least 5 feet (1.52 meters) wide by 7 feet 6 inches (2.29 meters) deep. Car doors shall have a clear opening of not less than 3 feet 8 inches (1.12 meters). Cars of all other required elevators shall have a minimum inside floor dimension of not less than 5 feet (1.52 meters). Car doors shall have a clear opening of not less than 3 feet (0.91 meter).

10.27 Mechanical Standards

Refer to applicable parts of Sections 7.31 and 9.2.L and M for these standards.

10.28 Electrical Standards

Refer to applicable parts of Sections 7.32 and 9.2.N for these standards.

11. PSYCHIATRIC HOSPITAL

▼ 11.1 General Conditions

11.1.A. Applicability
This section covers a psychiatric hospital intended for the care and treatment of inpatients and outpatients who do not require acute medical/surgical care services.

11.1.B. Functions
(See Section 1.1.F.)

11.1.C. Provisions for Handicapped
(See Section 1.3.)

11.1.D. Parking
In the absence of a formal parking study, the facility shall provide at least one space for each employee normally present during one weekday shift plus one space for every five beds or a total of 1.5 per patient. This ratio may be reduced when justified by availability of convenient public transportation and public parking. Additional parking may be required for outpatients or other services.

11.1.E. Swing Beds
Occupancy of a group of rooms within the facility may be changed to accommodate different patient groups based on age, sex, security level, or treatment programs.

11.1.F. Services
When the psychiatric facility is part of another facility, services such as dietary, storage, pharmacy, and laundry should be shared insofar as practical. In some cases, all ancillary service requirements will be met by the principal facility. In other cases, programmatic concerns and requirements may dictate separate services.

11.1.G. Environment
The facility should provide a therapeutic environment appropriate for the planned treatment programs. Security appropriate for the planned treatment programs shall be provided.

The unit should be characterized by a feeling of openness, with emphasis on natural light and exterior view. Interior finishes, lighting, and furnishings should suggest a residential rather than an institutional setting. These should, however, conform with applicable fire safety codes. Security and safety devices should not be presented in a manner to attract or challenge tampering by patients. Design, finishes, and furnishings should be such as to minimize the opportunity for residents to cause injury to themselves or others. Special design considerations for injury and suicide prevention shall be given to the following elements:

Visual control of nursing units and passive activity areas such as dayrooms and outdoor areas.

Hidden alcoves or enclosed spaces.

Areas secured from patients such as staff areas and mechanical space.

Door closers, latch handles, and hinges.

Door swings to private patient bathrooms.

Shower, bath, toilet, and sink plumbing fixtures, hardware and accessories including grab bars and toilet paper holders.

Windows including interior and exterior glazing.

Light fixtures, electrical outlets, electrical appliances, nurse call systems, and staff emergency assistance systems.

Ceilings, ventilation grilles, and access panels in patient bedrooms and bathrooms.

Sprinkler heads and other protrusions.

Fire extinguisher cabinets and fire alarm pull stations.

11.2 General Psychiatric Nursing Unit

Each nursing unit shall include the following (see Section 1.2 for exceptions to standards where existing conditions make absolute compliance impractical):

11.2.A. Patient Rooms
Each patient room shall meet the following standards:

11.2.A1. Maximum room capacity shall be two patients.

11.2.A2. Patient room areas, exclusive of toilet rooms, closets, lockers, wardrobes, alcoves, or vestibules, shall be at least 100 square feet (9.29 square meters) for single-bed rooms and 80 square feet (7.43 square meters) per bed for multiple-bed rooms. Minor encroachments, including columns and lavatories, *that do not interfere with functions* may be ignored when determining space requirements for patient rooms. The areas noted herein are intended as recognized minimums and do not prohibit use of larger rooms where required for needs and functions.

Security rooms may be included if required by the treatment program. Security rooms shall be single-bed rooms designed to minimize potential for escape, hiding, injury to self or others, or suicide. Access to toilets, showers, and wardrobes shall be restricted. Security rooms may be centralized on one unit or decentralized among units.

11.2.A3. Windows or vents in psychiatric units shall be arranged and located so that they can be opened from the inside to permit venting of combustion products and to permit any occupant direct access to fresh air in emergencies. The operation of operable windows shall be restricted. Where windows or vents require the use of tools or keys for operation, the tools or keys shall be located on the same floor in a prominent location accessible to staff. Windows in buildings designed with approved, engineered smoke-control systems may be fixed construction. Security glazing and/or other appropriate security features shall be used at all windows of the nursing unit and other patient activity and treatment areas to reduce the possibility of patient injury or escape.

11.2.A4. Each patient shall have access to a toilet room without having to enter the general corridor area.

(This direct access requirement may be disregarded if it conflicts with the supervision of patients as required by the treatment program.)

One toilet room shall serve no more than four beds and no more than two patient rooms. The toilet room shall contain a water closet and a handwashing fixture and the door should swing outward or be double acting. The handwashing fixture may be omitted from a toilet room if each patient room served by that toilet contains handwashing facilities.

11.2.A5. Each patient shall have within his or her room a separate wardrobe, locker, or closet suitable for hanging full-length garments and for storing personal effects. Adequate storage should be available for a daily change of clothes for seven days. Where treatment program indicates, shelves for folded garments may be used instead of hanging garments.

11.2.A6. There shall be a desk or writing surface in each room for patient use.

11.2.B. Service Areas

Provisions for the services noted below shall be located in or be readily available to each nursing unit. Each service area may be arranged and located to serve more than one nursing unit but, unless noted otherwise, at least one such service area shall be provided on each nursing floor. Where the words *room* or *office* are used, a separate, enclosed space for the one named function is intended; otherwise, the described area may be a specific space in another room or common area.

11.2.B1. Administrative center or nurse station.

11.2.B2. Office(s) for staff.

11.2.B3. Administrative supplies storage.

11.2.B4. Handwashing fixtures (see Section 7.2.B4).

11.2.B5. A separate charting area shall be provided with provisions for acoustical and patient file privacy.

11.2.B6. Toilet room(s) for staff.

11.2.B7. Staff lounge facilities.

11.2.B8. Securable closets or cabinet compartments for the personal effects of nursing personnel, conveniently located to the duty station. At a minimum, these shall be large enough for purses and billfolds.

11.2.B9. Clean workroom or clean holding room (see Section 7.2.B11).

11.2.B10. Soiled workroom (see Section 7.2.B12).

11.2.B11. Drug distribution station (see Section 7.2.B13).

11.2.B12. Clean linen storage (see Section 7.2.B14).

11.2.B13. Food service within the unit may be one or a combination, of the following:

    a. A nourishment station.

    b. A kitchenette designed for patient use with staff control of heating and cooking devices.

    c. A kitchen service within the unit including a sink equipped for handwashing, storage space, refrigerator, and facilities for meal preparation.

11.2.B14. Ice machine (see Section 7.2.B16).

11.2.B15. A bathtub or shower shall be provided for each six beds not otherwise served by bathing facilities within the patient rooms. Bathing facilities should be designed and located for patient convenience and privacy.

11.2.B16. At least two separate social spaces, one appropriate for noisy activities and one for quiet activities, shall be provided. The combined area shall be at least 25 square feet (2.32 square meters) per patient with at least 120 square feet (11.15 square meters) for each of the two spaces. This space may be shared by dining activities if an additional 15 square feet (1.39 square meters) per patient is added; otherwise, provide 20 square feet (1.86 square meters) per patient for dining. Dining facilities may be located off the nursing unit in a central area.

11.2.B17. Space for group therapy shall be provided. This may be combined with the quiet space noted above when the unit accommodates not more than 12 patients and when at least 225 square feet (20.90 square meters) of enclosed private space is available for group therapy activities.

11.2.B18. Patient laundry facilities with an automatic washer and dryer shall be provided.

11.2.B19. A secured storage area for patients' effects determined potentially harmful (razors, nail files, cigarette lighters, etc.). This area will be controlled by staff.

The following elements shall also be provided, but may be either within the psychiatric unit or immediately accessible to it unless otherwise dictated by the program:

11.2.B20. Equipment storage room.

11.2.B21. Storage space for wheelchairs may be outside the psychiatric unit, provided that provisions are made for convenient access as needed for handicapped patients.

11.2.B22. Examination and treatment room(s). The examination and treatment room(s) may serve several nursing units and may be on a different floor if conveniently located for routine use. Examination rooms shall have a minimum floor area of 120 square feet (11.15 square meters) excluding space for vestibule, toilets, and closets. The room shall contain a lavatory or sink equipped for handwashing; storage facilities; and a desk, counter, or shelf space for writing.

11.2.B23. Emergency equipment storage. Space shall be provided for emergency equipment that is under direct control of the nursing staff, such as a CPR cart. This space shall be in close proximity to a nurse station; it may serve more than one unit.

11.2.B24. Housekeeping room (see Section 7.2.B22).

11.2.B25. A visitor room for patients to meet with friends or family with a minimum floor space of 100 square feet (9.29 square meters).

11.2.B26. A quiet room for a patient who needs to be alone for a short period of time but does not require a seclusion room. A minimum of 80 square feet (7.43 square meters) is required. The visitor room may serve this purpose.

11.2.B27. Separate consultation room(s) with minimum floor space of 100 square feet (9.29 square meters) each provided at a room-to-bed ratio of one consultation room for each 12 psychiatric beds. The room(s) shall be designed for acoustical and visual privacy and constructed to achieve a level of voice privacy of 50 STC (which in terms of vocal privacy means that some loud or raised speech is heard only by straining, but is not intelligible). The visitor room may serve as a consultation room.

11.2.B28. A conference and treatment planning room for use by the psychiatric unit. This room may be combined with the charting room.

11.2.C. Seclusion Treatment Room

There shall be at least one seclusion room for up to 24 beds or a major fraction thereof. The seclusion treatment room is intended for short-term occupancy by violent or suicidal patients. Within the psychiatric nursing unit, this space provides for patients requiring security and protection. The room(s) shall be located for direct nursing staff supervision. Each room shall be for only one patient. It shall have an area of at least 60 square feet (5.6 square meters) and shall be constructed to prevent patient hiding, escape, injury, or suicide. Where restraint beds are required by the functional program, 80 square feet (7.43 square meters) shall be required. If a facility has more than one psychiatric nursing unit, the number of seclusion rooms shall be a function of the total number of psychiatric beds in the facility. Seclusion rooms may be grouped together. Special fixtures and hardware for electrical circuits shall be used. Doors shall be 3 feet 8 inches (1.12 meters) wide and shall permit staff observation of the patient while also maintaining provisions for patient privacy. Minimum ceiling height shall be 9 feet (274.32 centimeters). Seclusion treatment rooms shall be accessed by an anteroom or vestibule that also provides direct access to a toilet room. The toilet room and anteroom shall be large enough to safely manage the patient. The seclusion room door shall swing out.

Where the interior of the seclusion treatment room is padded with combustible materials, these materials shall be of a type acceptable to the local authority having jurisdiction. The room area, including floor, walls, ceilings, and all openings shall be protected with not less than one-hour-rated construction.

11.3 Child Psychiatric Unit

The standards of Section 11.2 shall be applied to child units with the following exceptions.

11.3.A. Patient Rooms

11.3.A1. Maximum room capacity shall be four children.

11.3.A2. Patient room (with beds or cribs) areas shall be 100 square feet (9.29 square meters) for single bedrooms; 80 square feet (7.43 square meters) per bed and 60 square feet (5.57 square meters) per crib in multiple-bed rooms.

11.3.A3. Storage space shall be provided for toys, equipment, extra cribs and beds, and cots or recliners for parents who might stay overnight.

11.3.B. Service Areas

11.3.B1. The combined area for social activities shall be 35 square feet (3.25 square meters) per patient.

11.4 Geriatric, Alzheimer's, and Other Dementia Unit

The standards of Section 11.2 shall be applied to geriatric units with the following exceptions.

11.4.A. Patient Rooms

11.4.A1. Patient room areas shall be 120 square feet (11.15 square meters) in single-bed rooms and 200 square feet (18.58 square meters) in multiple-bed rooms.

11.4.A2. A nurses call system shall be provided in accordance with standards contained in Section 7.32. Provisions shall be made for easy removal or for covering call button outlets.

11.4.A3. Each patient bedroom shall have storage for extra blankets, pillows, and linen.

11.4.A4. Door to patient room shall be a minimum of 3 feet 8 inches wide (1.12 meters).

11.4.B. Service Areas

11.4.B1. Patients shall have access to at least one bathtub in each nursing unit.

11.4.B2. The standards of Section 11.2.B16 shall apply for social spaces except that the combined area for social activities shall be 30 square feet (2.79 square meters) per patient.

11.4.B3. Storage space for wheelchairs shall be provided in the nursing unit.

11.5 Forensic Psychiatric Unit

The standards of Section 11.2 shall be applied to forensic units. Forensic units shall have security vestibules or sally ports at the unit entrance. Specialized program requirements may indicate the need for additional treatment areas, police and courtroom space, and security considerations. Children, juveniles, and adolescents shall be separated from the adult areas.

11.6 Radiology Suite

Radiology services are not required to be provided within a psychiatric hospital. If they are provided within the hospital, the radiology suite shall comply with Section 7.10.

11.7 Nuclear Medicine

Nuclear medicine services are not required to be provided within a psychiatric hospital. If they are provided within the hospital, the nuclear medicine area shall comply with Section 7.11.

11.8 Laboratory Suite

Required laboratory tests may be performed on-site or provided through a contractual arrangement with a laboratory service.

Provisions shall be made for the following procedures to be performed on-site: urinalysis, blood glucose, and electrolytes. Provisions shall also be included for specimen collection and processing.

Minimum facilities on-site shall include a defined area with a laboratory lab counter, sink with water, refrigerated storage, storage for equipment and supplies, clerical area, and record storage.

11.9 Rehabilitation Therapy Department

11.9.A. General
Rehabilitation therapy in a psychiatric hospital is primarily for the diagnosis and treatment of mental functions but may also seek to address physical functions in varying degrees. It may contain one or several categories of services. If a formal rehabilitative therapy service is included in a project, the facilities and equipment shall be as necessary for the effective function of the program. Where two or more rehabilitative services are included, items may be shared, as appropriate.

11.9.B. Common Elements
Each rehabilitative therapy department shall include the following, which may be shared or provided as separate units for each service.

11.9.B1. Office and clerical space with provision for filing and retrieval of patient records.

11.9.B2. Where reception and control station(s) are required by the program, provision shall be made for visual control of waiting and activity areas. (This may be combined with office and clerical space.)

11.9.B3. Patient waiting area(s) out of traffic, with provision for wheelchairs. Patient waiting time for rehabilitation therapy should be minimized in a psychiatric hospital. The waiting area may be omitted if not required by the program.

11.9.B4. Patient toilets with handwashing facilities accessible to wheelchair patients.

11.9.B5. A conveniently accessible housekeeping room and service sink for housekeeping use.

11.9.B6. A secured area or cabinet within the vicinity of each work area for securing staff personal effects.

11.9.B7. Convenient access to toilets and lockers.

11.9.B8. Access to a demonstration-conference room.

11.9.C. Physical Therapy
The physical health of a person can have a direct effect on his or her mental health. Therefore, physical therapy may be desirable in a psychiatric hospital, especially for long-term care patients and elderly patients.

If physical therapy is part of the service, the following, at least, shall be included.

11.9.C1. Individual treatment area(s) with privacy screens or curtains. Each such space shall have not less than 60 square feet (5.57 square meters) of clear floor area.

11.9.C2. Handwashing facilities for staff either within or at each treatment space. (One handwashing facility may serve several treatment stations.)

11.9.C3. Exercise area and facilities.

11.9.C4. Clean linen and towel storage.

11.9.C5. Storage for equipment and supplies.

11.9.C6. Separate storage for soiled linen, towels, and supplies.

11.9.C7. Dressing areas, showers, and lockers for outpatients to be treated.

11.9.C8. Provisions shall be made for thermotherapy, diathermy, ultrasonics, and hydrotherapy when required by the functional program.

11.9.D. Occupational Therapy
Occupational therapy may include such activities as woodworking, leather tooling, art, needlework, painting, sewing, metal work, and ceramics. The following, at least, shall be included:

11.9.D1. Work areas and counters suitable for wheelchair access.

11.9.D2. Handwashing facilities.

11.9.D3. Storage for supplies and equipment.

11.9.D4. Secured storage for supplies and equipment potentially harmful.

*11.9.D5. A separate room or alcove for a kiln.

11.9.D6. Remote electrical switching for equipment potentially harmful.

11.9.D7. Work areas should be sized for one therapy group at a time.

*11.9.D8. (See Appendix A.)

11.9.E. Vocational Therapy
Vocational therapy assists patients in the development and maintenance of productive work and interaction skills through the use of work tasks. These activities may occur in an industrial therapy workshop in another department or outdoors. If this service is provided, the following, at least, shall be included:

11.9.E1. Work areas suitable for wheelchair access.

11.9.E2. Handwashing facilities if required by the program.

11.9.E3. Storage for supplies and equipment.

11.9.E4. Secured storage for supplies and equipment potentially harmful.

11.9.E5. Remote electrical switching for equipment potentially harmful.

11.9.E6. Group work areas should be sized for one therapy group at a time.

11.9.F. Recreation Therapy
Recreation therapy assists patients in the development and maintenance of community living skills through the use of leisure-time activity tasks. These activities may occur in a recreation therapy department, in specialized facilities (e.g., gymnasium), multipurpose space in other areas (e.g., the nursing unit), or outdoors. The following, at least, shall be included:

11.9.F1. Activity areas suitable for wheelchair access.

11.9.F2. Handwashing facilities if required by the program.

11.9.F3. Storage for supplies and equipment.

11.9.F4. Secured storage for supplies and equipment potentially harmful.

11.9.F5. Remote electrical switching for equipment potentially harmful.

11.9.G. Education Therapy
Education therapy may be a program requirement, especially for children and adolescents. If the service is provided, the following, at least, shall be included.

11.9.G1. Classroom with student desks with 30 square feet (2.79 square meters) per desk with at least 150 square feet (13.94 square meters) per classroom.

11.9.G2. Desk and lockable storage for the teacher.

11.9.G3. Storage for supplies, equipment, and books.

11.10 Pharmacy

11.10.A. General
As described in the functional program, the size and type of services to be provided in the pharmacy will depend on the type of patients and illnesses treated, type of drug distribution system used, number of patients to be served, and extent of shared or purchased services. This shall be described in the functional program. The pharmacy room or suite shall be located for convenient access, staff control, and security. Facilities and equipment shall be as necessary to accommodate the functions of the program and shall include provisions for procurement, storage, distribution, and recording of drugs and other pharmacy products. (Satellite facilities, if provided, shall include those items required by the program.)

11.11 Dietary Facilities

(See Section 7.17.)

11.12 Administration and Public Areas

(See Section 7.18.)

11.13 Medical Records

(See Section 7.19.)

11.14 Central Services

If only primary medical care is provided, central services may not be required or may be provided by countertop sterilizing/cleaning equipment. If decontamination and sterilization are required on-site, full central services shall be provided (see Section 7.20).

11.15 General Storage

General storage room(s) with a total area of not less than 4 square feet (0.37 square meters) per inpatient bed shall be provided. Storage may be in separate, concentrated areas within the institution or in one or more individual buildings on-site. A portion of this storage may be provided off-site.

11.16 Linen Services

(See Section 7.22.)

11.17 Facilities for Cleaning and Sanitizing Carts

(See Section 7.23.)

11.18 Employee Facilities

(See Section 7.24.)

11.19 Housekeeping Room

(See Section 7.25.)

11.20 Engineering Service and Equipment Area

(See Section 7.26.)

11.21 Waste Processing Services

(See Section 7.27.)

11.22 General Standards for Details and Finishes

The standards of Section 11.22 shall comply with Section 7.28 with the following exceptions.

11.22.A.
The minimum door width for patient use access in new work shall be at least 3 feet (.91 meters).

11.22.B.
Where grab bars are provided the space between the bar and the wall should be filled to prevent a cord being tied around it for hanging. Bars, including those which are part of such fixtures as soap dishes, shall be sufficiently anchored to sustain a concentrated load of 250 pounds (113.4 kilograms).

11.23 Design and Construction, Including Fire-Resistive Standards

(See Section 7.29.)

11.24 Elevators

The standards of Section 11.24 shall comply with Section 7.30 with the following exception: Hospital-type elevators are not required, but at least one passenger-type elevator in a multifloor building must be sized to accommodate a gurney.

11.25 Mechanical

(See Section 7.31.)

11.26 Electrical

▲ (See Section 7.32.)

12. MOBILE, TRANSPORTABLE, AND RELOCATABLE UNITS

▼ 12.1 General

12.1.A. Application
This section applies to mobile, transportable, and relocatable structures. The size of these units limits occupancy, thereby minimizing hazards and allowing for less stringent standards. Needed community services can therefore be provided at an affordable cost. These facilities shall be defined as space and equipment service for four or fewer workers at any one time. Meeting all provisions of Section 9.2 for general outpatient facilities is desirable, but limited size and resources may preclude satisfying any but the basic minimums described. Specifically described are:

12.1.A1. Mobile units.

12.1.A2. Transportable units.

12.1.A3. Relocatable units.

12.1.B. Definitions

12.1.B1. Mobile unit.

Any premanufactured structure, trailer, or self-propelled unit, equipped with a chassis on wheels and intended to provide shared medical services to the community on a temporary basis. These units are typically 8 feet wide by 48 feet long (2.44 meters by 14.63 meters) (or less), some equipped with expanding walls, and designed to be moved on a daily basis.

12.1.B2. Transportable unit.

Any premanufactured structure or trailer, equipped with a chassis on wheels, intended to provide shared medical services to the community on an extended temporary basis. The units are typically 12 feet wide by 60 feet long (3.66 meters by 18.29 meters) (or less) and are designed to move periodically, depending on need.

12.1.B3. Relocatable unit.

Any structure, not on wheels, built to be relocated at any time and provide medical services. These structures vary in size.

12.1.C. Classification
The classifications of these facilities shall be Business Occupancy as listed in the building codes and NFPA 101 Life Safety Code, chapter 26.

Units shall comply with chapter 12-6, "Ambulatory Health Care Centers," of NFPA 101, where patients incapable of self-preservation or those receiving inhalation anesthesia are treated.

12.1.D. Common Elements for Mobile, Transportable, and Relocatable Units

12.1.D1. Site conditions.

a. Access for the unit to arrive shall be taken into consideration for space planning. Turning radius of the vehicles, slopes of the approach (6 percent maximum), and existing conditions shall be addressed.

b. Gauss fields of various strengths of Magnetic Resonance Imaging (MRI) units shall be considered for the environmental effect on the field homogeneity and vice versa. Radio frequency interference shall be considered when planning site.

c. Sites shall be provided with properly sized power, including emergency power, water, waste, telephone, and fire alarm connections, as required by local and state building codes.

d. Sites shall have level concrete pads or piers and be designed for the structural loads of the facility. Construction of pads shall meet local, state, and seismic codes. Concrete-filled steel pipe bollards are recommended for protection of the facility and the unit.

e. Sites utilizing MRI systems shall consider providing adequate access for cryogen-servicing of the magnet. Cryogen dewars are of substantial weight and size. Storage of dewars also shall be included in space planning.

f. It is recommended that each site provide a covered walkway or enclosure to ensure patient safety from the outside elements.

g. Consideration shall be given to location of the unit so that diesel exhaust of the tractor and/or unit generator is kept away from the fresh air intake of the facility.

h. It is recommended that each facility provide a means of preventing unit movement, either by blocking the wheels or by providing pad anchors.

i. Sites shall provide hazard-free drop-off zones and adequate parking for patients.

j. The facility shall provide waiting space for patient privacy and patient/staff toilets as close to the unit docking area as possible.

k. Each site shall provide access for wheelchair/stretcher patients to the unit.

l. Mobile units shall be provided with handwashing facilities unless each site can provide handwashing facilities within a 25-foot (7.47 meter) proximity to the unit. Transportable and relocatable units shall be provided with handwashing facilities.

m. It is recommended that each site requiring water and waste services to the unit provide a means of freeze protection in geographical areas where freezing temperatures occur.

12.1.D2. Site considerations—relocatable units.

Seismic force resistance for relocatable units shall comply with Section 1.4 and shall be given an importance factor of one when applied to the seismic design formulas. These units shall meet the structural requirements of the local and state building codes.

12.1.E. General Standards for Details and Finishes for Unit Construction

12.1.E1. Existing facilities.

Existing facilities shall comply with applicable requirements of the existing Business Occupancies, Chapter 27, of NFPA 101; and where there are patients incapable of self-preservation receiving inhalation anesthesia, existing Ambulatory Health Care Centers, Chapter 13-6, shall apply.

12.1.E2. Details and finishes.

Requirements below apply to all units unless noted otherwise:

a. Horizontal sliding doors and power-operated doors shall comply with NFPA 101, Section 5-2.

b. Units shall be permitted a single means of egress as permitted by NFPA 101, Chapter 26-2.

c. All glazing in doors shall be safety or wire glass.

d. Stairs for mobile and transportable units shall be in accordance with the following table:

New units

Minimum width clear of all obstructions, except projections not exceeding 3½ inches at or below handrail height on each side	34 inches (86.36 centimeters)
Minimum headroom	6 ft. 8 inches (2.03 meters)
Maximum height of risers	9 inches (22.86 centimeters)
Minimum height of risers	4 inches (10.16 centimeters)
Minimum tread depth	9 inches (22.86 centimeters)
Doors opening immediately onto stairs without a landing	NO

Existing units

Minimum width clear of all obstructions, except projections not exceeding 3½ inches at or below handrail height on each side	27 inches (.69 meters)
Minimum headroom	6 ft. 8 inches (2.03 meters)
Maximum height of risers	9 inches (22.86 centimeters)
Minimum height of risers	4 inches (10.16 centimeters)
Minimum tread depth	7 inches (17.78 centimeters)
Doors opening immediately onto stairs without a landing	YES

There shall be no variation exceeding ³⁄₁₆ inch in depth of adjacent treads or in the height of adjacent risers, and the tolerance between the largest and smallest tread shall not exceed ⅜ inch in any flight.

Exception: Where the bottom riser adjoins a public way, walk, or driveway having an established grade and serving as a landing, a variation in height of not more than 3 inches (0.08 meter) in every 3 feet (0.91 meter) and fraction of thereafter is permitted. Adjustable legs at the bottom of the stair assembly shall be permitted to allow for grade differences.

Stairs and landings for relocatable units shall comply with NFPA 101.

e. Handrails shall be provided on at least one side. Handrails shall be installed and constructed in accordance with NFPA 101, 5-2.2.4.2, with the following exception: Provided the distance from grade to unit floor height is not greater than 4 feet 5 inches (1.35 meters), one intermediate handrail, having clear distance between rails of 19 inches (0.48 meter) maximum, shall be permitted. Exception: Existing units having a floor height of 63 inches (1.60 meters) maximum.

f. All units shall be equipped with an automatic sprinkler system or other automatic extinguishing equipment as defined in NFPA 101, Section 7-7. In addition, manual fire extinguishers shall be provided in accordance with NFPA 101, Sections 26-3.5 and 12-6.3.5.2. Exception: Existing units equipped with portable fire extinguishers.

g. Fire detection, alarm, and communications capabilities shall be installed and connected to facility central alarm system on all new units in accordance with NFPA 101, Section 7-6.

h. Radiation protection for X-ray and gamma ray installations shall be in accordance with NCRP reports numbers 49 and 91 in addition to all applicable local and state requirements.

i. Interior finish materials shall be class A as defined in NFPA 101, Section 6-5.

j. Textile materials having a napped, tufted, looped, woven, nonwoven, or similar surface shall be permitted on walls and ceilings provided such materials have a class "A" rating and rooms or areas are protected by automatic extinguishment or sprinkler system.

k. Fire retardant coatings shall be permitted in accordance with NFPA 101, Section 6-5.6.

l. Curtains and draperies shall be noncombustible or flame retardant and shall pass both the large and small scale tests required by NFPA 101.

12.1.F. Mechanical Standards

12.1.F1. Air conditioning, heating, ventilating, ductwork, and related equipment shall be installed in accordance with NFPA 90A, Standard for the Installation of Air Conditioning and Ventilation systems.

12.1.F2. All other requirements for heating and ventilation systems shall comply with Section 9.2.I.

12.1.G. Plumbing Standards

12.1.G1. Plumbing and other piping systems shall be installed in accordance with applicable model plumbing codes, unless specified herein.

12.1.G2. Mobile Units, requiring sinks, shall not be required to be vented through the roof. Ventilation of waste lines shall be permitted to be vented through the sidewalls or other acceptable locations. Transportable and relocatable units shall be vented through the roof per model plumbing codes.

12.1.G3. All waste lines shall be designed and constructed to discharge into the facility sanitary sewage system.

12.1.G4. Backflow prevention shall be installed at the point of water connection on the unit.

12.1.G5. Medical gases and suction systems, if installed, shall be in accordance with NFPA 99.

12.1.H. Electrical Standards

12.1.H1. Refer to Section 9.2.N for applicable electric standards.

12.1.I. Environmental Standards

All mobile, transportable, and relocatable units shall be sited in full compliance with such federal, state, and local environmental laws and regulations as may apply,
▲ for example, those listed in Section 3.3.

APPENDIX A

▼ This Appendix is not part of the requirements of these Guidelines, but is included for information purposes only.

The following notes, bearing the same number as the text of the *Guidelines* to which they apply, contain useful explanatory material and references.

A1.4

Owners of existing facilities should undertake an assessment of their facility with respect to its ability to withstand the effects of regional natural disasters. The assessment should consider performance of structural and critical nonstructural building systems, and the likelihood of loss of externally supplied power, gas, water, and communications under such conditions. Facility master planning should consider mitigation measures required to address conditions that may be hazardous to patients and conditions that may compromise the ability of the facility to fulfill its planned postemergency medical response. Particular attention should be paid to seismic considerations in areas where the effective peak acceleration coefficient, Aa, of ASCE 7-92 exceeds 0.15.

A1.4.A. The ASCE 7-92 seismic provisions are based on the National Earthquake Hazards Reduction Program (NEHRP) provisions (1988 edition) developed by the Building Seismic Safety Council (BSSC) for the Federal Emergency Management Agency (FEMA).

A study by the National Institute of Standards and Technology (NIST) found that the following seismic standards were essentially equivalent to the NEHRP (1988) provisions:

1991 ICBO Uniform Building Code

1992 Supplement to the BOCA National Building Code

1992 Amendments to the SBCC Standard Building Code

Executive Order 12699, dated January 5, 1990, specified the use of the maps in the most recent edition of ANSI A58 for seismic safety of Federal and Federally Assisted or Regulated New Building Construction. The ASCF 7 standard was formerly the ANSI A58 standard. Public Law 101-614 charged FEMA to "…prepare and disseminate widely …information on building codes and practices for buildings…." The NEHRP provisions were developed to provide this guidance.

A4.2.C1. Examples of movable equipment include operating tables, treatment and examination tables, laboratory centrifuges, food service trucks and other wheeled carts, and patient room furnishings.

A4.3 Major Technical Equipment

Examples of major technical equipment are X-ray and other imaging equipment, radiation therapy equipment, lithotripters, audiometry testing chambers, laundry equipment, computers, and similar items.

A7.3.A9. If a central station is provided, partial enclosure with glass is recommended to minimize sound transmission to patients and to provide consultative privacy to the staff while maintaining visualization of patients.

A7.3.A15.g. Equipment storage room or alcove. Appropriate room(s) or alcove(s) should be provided for storage of large items of equipment necessary for patient care and as required by the functional program. Its location should not interfere with the flow of traffic. Work areas and storage of critical care supplies should be in locations such that they are readily accessible to nursing and physician staff. Shelving, file cabinets, and drawers should be located so that they are accessible to all requiring use. Separate areas need to be designed for the unit secretary and staff charting. Planning should consider the potential volume of staff (both medical and nursing) that could be present at any one time and translate that to adequate charting surfaces. The secretarial area should be accessible to all. However, the charting areas may be somewhat isolated to facilitate concentration. Storage for chart forms and supplies should be readily accessible. Space for computer terminals and printer and conduit for computer hook-up should be provided when automated information systems are in use or planned for the future. Patient records should be readily accessible to clerical, nursing, and physician staff. Alcoves should be provided for the storage and rapid retrieval of crash carts and portable monitor/defibrillator units. Grounded electrical outlets should be provided in sufficient numbers to permit recharging stored battery-operated equipment.

A7.3.A15.i. A stat laboratory should be available on the periphery of the critical care unit if the main laboratory is not in close proximity, or if it is not accessible via a specimen transport system, or if it provides less than 24-hour service.

A7.3.A16.d. Critical care units of more than 12 beds should have a separate reception area which should be located next to the visitor lounge/waiting facility. It should be linked to the critical care unit by telephone and the intercommunications system. It is desirable to have separate visitor and professional entrances to the unit. The reception area should be situated so that it can control access to the critical care unit(s). It should be strategically located so that all visitors must pass by the receptionist area for verification and notification of the nursing staff as appropriate. One-and-a-half to two seats per critical care bed are recommended. House and public telephones should be provided. Windows are desirable. The area should have a desk or counter at the entrance to the critical care facility. It should be planned so that the placement shields the interior of the unit. A private family consultation room and sleep/rest cubicles are desirable, and shower facilities are optional.

A7.3.E4. It is recommended that the NICU be located in an area of low traffic volume, preferably in a closed corridor with no through traffic. Exits must meet national, state, and local fire code regulations. Traffic patterns should encourage family visitation and discourage casual use.

A7.3.E6. Whenever possible, supplies should flow through special supply entrances from external corridors so that penetration of the semisterile zone by non-nursery personnel is unnecessary. Soiled materials should be sealed and stored in a soiled holding area until removed. This holding area should be located where there will be no need to pass back through the semisterile zone to remove the soiled materials.

A7.3.E7. Windows should be provided in patient care areas whenever possible.

A7.3.E9. General lighting in the nursery should not exceed 100 footcandles measured at mattress level. The lighting fixture layout should be designed to avoid a fixture directly above or over the neonate. Whenever possible, general lighting as well as supplemental examination lights should be designed to be controlled from each incubator position. A master switch is also desirable to simultaneously control all lights in special situations.

A7.3.E13. Intercom systems with volume control between the NICU, term nursery, and labor and delivery area are desirable. "Hands-free" telephone and intercoms are encouraged.

A7.4

There should be a breastfeeding/pumping room readily available for mothers of NICU babies to pump breastmilk. (See Section 7.2.)

A7.4.D.
When the functional program includes a mother-baby couplet approach to nursing care, the workroom functions described above may be incorporated in the nurse station that serves the postpartum patient rooms.

A7.8.A.
Obstetrical program models vary widely in their delivery methodologies. The models are essentially three types. The following narrative describes the organizational framework of each model.

A7.8.A1. The Traditional Model

Under the traditional model, labor, delivery, recovery, and postpartum occur in separate areas. The birthing woman is treated as the moving part. She is moved through these functional areas depending on the status of the birth process.

The functional areas are separate rooms consisting of the labor room, delivery room, recovery room, postpartum bedroom, and infant nurseries (levels determined by acuity).

A7.8.A2. The Labor-Delivery-Recovery Model

All labor-delivery-recovery rooms (LDRs) are designed to accommodate the birthing process from labor through delivery and recovery of mother and baby. They are equipped to handle most complications, with the exception of caesarean sections.

The birthing woman moves only as a postpartum patient to her bedroom or to a caesarean section delivery room (surgical operative room) if delivery complications occur.

After the mother and baby are recovered in the LDR, they are transferred to a mother-baby care unit for postpartum stay.

A7.8.A3. The Labor-Delivery-Recovery-Postpartum Model

Single room maternity care in labor-delivery-recovery-postpartum rooms (LDRPs) adds a "P" to the LDR model. Room design and capability to handle most emergencies remain the same as the LDRs. However, the LDRP model eliminates a move to postpartum after delivery. LDRP uses one private room for labor, delivery, recovery, and postpartum stay.

Equipment is moved into the room as needed, rather than moving the patient to the equipped room. Certain deliveries are handled in a caesarean section delivery room (surgical operative room) should delivery complications occur.

A7.9.A2. Classification of emergency departments/services (from the *Accreditation Manual for Hospitals.* The Joint Commission on Accreditation of Healthcare Organizations, 1991, pp. 32-33):

Level I: provides comprehensive emergency care 24 hours a day, with a physician experienced in emergency care on duty at all times. Must include in-hospital physician coverage of medical, surgical, orthopedic, obstetric/gynecologic, pediatric, and anesthesia services. Other specialty coverage must be available within approximately 30 minutes. Physical and related emotional problems must be provided in-house.

Level II: provides emergency care 24 hours a day, with a physician experienced in emergency care on duty at all times, and specialty consultation available within approximately 30 minutes. Physical and related emotional problems must be provided in-house, with transfer provisions to another facility when needed.

Level III: provides emergency care 24 hours a day, with at least one physician available within approximately 30 minutes. Specialty consultation available per medical staff request or by transfer to a designated hospital where definitive care can be provided.

Level IV: provides reasonable care in assessing if an emergency exists and in performing lifesaving first aid, with appropriate referral to the nearest hospital capable of providing needed services. Physician coverage is defined by the local medical staff.

More detailed descriptions of emergency service categories may be available from the Committee on Trauma of the American College of Surgeons and the American College of Emergency Physicians.

A7.9.D8. Access needs to be convenient to ambulance entrance.

A7.9.D16.a. Disposal space for regulated medical waste, e.g., gauzes/linens soaked with body fluids, should be separate from routine disposal space.

A7.9.D21. A security station and/or system should be located to maximize visibility of the treatment areas, waiting areas, and key entrance sites. This system should include visual monitoring devices installed both internally in the emergency department as well as externally at entrance sites and parking lots. Spatial requirements for a security station should include accommodation for hospital security staff, local police officers, and monitoring equipment. Design consideration should include installation of silent alarms, panic buttons, and intercom systems, and physical barriers such as doors to patient entry areas.

The security monitoring system should be included on the hospital's emergency power back-up system.

A7.9.D23. A family room to provide privacy for families of critically ill or deceased patients should be located away from the main traffic and treatment areas. An enclosed room with space for comfortable seating of six to ten persons should be provided; telephone access is essential. A salon- or parlor-type ambience and incandescent lighting is preferred.

A7.9.E. Other Space Considerations
When the functional program defines the need, there should be additional space considerations as noted:

A7.9.E1. A decontamination room for both chemical and radiation exposure. This room should have a separate entrance to the emergency department, and an independent, closed drainage system. A negative air flow and ventilation system separate and distinct from the hospital system should be provided. Spatial requirements should allow for at least one stretcher, several hospital staff, two shower heads and an adjacent locked storage area for medical supplies and equipment. Solid lead-lined walls and doors should meet regulatory requirements.

A7.9.E2. A separate pediatric emergency area. This area should include space for registration, discharge, triage, waiting, and a playroom. An area for the nurse station and physician station, storage for supplies and medication, and one to two isolation rooms should also be included. Each examination/treatment room should be 100 square feet (9.29 square meters) of clear floor space, with a separate procedure/trauma room of 120 square feet (11.15 square meters) of clear floor space; each of these rooms should have handwashing facilities, vacuum, oxygen, and air outlets, examination lights, and wall/column mounted ophthalmoscopes/otoscopes. At least one room for pelvic examinations shall be included. X-ray illuminators shall be available.

A7.9.E3. Observation/holding units for patients requiring observation up to 23 hours or admission to an inpatient unit. This area should be located separately but near the main emergency department. The size will depend upon the function (observation and/or holding), patient acuity mix, and projected utilization. As defined by the functional plan, this area should consist of a centralized nurse station; 100 square feet (9.29 square meters) of clear floor space for each cubicle, with vacuum, oxygen, and air outlets, monitoring space, and nurse call buttons. A patient bathroom should be provided. Storage space for medical and dietary supplies should be included. X-ray illuminators shall be available.

A7.9.E4. A separate fast track area when annual emergency department visits exceed 20-30,000 visits should be considered. This area should include space for registration, discharge, triage, and waiting, as well as a physician/nurse workstation. Storage areas for supplies and medication should be included. A separate treatment/procedure room of 120 square feet (11.15 square meters) of clear floor space should be provided. Examination/treatment areas should be 100 square feet (9.29 square meters) of clear floor space, with handwashing facilities, vacuum, oxygen, and air outlets, and examination lights. At least one treatment/examination room should be designated for pelvic examinations.

A7.10.C3. Some equipment may require additional air conditioning for the computer room.

A7.10.D1. Radiography rooms should be a minimum of 180 square feet (7.43 square meters). (Dedicated chest X-ray may be smaller.)

A7.10.D2. Tomography and Radiography/ Fluoroscopy (R&F) rooms should be a minimum of 250 square feet (23.23 square meters).

A7.10.D3. Mammography rooms should be a minimum of 100 square feet (9.29 square meters).

A7.10.E4. When provided, space should be a minimum of 50 square feet (4.65 square meters) to accommodate two large dewars of cryogen.

A7.10.H. Cardiac Catheterization Lab (Cardiology)

A7.10.H1. The cardiac catherization lab is normally a separate suite located near surgery, but may be a part of imaging provided that the appropriate sterile environment is provided. It can be combined with angiography in low usage situations. Equipment and space shall be as necessary to accommodate the functional program and is generally a minimum of 400 square feet (37.16 square meters). Layouts should be developed in accordance with manufacturer's recommendations.

A7.10.H2. A certified physicist representing the owner or appropriate state agency shall specify the type, location, and amount of radiation protection to be installed following the final approved department layout and equipment selections. The architect should incorporate radiation protection requirements into the specifications and building plans.

A7.10.H3. A control room should be provided and should be a minimum of 150 square feet (13.94 square meters) to accommodate physiological monitoring equipment. A view window should be provided to permit full view of the patient.

A7.10.H4. A viewing area should be provided with space for processing, individual countertop projection equipment (cine) and film boxes (a minimum of 10 feet [3.05 meters] in length) with illumination to provide light of the same color value and intensity for appropriate comparison of several adjacent films. (When the procedure room is combined with angiography, cine can be included in the viewing area for angiography.)

A7.10.H5. A scrub sink located outside the staff entry to the special procedure room should be provided for staff use.

A7.10.H6. A patient holding area for prep and hold shall be provided to accommodate stretchers. Its size should be based upon the number of exams expected.

A7.10.H7. Soiled holding and contaminated holding should be provided with handwashing facilities.

A7.10.H8. Storage space should be provided for portable equipment, defibrillators, catheters, and other supplies.

A7.10.H9. When the suite is located outside of the imaging suite, a separate scheduling and staff work space, cardiologist's office, and staff toilet should be provided.

A7.11.G1. Space shall be provided as necessary to accommodate the functional program. PET scanning is generally used in experimental settings and requires space for a scanner and for a cyclotron. The scanner room should be a minimum of 300 square feet (27 square meters).

A7.11.G2. Where a cyclotron room is required, it should be a minimum of 225 square feet (20.90 square meters) with a 16 square foot (4.88 square meter) space safe for storage of parts which may need to cool down for a year or more.

A7.11.G3. Both a hot (radioactive) lab and a cold (nonradioactive) lab may be required, each a minimum of 250 square feet (23.23 square meters).

A7.11.G4. A blood lab of a minimum of 80 square feet (7.43 square meters) should be provided.

A7.11.G5. A patient holding area to accommodate two stretchers should be provided.

A7.11.G6. A gas storage area large enough to accommodate bottles of gas should be provided. Each gas will be piped individually and may go to the cyclotron or to the lab. Ventilation adequate for the occupancy is required. Compressed air may be required to pressurize a water circulation system.

A7.11.G7. Significant radiation protection may be required since the cyclotron may generate high radiation.

A7.11.G8. Special ventilation systems together with monitors, sensors, and alarm systems may be required to vent gases and chemicals.

A7.11.G9. The heating, ventilating, and air conditioning system will require particular attention; highest pressures should be in coldest (radiation) areas and exhaust should be in hottest (radiation) areas. Redundancy may be important.

A7.11.G10. The cyclotron is water cooled with de-ionized water. A heat exchanger and connection to a compressor or connection to chilled water may be required. A redundant plumbing system connected to a holding tank may be required to prevent accidental leakage of contaminated water into the regular plumbing system.

A7.11.I4. Minimum size should be 260 square feet (24.15 square meters) for the simulator room. Minimum size, including the maze, should be 680 square feet (63.17 square meters) for accelerator rooms and 450 square feet (41.81 square meters) for cobalt rooms.

A7.20.A2. Clean Assembly/Workroom

Access to sterilization room should be restricted. This room should contain Hi-Vacuum or gravity steam sterilizers and sterilization equipment to accommodate heat-sensitive equipment (ETO sterilizer) and ETO aerators. This room is used exclusively for the inspection, assembly, and packaging of medical/surgical supplies and equipment for sterilization. Area should contain worktables, counters, a handwashing fixture, ultrasonic storage facilities for backup supplies and instrumentation and a drying cabinet or equipment. The area should be spacious enough to hold sterilizer cars for loading of prepared supplies for sterilization.

A7.27.B4. When incinerators are used, consideration shall be given to the recovery of waste heat from on-site incinerators used to dispose of large amounts of waste materials.

A7.27.B5. Incinerators should be designed in a manner fully consistent with protection of public and environmental health, both on-site and off-site, and in compliance with federal, state, and local statutes and regulations. Toward this end, permit applications for incinerators and modifications thereof should be supported by Environmental Assessments and/or Environmental Impact Statements (EISs) and/or Health Risk Assessments (HRAs) as may be required by regulatory agencies. Except as noted below, such assessments should utilize standard U.S. EPA methods, specifically those set forth in U.S. EPA (1990), and shall be fully consistent with U.S. EPA guidelines for health risk assessment (U.S. EPA 1987). Under some circumstances, however, regulatory agencies having jurisdiction over a particular project may require use of alternative methods.

A7.31.D1. One way to achieve basic humidification may be accomplished by a steam jacketed manifold type humidifier, with a condensate separator that delivers high-quality steam. Additional trim humidification may also be provided by steam jacketed humidifiers for each individually controlled area. Steam to be used for humidification may be generated in a separate steam generator. The steam generator feedwater may be supplied either from soft or reverse osmosis water. Provisions should be made for periodic cleaning.

Appendix A

A9.7.

The birth center was conceptualized as small (intimate), home-like service units serving a population of healthy childbearing families approaching pregnancy and birth as a normal family event and seeking care in a safe environment outside of, but with access to, the acute-care hospital setting when needed. The freestanding birth center may be a separate outpatient facility.

A9.8.A.

The range of services provided in these facilities is very dynamic and growing, including diagnostic cardiac catheterization, general radiography, fluoroscopy, mammography, CT scanning, magnetic resonance imaging (MRI), ultrasound, radiation therapy, and IV therapies. Facilities may specialize in only one of these areas or may provide a mix of services.

A11.9.D5. Exposure to some art materials, such as solvents and ceramic glazes, is associated with adverse health effects. Such risks should be controlled by adopting methods recommended in appropriate instructional manuals.

A11.9.D8. Display areas for patients' work such as
▲ shelves or wall surfaces should be provided.

APPENDIX B

Energy Conservation Considerations

B1 General

Hospital energy consumption ranges from 200,000–800,000 Btu per square foot per year and can be approximately three times that used in large office buildings. For the average hospital, energy costs are between 3 and 8 percent of its total budget. Hospitals are unique in terms of occupant demands and needs: many areas of hospitals are occupied 24 hours a day, 7 days a week; they provide services which may require energy-consuming technology; and they must provide services in an environment controlled for patient health and safety. Effective energy management requires close, consistent control of all energy-consuming systems and components.

Providing for an acceptable environment for appropriate patient care is a major part of energy consumption by a hospital. Heating, cooling, domestic hot water, and lighting systems for occupant needs are generally responsible for approximately 80 percent of energy consumed. Support functions, such as food service, and equipment account for the remaining 20 percent.

The quality of hospital environment is supportive of patients. When energy resources were plentiful and inexpensive compared to present-day costs, hospitals, like all other buildings, were designed and constructed for maximum comfort without careful consideration of the impact on operating costs. As energy resources become more expensive and the future supply of fossil fuel uncertain, energy conservation and life-cycle cost considerations become increasingly important to designers and administrators. However, opportunities for conserving energy resources and dollars must be carefully weighed against the benefits of energy use, i.e., patient health and safety. Functional requirements may outweigh the need to conserve energy. Maintaining this consideration as a first priority, individuals responsible for energy management have found that through the installation of various new equipment, e.g., heat recovery systems, new lighting, energy efficient chillers, and boiler modifications, substantial savings have been obtained.

The intent is to promote energy conservation without reducing indoor environmental quality below acceptable levels. For the last few years, a common belief has developed that energy conservation implies a degradation of environmental quality. Sufficient evidence now exists to indicate that degradation is not a necessary effect of energy conservation, but that it can easily occur if care is not taken in the selection and implementation of appropriate measures. Conversely, hospitals as well as other buildings can be designed and managed so that improved environmental quality can be achieved at reduced energy consumption.

Recommendations for design, construction, and operation which are intended to decrease energy consumption and minimize life-cycle costs without decreasing environmental quality below initial conditions are discussed.

B2 Life-Cycle Cost Analysis of Energy Conservation Investments

The construction and operation of hospitals requires the commitment of a great many dollars—not only in the initial planning, design, and construction of facilities, but also throughout their lives.

Once occupied, a facility must be heated, cooled, cleaned, and secured; its environmental control systems demand not only energy to fuel them but also people to watch over and maintain them; building surfaces must be cleaned, resealed, repainted, and refinished; grounds must be cared for; and, from time to time, individual elements within the building must be renewed or replaced. If money was borrowed to finance the initial investment, its repayment also becomes a continuing cost.

Design plays a key role in determining both initial and continuing costs. Furthermore, these costs may often be traded off against each other: extra initial investment in a more efficient HVAC system, or in finishes which do not have to be frequently replaced, or in facade design which makes windows easier to clean, or in lobby design which minimizes the need for security personnel. All may reap dividends that can keep paying off—year after year.

Life-cycle cost (LCC) analysis provides architects, consultants, and their clients with a straightforward and usable technique to assist in determining these trade-offs, and in making them when they count, during the planning and early design phases. The technique allows, and in fact encourages, the architect to consider all of the relevant economic consequences of design decisions, both in terms of the dollars to be spent today and the dollars required tomorrow.

LCC analysis is a method of economic evaluation of alternatives which considers all relevant costs and benefits associated with each alternative activity or project over its life. As applied to energy conservation projects in buildings, LCC analysis provides an evaluation of the net effect, over time, of reducing fuel costs by purchasing, installing, maintaining, operating, repairing, and replacing energy-conserving features. The use of LCC analysis has become widespread and almost essential in the evaluation of alternative energy conservation measures applicable to both new buildings in design and to existing buildings where retrofit for energy efficiency is under consideration.

LCC analysis is primarily suited for the economic comparison of alternatives. Its emphasis is on determining how to allocate a given budget among competing projects so as to maximize the overall net return from that budget. The LCC method is used to select energy conservation projects for which budget estimates must be made; however, the LCC cost estimates are not appropriate as budget estimates, because they are expressed in constant dollars (excluding inflation) and all dollar cash flows are converted to a common point in time. Hence, LCC estimates are not necessarily equivalent to the obligated amounts required in the funding years.

The results of LCC analyses are usually expressed in either present value dollars, uniform annual value dollars, as a ratio of present or annual value dollar savings to present or annual value dollar costs (referred to here as the savings-to-investment ratio or SIR), or as a percentage rate of return on the investment.

Although it is not in a strict sense an LCC measure, the time until the initial investment is recouped (payback) is another form that is sometimes used to report the results of an LCC analysis. A simple payback period of 3-5 years is generally considered to be cost effective. To derive any of these measures, it is important to adjust for differences in the timing of expenditures and cost savings. This time adjustment can be accomplished by a technique called "discounting."

The major steps for performing an LCC analysis of energy conservation investments are the following:

B2.A.
Identify the alternative approaches to achieve the objective of reducing consumption of nonrenewable energy, as well as any constraints that must be imposed, such as the level of thermal comfort required.

B2.B.
Establish a common time basis for expressing LCC values, a study period for the analysis, and the economic lives of major assets.

B2.C.
Identify and estimate the cost (and benefit) parameters to be considered in the analysis.

B2.D.
Convert costs and savings occurring at different times to a common time.

B2.E.
Compare the investment alternatives in terms of their relative economic efficiencies in order to select the energy conservation projects that will result in the largest savings of nonrenewable energy costs possible for a given budget and constraints.

B2.F.
Analyze the results for sensitivity to the initial assumptions.

LCC is the best method for evaluating the economics of alternative capital investments. Other methods are still in common use but sometimes give erroneous results. The payback method is probably the most popular, but it has the following disadvantages: it does not allow for the difference in length of life for various investments, it does not adequately consider the effects of uneven cash flows from one year to the next, and finally, it does not account for any expenses or revenues that may occur after the end of the payback period when the investment may still be in operation.

B3 Energy Conservation Measures

Opportunities for energy conservation exist in all aspects of hospital design, construction, and operation—from initial site selection and landscaping to equipment selection. This section provides guidelines for building orientation and building envelope construction in the interest of energy conservation as well as HVAC systems requirements for effective utilization of energy.

B3.A. Architectural Design Considerations

B3.A1. Land Planning

Planning of the site should take advantage of existing natural resources such as: existing groundwater formation and rainwater collection for use as heat sinks, prevailing wind direction and air quality for natural ventilation, vegetation and land forms which may be used as wind breaks in colder climates, the location and type of vegetation to provide summer shading, and the use of slopes for subterranean building opportunities. Careful evaluation of the site should also include adjacent public transportation routes. The microclimate of the site should be analyzed to take advantage of or protect against the impacts of prevailing winds, secondary currents, and weather movement.

B3.A2. Civil/Site Engineering

a. Building orientation. In climates that primarily require cooling, the building should be oriented with major glass portions to the north. Where possible, minimum glazing or solar shading should be used on southern exposures. In climates that primarily require heating, a southern orientation would reduce the heating load. Proper shading devices should be used on south-facing glazing during appropriate seasons. Natural wind breaks, existing adjacent structures, or locating the primary building axis into the prevailing wind direction may be used to reduce the wind load and cooling effect on the facility.

b. Partially buried building. Partially buried buildings may be considered for nonpatient sleeping areas of hospitals. This approach should consider the additional cost related to structure, excavation, and water protection.

c. Underground energy sources. A system of piping buried in the ground for ground-to-water (or air) transfer of energy from the ground to the building for heating by means of a heat pump can be advantageous. The application must consider the availability of land, cost effectiveness, and potential building expansion. Where feasible, consideration should also be given to the utilization of underground hot springs for heating and underground water for cooling or heating by means of a heat pump.

B3.A3. Landscape Design

a. General landscaping. To reduce the reflected radiation on the ground surface by such materials as concrete, asphalt, water, gravel, metal, and sand, the ground surfaces surrounding the building within the reflective zone of the sun should be designed with less reflective materials such as trees, shrubs, grass, ground cover, or mulch.

b. Vegetation. In cold climates plants can manage snow accumulation and serve as windblocks for buildings. In mild and hot climates, plants can be used to shade the building to reduce solar heat gain, and at the same time, permit air circulation.

B3.A4. Building Architecture

a. Orientation

i. Daylighting. Natural lighting and ventilation should be considered. Windows can be used for both ventilation and lighting to reduce heat gain. Energy consumption for lighting can be reduced by developing a building configuration and envelope which maximizes the natural light available to the interior spaces. For example, the exterior surface exposed to light may be increased by use of atria. The space could be used as a thermal buffer, unoccupied and unconditioned, by using skylights and interior glass walls.

Lightwells and atria, in conjunction with side-lighting from the windows, raise the overall level of natural light. The use of natural lighting can also reduce energy consumption for cooling, in some cases, due to lower internal heat gains from reduced use of artificial lighting. An increase in energy consumption for heating may also result and should be considered in the analysis.

ii. Solar shading. Solar shading to reduce undesirable heat gain may be accomplished by use of site conditions such as trees, adjacent structures, or other materials. Additionally, solar shading may be achieved by using solar shading devices at each window requiring shade.

iii. Massing. Building systems which provide mass to delay heat transfer into the facility may be used to reduce peak cooling loads during the peak cooling season. The system may also reduce night perimeter heating during heating seasons.

iv. Interior transportation. Interior transportation systems for people and materials are typically required in hospitals. The electrical energy consumption for interior transportation is a small portion of the total consumption of the building, but savings can be realized in this area.

Energy consumption for transportation can be minimized by arranging the spaces to reduce the need for moving people and materials vertically, if possible, and by maximizing the efficiency of the system through controls. Additionally, the type of drive system can affect consumption.

aa. Architectural considerations. Reducing the number of floors or arranging the spaces to encourage the use of stairs by the staff and reducing the floor elevation of material storage areas or other material handling requirements will reduce the need for vertical transportation systems.

bb. Optimize cab type and number. Traffic patterns should be analyzed and the system designed to provide the heaviest loadings. Reduction of the number of stops per elevator, as with various skip-stop schemes, reduces starting and stopping energy requirements to the elevator system. Design should provide the required unoccupied period capacity using the minimum practicable number of cabs.

cc. Optimizing controls. Optimizing controls ensure that transportation tasks are achieved with minimum elevator travel. The controls respond to any particular demand situation by dispatching the cab that is already loaded while preventing an unloaded cab from responding. In addition to avoiding unnecessary travel by unoccupied cabs, the improved response allows the elevator demand to be met with a reduced number of cabs, over a system with simple demand controls. An elevator system utilizing group supervisory operation can be preprogrammed to react to all levels of elevator demand: heavy up, heavy down, heavy balanced, off hours, etc. In addition, the system can be programmed to selectively turn off elevators as demand lessens. Energy savings of up to 45 percent can be realized using this type of system. A survey of elevator demand and use after occupancy should be part of a contract.

b. Exterior envelope (walls, floor, glass, and roof)

i. Exterior envelope—heating and cooling. The exterior shell of a building should be designed to minimize winter heat loss and summer heat gain. The selection of heat transmission factor "U" (Btu/hour/square foot/°F) is made by comparing heating and cooling criteria requirements and selecting the most restrictive value, i.e., the lower value of the two.

aa. Heating design criteria. The heat transmission factors for walls, roof, and floors should not exceed the values suggested in Table B-1. (No interpolation for intermediate degree days values should be used.) Glass selection for all buildings should be based on economics, but in no case should the overall heat transfer coefficient value

(U_O) shown in table 1 be exceeded when used in conjunction with the following equation:

$$U_O A_O = U_W \times A_W + U_G \times A_G + U_D \times A_D$$

$$U_O = \frac{U_W \times A_W + U_G \times A_G + U_D \times A_D}{A_O}$$

where U_O = the average thermal transmittance of the gross wall; A_O = a unit area of gross wall; U_W = thermal transmittance of opaque (net) wall area; A_W = ratio of opaque (net) wall area to gross wall area; U_G = thermal transmittance of window or glass; A_G = ratio of window area to gross wall area; U_D = thermal transmittance of door; and A_D = ratio of door area to gross wall area.

bb. Perimeter insulation. Where heated spaces are adjacent to exterior walls in slab-on-grade construction, perimeter insulation should be installed on the interior of foundation walls as follows: 1 inch thick when annual heating degree days aggregate from 3,500 to 4,500 and 2 inches thick when the annual heating degree days are 4,500 and over. Installation of the insulation should be in accordance with the ASHRAE Guide.

cc. Condensation control—heating. The building envelope should be designed to provide protection against cold weather water-vapor condensation on or in roofs, attics, walls, windows, doors, and floors. For opaque areas of ceilings, roofs, floors, and walls contained for thermal insulation, a continuous vapor barrier having a water vapor permeance not exceeding 0.5 perm [grains/hr ft² (in.-Hg.)] is recommended on the wintertime warm side of the insulation. Slab-on-grade floors should have vapor barrier with lapped joints under the slab not exceeding 0.1 perm. A vapor barrier not exceeding 0.1 perm should cover the ground area of a crawl space beneath floors. There should be thermal breaks to prevent excessive heat transmission through framing members of windows, ceiling, roof, floor, and wall construction. Overall heat transfer coefficient for windows in sensitive areas requiring winter humidity control should be sufficient to avoid condensation when the outdoor dry-bulb temperature is at or above the minimum temperature for 97.5

percent of the hours occurring in any one heating month as noted in the ASHRAE *Handbook of Fundamentals.*

dd. Cooling design criteria. Wall (net area) and roof heat gain should not exceed 2.0 Btu/h per square foot at design conditions. All glass, except north glass, should have a shading device (e.g., shades, venetian blinds, draperies, awnings, eyebrow reveals, or vertical/horizontal fins), and maximum instantaneous transmission and solar gain through glass should not exceed 70 Btu's per square foot as an average for the entire building (i.e., block load figure). This average of maximum instantaneous solar and transmission factors includes shading factor. Thermal storage effect due to mass of building must be accounted for to produce the properly sized system, capable of balancing the actual loads. For buildings that are cooled, only the overall thermal transmittance U_O for the gross wall should not exceed 0.38.

c. Vestibules. Vestibules and/or windshields should be used at entries to provide protection against prevailing winds.

d. Textures and materials. Exterior materials, colors, and textures should be selected for the effect on the solar heat gains and reflective lighting.

B3.A5. Structural Engineering

a. Roofs and walls. Where active solar system might be installed in the future, the design of roof and wall systems should include increased loading to carry active solar equipment such as solar panels to ensure that the increased dead load, penetrations, and maintenance are provided.

b. Subterranean building. The effects of hydrostatic pressure on the floor and exterior walls should be considered in the design of subterranean and "berm" structures.

B3.B. Mechanical Design Considerations

B3.B1. General

a. Even though much of the energy use of a hospital is determined by the architectural design and internal building activity, the achievement of energy efficiency within a health facility will depend largely upon the design and operation of the mechanical systems. The design process should include comparative analysis of appropriate systems, equipment, and control strategies for energy use characteristics, including thermal and

Table B-1

Maximum Wall, Roof, Floor, and Overall Transmission Factors for Hospital Facilities[1]

Heating degree days[2]	Gross wall[3,4] (UO)	Walls[5] (UW)	Ceiling/roof[6] (UR)	Floor[7] (UF)	Floor[8] (UF)
Less than 1,000	0.38	0.15	0.05	0.10	0.29
1,000–2,000	0.38	0.15	0.05	0.08	0.24
2,001–3,000	0.36	0.10	0.04	0.07	0.21
3,001–4,000	0.36	0.10	0.03	0.07	0.18
4,001–6,000	0.31	0.08	0.03	0.05	0.14
6,001–8,000	0.28	0.07	0.03	0.05	0.12
Over 8,000	0.28	0.07	0.03	0.05	0.10

Table B-1 Notes: *Value of U for wall, roof, and floor should not be greater than the following values corresponding to 97.5 percent (99 percent for sensitive areas)[9] winter ambient design temperatures (i.e., use the lowest of the two values obtained, one based on degree day criteria and the other on winter ambient design criteria):*

Temperature (°F)	Walls	Floor
-40 to -10	.07	.05
-9 to +10	.10	.07
+11 to +50	.15	.10

1 Heat transmission values are expressed in $Btu/hr/ft^3/°F$.

2 Degree days value from the latest edition of ASHRAE System Manual shall be used.

3 Gross wall value includes all doors and windows, window frames, metal ties through walls, structural steel members that protrude through all insulation to the exterior or adjacent to the exterior, and continuous concrete or masonry walls or floors that extend from inside heated spaces through the building envelope to the exterior, e.g., fire walls that extend above the roof and concrete floor slabs that extend beyond the exterior wall to form a balcony or terrace.

4 Maximum U_O value will put a limitation on the allowable percentage of glass to gross wall area in a building. Insulating glass on the building will allow higher percentage of glass in comparison with single glass.

5 Wall U_W is the thermal transmittance of all elements of the opaque wall area. U_W values are to be used for upgrade of existing facilities where the alteration of walls and resizing of window glazing to meet gross wall is not cost-effective.

6 Ceiling/roof U_R values are for ceiling/roof areas where adequate space exists for insulation to be applied above ceiling and/or below roof structure. Built-up roof assemblies and ceiling assemblies in which the finished interior surface is essentially the underside of the roof deck shall have a maximum U_R value of 0.05 for a heating degree day area. On existing buildings, use the maximum U_R value practical to accommodate the existing roof conditions where the life-cycle cost analysis indicates a higher life-cycle cost to implement U_R values required by table B-1. The values are as follows: (a) cost of providing additional structural support to accommodate additional dead loads of new insulation and roofing system, and additional live loads from greater accumulations of snow (snow will melt slower due to increased insulation); (b) cost of raising roof curbs; (c) cost of raising cap flashings; (d) cost of raising roof drains.

7 Floor U_F values are for floors of heated space over unheated areas such as garages, crawl spaces, and basements without a positive heat supply to maintain a minimum of 50°F.

8 Floor U_F values are for slab-on-grade insulation around the perimeter of the floor.

9 Sensitive areas are defined as operating rooms, obstetrical delivery rooms, nurseries, recovery rooms, emergency operating and treatment rooms, central sterile supply rooms, ICU and CCU units, neopsychiatric seclusion units, allergy suite and those technical equipment areas, e.g., automatic data processing, radiology, and nuclear magnetic resonance, where accurate temperature and humidity control is vital to the function of the equipment or the success of medical procedure performed. Related working areas, lounges, locker rooms, etc., should not be designed on the 99 percent criteria.

mechanical efficiencies, and consideration of the interface between mechanical and electrical loads.

b. Pursuit of maximum efficiency in mechanical system design should be exercised to a degree that does not impair health care operations and cost objectives.

B3.B2. Heating, Ventilating and Air Conditioning (HVAC)

a. General. Three types of HVAC systems are commonly applied to health facilities: all-air, air and water, and unitary air conditioning equipment.

b. All-air systems

i. In all-air systems the air supplied to the spaces served provide the cooling, and possibly heating, capacity necessary to produce the desired temperature and humidity levels for comfort or process control.

ii. The fan energy required for the distribution of the air can be quite significant and is dependent upon (a) the quantity of the air, (b) pressure resistance of the conditioning equipment and ductwork, (c) fan and drive efficiencies, and (d) hours of operation.

iii. Although ventilation for reduction of contaminants may govern, the quantity of air is usually determined by and is proportional to the space-sensible cooling or heating load and inversely proportional to the difference between room and supply air temperatures. Consequently, reduction in space cooling load through prudent design of the building envelope and lighting will produce a reduction in the required fan energy. The air quantity and fan energy can be further minimized by designing with as high a room supply air temperature difference as considerations of refrigeration design, duct heat gain, and room air distribution will permit.

iv. Air system resistance

aa. Fan energy is proportional to the conditioning equipment and duct resistance and, therefore, can be minimized by thoughtful selection of components and duct design.

bb. Air-handling equipment including intake and exhaust louvers, filters, and heating and cooling coils can be optimized by selection at a conservative face velocity. Since the pressure drop of these components generally varies as the square of the face velocity, selection at 300 to 400 feet per minute, instead of the customary

500 feet per minute can often be justified by life-cycle cost analysis, especially for continuously operating systems.

cc. Filter life may be improved by reducing face velocity, permitting an economically justifiable lower final pressure drop (before replacement).

dd. Lower cooling coil face velocities may reduce the required depth (number of rows) in the coil bank giving an additional pressure drop improvement.

ee. Where return air and outdoor air are both conditioned by the air-handling unit, the effectiveness of the blending of the two air streams can have impact upon both actual operating pressure losses and the stability of the supply air temperature control.

ff. Where desirable to have the supply (or other fans) discharge into a plenum, the fan discharge transition should be gradual for proper fan performance and minimal fan energy use.

gg. Simpler, shorter duct systems designed with conservatively low duct velocities are likely to be consistent with energy efficiency objectives. High loss fittings, such as mitered elbows, abrupt transitions and take-offs; and internal obstructions, such as damper frames, should be avoided. Long duct runs, if necessary, should be designed with special consideration of pressure loss since the maximum loss for any run will be imposed upon the entire fan system.

hh. Sound attenuators should be selected for low-velocity pressure losses. High-velocity selection may, in addition to incurring undesirable pressure loss, result in internally generated noise.

ii. Terminals, such as mixing boxes and variable-air-volume devices, should be selected for low pressure loss.

v. Leakage of air from supply ducts robs system capacity and wastes energy. Sealing seams and joints of supply ducts will minimize this loss.

vi. Fan type and size and its motor drive should be selected for good mechanical efficiency. (See Section 1.3C(5) of this Appendix for high-efficiency motors.) Special design investigation of existing conditions may be necessary in renovation projects.

vii. Supply and exhaust air systems should serve spaces having similar operating characteristics. Spaces with different periods of occupancy or substantially different ventilation requirements generally should not be combined on the same system.

viii. Dedicating air systems to specific medical departments can often provide proper grouping of spaces with similar occupancy characteristics and environmental performance requirements and simplify the duct distribution systems. Supplying perimeter and interior building spaces (because of differing load characteristics) from separate systems will permit use of energy-saving control strategies.

ix. Humidification. During the heating season, humidification systems vaporize water into the dry ventilating air to increase moisture and achieve the desired humidity within the building. The volume of moisture required to maintain a desired level of relative humidity is proportional to the amount of outdoor air entering the building, its dryness, and the natural moisture contributed by occupants.

Humidification systems are often designed not only to maintain the comfort and health of occupants, but to preserve materials, furnishings, and equipment.

Over-humidification can be avoided by: (1) high limit control of air supply stream; (2) proper sizing of humidifier; (3) selecting humidifiers for stepped capacity and sequence control; (4) avoiding placing objects (e.g., filters) downstream of steam humidifiers; (5) providing positive shut off of steam humidifiers, including jacket when air supply is off and when seasonably not required; and (6) providing concealed adjustment for room humidistats. Humidifiers should be shut off during unoccupied periods. No additional humidification should be provided in unoccupied spaces unless it is justified to be critical, such as to avoid static electricity for electronic components or computer rooms.

x. Variable air volume. Variable-air-volume (VAV) systems offer opportunities for savings and can be used in health care facilities if environmental requirements (including minimum outdoor air ventilation) for the space being served are continually met during occupancy. VAV control should not be used for areas which require outward air movement to control contamination and odors (Table 3), nor should VAV control be used for areas which require inward air movement unless an acceptable alternate source of makeup air is provided for exhaust to maintain the minimum number of total air changes (Table 3). Although it may be possible to design a VAV system which satisfies air quality requirements for these spaces, complexities of controls could make such a system unreliable and difficult to maintain. VAV systems for areas which require positive air movement should be used only after careful consideration that the control reliability is adequate to justify the achievable energy savings.

Modified variable-air-volume systems designed to provide not less than a preset minimum total air change rate required to ensure continuous control of air flow direction may be used in critical care areas (i.e., surgery, nurseries, recovery, and intensive care). In addition, outdoor air and total air change rates, including those of sensitive areas, may be reduced when space is unoccupied or unused. Care should be taken to ensure that control of air flow direction created by use of exhaust fans in adjacent areas does not cause undesired movement of air from soiled areas to clean areas.

xi. Room air distribution. The room air-distribution system must be responsive to the thermal loads in the space, the indoor air quality requirements, and the acoustic room criteria. To meet all of these criteria simultaneously, care is required in the selection and placement of the supply and return air terminals.

aa. To provide thermally acceptable conditions in the functional areas, the supply air diffusers should be sized and located within the rooms according to the air diffusion performance index (ADPI) procedure described in chapter 32 of the ASHRAE *Handbook of Fundamentals*. It should be noted that this procedure does not specify the amount of supply air to be delivered to the room, but only how that air should be distributed within the room.

bb. To provide acoustically acceptable conditions in the functional areas, the supply and return air terminal devices should be selected to meet the appropriate noise criteria (NC) or room criteria (RC) described in chapter 7 of the ASHRAE *Handbook of Fundamentals*. These noise criteria should be complied with in addition to the ADPI requirements.

cc. To provide acceptable indoor air quality in the functional areas, the location of the return air terminal devices should be carefully considered. The common practice of locating both supply and return air devices in the ceiling or on opposing high sidewalls can materially reduce the effectiveness of the ventilation and the heating/cooling capability by short-circuiting the supply air directly to the return device. The air-distribution pattern within an occupied space is at least as important as the amount of ventilation air supplied to the room. In areas where variable-volume systems are installed, special care is needed to ensure that sufficient room ventilation air reaches the occupants. For example, high-occupancy density and a moderate lighting load in a perimeter zone may offset the heat loss through the walls and windows of a space during the heating season. Thus, with a variable-air-volume system the room thermostat may be satisfied, resulting in minimum supply air to the space at the time when the ventilation requirements may be at a maximum. To compensate for this type of problem, it may be necessary to provide a separate ventilation system or to use a reset control strategy on the mixed-air control system.

c. Air and water systems

i. Air and water systems are those where air and water distributed to the spaces served provide the cooling and, commonly, heating capacity necessary to produce the desired temperature and humidity level. Less than half as much air is generally circulated to the spaces compared with all-air systems. Water can transfer energy more efficiently than air systems. Consequently, distribution energy use is less a factor. However, design guidelines for the all-air systems are also appropriate to the air side of air and water systems.

ii. Water distribution piping should be sized to minimize heat loss following ASHRAE recommendations (*Handbook of Fundamentals*).

iii. Air and water systems are categorized as two-pipe, three-pipe, or four-pipe systems. Two-pipe systems derive their name from the water-distribution system which consists of one supply pipe and one return pipe. Three-pipe systems have a cold water supply, warm water supply, and a common return. Four-pipe systems connect a chilled water supply, chilled water return, warm water supply, and warm water return to each terminal unit. Controls for room terminals connected to four-pipe distribution systems should be sequenced to avoid simultaneous heating and cooling with provisions for an adjustable dead band between cooling and heating modes. Systems pressures for all these systems should be limited by design, or controlled to avoid pressure differentials across terminal control valves that would prevent them from closing.

iv. Pumps dedicated to cooling or heating should be automatically controlled to shut off when their function is unnecessary.

v. Piping systems should be zoned by exposure, where such zoning will avoid over-cooling or over-heating of spaces served that could occur if supplied with water at a common temperature.

d. Unitary equipment

i. Unitary air conditioning equipment within, or in the proximity of, the spaces served for the purpose of environmental control should be evaluated for their seasonal energy efficiency and energy cost effectiveness. The energy use of such systems may be more or less than central air conditioning systems depending upon application factors and component performance characteristics. Unitary systems and central systems should be compared in terms of energy efficiency, cost effectiveness, and compliance with applicable state codes.

ii. Both air and water source heat pumps require compressor operation during the heating mode. Emergency power will be necessary to maintain the minimum heating capability in the event of interruption to the normal electrical power supply.

B3.B3. Refrigeration

a. Because refrigerating equipment serving HVAC systems can be selected over a varying range of full- and partial-load operating efficiencies (coefficient of performance), purchasing decisions for such equipment should be based upon life-cycle cost evaluation.

b. Partial-load performance of water chillers, as well as reliability, will be improved by selecting multiple refrigeration units arranged to operate in series or parallel, whichever is best suited to the performance objectives of the chilled water system.

c. In some climates "free cooling" of chilled water can be obtained with reduced energy use during cool weather by utilizing the cooling capability of the cooling tower. Evaluation of the feasibility of this technique, including possible contamination of the cooled water, is suggested for central refrigeration plants.

d. The feasibility of employing heat rejected by the refrigeration plant for service hot water pre-heating, air conditioning reheat, or other cooling season uses should be considered. Year-round cooling loads can be converted by the refrigeration equipment or a dedicated elevated temperature heat pump for process or building heating.

e. Separate refrigeration should be considered for laboratories and surgical suites and other spaces where space temperature control is essential. This provision will permit mechanical cooling of critical spaces independent of the central refrigeration plant serving the total hospital.

B3.B4. Economizer Cycles, Air (See glossary for definition)

Air-economizer cycles which use filtered outside air for cooling may be used when the energy to be exhausted may not be usefully recaptured for heating or cooling the incoming air or another use, such as hot water heating.

B3.B5. Heat-Generating Plants

a. Hot water and steam boilers should be selected for both full- and partial-load thermal efficiency.

b. Efficient part-load performance can be obtained through modulating burner controls and sequence firing of multiple boilers. This is of special significance where the boilers of medical facilities must be oversized for standby and future growth considerations.

c. Reduced summer loads frequently can be provided most economically by a small heat generator sized for the load or individual generators at the points of use.

d. The versatility of having boilers capable of burning different fuels (oil, gas, coal, combustible waste) often can prove cost effective as the comparative costs and availability of fuels change.

e. Heat exchangers for the recovery of heat from the flue gas for feed water or combustion air preheating should be evaluated for boiler efficiency improvement especially in larger, high pressure boilers.

f. Analysis of boiler and stack performance for automatic adjustment of fuel-air proportions can be of positive value in obtaining optimum efficiency performance.

g. Recovery of heat from boiler blowdown can be both cost effective and reduce the temperature of wastewater to a more acceptable level prior to discharge to the sewerage system.

B3.B6. Heat Distribution Systems

a. Energy losses from steam and hot water distribution networks can be substantial. Life-cycle cost evaluation should be used to determine the type and thickness of insulation.

b. Unnecessarily high steam pressures or hot water temperatures in the distribution piping will aggravate energy losses and should be avoided where practical.

c. Flash steam resulting from high-pressure steam condensate should be collected for supply to low-pressure steam mains.

d. Steam traps should be selected for their intended use. Selection should be based upon the maximum design load plus an allowance for warm-up and the estimated inlet and outlet pressures.

e. Heating elements in building heating systems should be parallel connected and controlled sequentially with the cooling system supply with provision for adjustable dead band to avoid simultaneous heating and cooling.

f. The hot water temperature of building heating systems should be automatically or manually adjustable for reset of heating capacity to match changes in load.

B3.B7. Service Hot Water Systems

a. The temperature of the hot water supply should be limited to maximum system requirements.

b. Recirculation of hot water should be minimal.

c. Decentralized generation or booster heating of hot water should be considered for remote fixtures and for those requiring high temperatures, such as dishwashing, laundry, etc.

B3.B8. Heat Reclamation

Heat reclamation is the recovery and utilization of heat energy that is otherwise rejected as waste. Sources of this waste heat include lights, equipment, and people. Heat-reclamation systems recover waste heat to satisfy part of the heat energy needs for heating, cooling, and domestic hot water systems. Heat recovery conserves energy, reduces operating costs, and reduces peak loads.

The performance of any heat recovery system depends upon the following factors: temperature difference between the heat source and heat sink; latent heat difference (where applicable) between the heat source and sink; mass flow multiplied by specific heat of each source and sink; efficiency of the heat-transfer device; extra energy input required to operate the heat recovery device; and fan or pump energy absorbed as heat by the heat transfer device, which can enhance or detract from the performance.

a. Methods. The basic principles of heat recovery can be implemented by various methods using different devices applicable to different systems or situations. Heat-recovery devices reduce the peak heating and cooling loads when used with outdoor air systems. Other devices reduce or completely eliminate the requirements for heating and/or cooling equipment in major building expansions. Consideration of cross contamination should be exercised in the application of heat-recovery methods. The following are some of the most frequently used methods for heat recovery:

i. Thermal wheels. A thermal or heat wheel is a rotating heat exchanger driven by an electric motor with a high-thermal inertia core. Such wheels are capable of transferring energy from one air stream to another and, in very large boiler plants, from flue gas to air. The hot and cold air streams must be immediately adjacent and parallel to permit installation of the heat wheel. Duct modifications may be necessary. Two types of thermal wheels are available. The first type transfers sensible heat only and the second transfers both sensible and latent heat.

ii. Runaround system. This system is comprised of two or more extended surface fin coils installed in air ducts and interconnected by piping. The heat-exchanger fluid, consisting of ethylene glycol and water, is circulated through the system by a pump, removing heat from the hot air stream and rejecting it into the cold air stream. A runaround-coil system may be used in winter to recover heat from warm exhaust air for use in preheating cold outdoor air, and in summer to cool hot outdoor air by rejecting heat into cooler exhaust air.

iii. Heat pipe systems. Heat pipe systems are comprised of extended surface finned tubes extending between adjacent air ducts. The tubes are continuous from one duct to the other on the same horizontal plane. Each tube contains liquid refrigerant, which evaporates at the warm end, absorbing heat from the water air stream, and migrates as a gas to the cold end where it condenses and releases heat into the cold air stream. The condensed liquid then runs back to the hot end of the tube to complete the cycle.

iv. Air-to-air heat exchangers. Air-to-air heat exchangers transfer heat directly from one air stream to another through direct contact on either side of a metal heat-transfer surface. This surface may be either convoluted plate (more common for low-temperature use in an HVAC system) or tube (more common for boiler flue gas-heat transfer).

v. Heat pump as heat exchanger. Heat pumps are actually heat-transfer devices and, unlike those previously described, upgrade the temperature by as much as a factor of 3 to 1. This feature makes them particularly attractive for use with low-temperature heat sources. They also have the capacity to transfer latent heat as well as sensible heat.

vi. Shell and tube heat exchangers. Shell and tube heat exchangers consist of tubular shell with a flange, in which a tube bundle of U-bend construction is inserted. This device transfers heat between two physically separated fluids, one circulating through the tubes while the other passes through the shell.

vii. Waste incineration. Incinerators burning solid waste, which generally has a heating value of 6,000 Btu/lb, can be designed to produce significant steam. Special heat-recovery incinerators are now available with exit gas temperatures as low as approximately 450°F (232°C), which can be used in a heat exchanger as a source of high- and low-temperature heat.

viii. Heat-of-light system. The major advantage of a "heat-of-light" system lies in its reduction of heating, cooling, and HVAC system and distribution loads, rather than in savings in electrical energy for lighting. However, slightly higher lamp efficiencies will result as the cooling effect on the lamps increases their output. The two types of heat-of-light systems, "dry" and "wet," provide the following three advantages: Excess heat from interior areas of the building can be collected and distributed to perimeter areas; the sensible room heat component of the cooling load is decreased, permitting a reduction in the quantity of air required for cooling (thus saving fan horsepower); and, in the case of wet heat-of-light systems, the cooling load is reduced and less power is required for the refrigeration units.

ix. Thermal storage. Thermal-storage system is any storage vessel in which water, ice, or water and ice are stored (charged) and made available to produce the desired heating or cooling effect when the demand occurs. Storage is accomplished by circulating water from storage tanks to heat-reclaim or double-bundle heat-recovery machines. The storage tanks may be utilized in several different ways, such as: (1) to store chilled water, or combination of ice and water to minimize peak demand; (2) installing an electric resistance heater to provide supplementary heat after the tanks are depleted; (3) charging the tanks at night using low-cost electrical energy; and (4) with sufficiently high storage temperatures, the tanks can supply building heat directly, thereby reducing the operating time of the booster heater. To optimize tank size for capacity and size, the tank should be located so that it receives the hottest water from the heating circuit and the coldest water from the chilled-water circuit. This same location will also be desirable from the hydraulic standpoint, since it will minimize pressure in the storage system. In multiple-tank installations, series piping of the tanks will decrease balancing problems.

x. Cogeneration. Broadly defined, cogeneration is the simultaneous production of electrical or mechanical energy in conjunction with useful thermal energy, typically in the form of hot gases or fluids. This concept was particularly popular with industry around the turn of the century. However, with the advent of low-cost, reliable electricity, the interest in such systems began to decline significantly, from a peak in 1940 to less than 10 percent of U.S. industrial energy in 1976. Because of the dramatic increases in the cost of fuel and electricity, the idea of cogeneration is once again receiving serious consideration as a means of reducing costs and assuring a reliable supply of energy.

Cogeneration systems applicable to a hospital setting would consist of a generator fueled by steam, natural gas, or diesel. It could be sized to produce electricity for baseload purposes or for peak shaving. The on-site production of electricity alone is usually not cost effective but with the recovery of the waste heat for useful purposes, the system efficiency may exceed 75 percent and become cost effective. The recovered heat may be used to augment building heating or hot water heating or to fire an absorption chiller for building cooling.

Hospitals have a special opportunity for cogeneration that does not exist in many other types of buildings because hospitals are usually equipped with emergency generators. The opportunity exists to use these generators for other than emergency situations. It is possible that when electricity is generated and the waste heat is recovered for useful purposes that the overall cost of on-site electricity will be lower than electricity purchased from the utility. This can be particularly attractive if the generator is used for peak-shaving purposes—to reduce the extent of electrical demand during peak conditions. In these situations, the hospital can save not only electrical consumption charges but also electrical demand charges. By extracting more utility from equipment that is required to meet power outages, the economics of cogeneration can be very beneficial.

b. Applications

i. Transfer energy between exhaust and outdoor air ducts when there is more than 4,000 cfm being exhausted.

When there are more than 3,500 heating degree days and/or more than 8,000 cooling degree hours above 78°F (26°C) dry-bulb temperature, consider thermal wheels, heat pipes, and other devices. Where supply and exhaust ducts are remote from each other and cannot be brought together, consider systems other than heat pipes and thermal wheels.

Install a thermal wheel or heat pump to recover both sensible and latent heat in locations with more than 12,000 wet-bulb degree hours above 66°F (19°C) wbt.

When justified for the heating mode only, install an air-to-water-air heat pump to transfer energy from the exhaust air stream to the fresh air stream.

Utilize exhaust-air heat energy to temper make-up air and preheat combustion air, or use this system for space heating via heat pumps.

ii. Recover waste heat from the boiler flue gases whenever the stack temperature is greater than 350°F (177°C).

Install a heat pipe or an air-to-air exchanger to transfer energy from the hot flue gas to temper ventilation air, preheat domestic hot water, heat space, or preheat combustion air.

Take into account the corrosive effect of flue gas when selecting materials.

Allow for change-of draft conditions caused by a heat exchanger.

Provide an alternative source of combustion air when heat exchanger dampers are closed for cleaning.

iii. Recover heat from laundry and/or kitchen wastewater:

When more than 30,000 gal/week of water at temperatures above 120°F (49°C) is discharged to waste, use it as a heat source for heat pump or other HVAC system requirements. Use of water discharged at lower temperatures would not be as economical.

Consideration must be given to the characteristics of the wastewater, particularly the soap/detergent content of laundry wastewater and the grease content of kitchen wastewater. Piping and/or material modifications may be necessary to enable the heat exchanger to handle water with high concentrations of these impurities. In addition, a holding tank may be required to maintain a steady flow rate through the heat exchanger when water is being sporadically discharged.

Waste heat thus recovered may be used by any system requiring hot water, such as domestic hot water and heating systems.

iv. Recover heat from engine or combustion turbine exhaust and cooling systems:

On engines larger than 50 hp., exhaust gas heat recovery is restricted by the practical limitations of the heat exchanger plus the prevention of flue gas condensation. The recommended minimum exhaust temperature is approximately 250°F (121°C). Depending on the initial exhaust temperature, 50 percent to 60 percent of the available exhaust heat can be removed.

v. Recover heat from incinerators if the quantity of solid waste exceeds 1,000 lbs/day.

vi. Recover heat from condensate-return systems when district heat steam condensate is discharged to waste, or when steam condensate from equipment supplied by on-site boilers is at a temperature of 180°F (82°C) or greater.

vii. Recover heat from refrigeration-system hot gas where there is a steady and concurrent demand for refrigeration and waste heat and where the refrigeration systems operate 1,000 hours or more per year.

Do not reduce superheat to the point where liquid slugging occurs.

The heat exchanger must be located after the hot gas bypass or other unloading devices. If located outdoors, drains must be provided to prevent freezing.

viii. Recover heat from condenser water systems:

Install a heat exchanger or heat pipe in the hot condenser water line to temper outdoor air, preheat domestic hot water, or modify the piping in air-handling units to utilize hot condenser water to heat air.

Install a coil to extract heat from the hot condenser water line to heat intake air in an air-cycle heat pump, which can then transfer its condenser heat to the space requiring it. (Generally, it is not economical to replace existing condensers by double-bundle condensers; however, in the event that replacement is being contemplated due to age or the installation of new refrigeration equipment, give consideration to a double-bundle condenser.)

ix. Utilize heat from internal spaces to charge thermal storage tanks:

Install thermal storage tanks to store hot condenser water from daytime cooling for nighttime heating. This water can be used either directly for space heating or as a heat source for a heat pump system.

B3.C. Lighting and Electrical Design Considerations
The following design considerations have been identified and recommended as areas of design opportunity for minimizing or conserving energy consumption in new hospitals. Special applications are left to the discretion of the designer.

B3.C1. Lighting Equipment and Systems

a. General. Lighting design for hospitals should focus on equipment (including lamp source and luminaire) and on system design. Efficiency can be maximized by incorporating the high-efficiency lighting products available with design that will best utilize the equipment. Additionally, consideration should be given to the use of natural light when designing systems (see Section 1.3.A4). Attention should be paid to both lighting levels and power consumption on a per-square-foot basis.

b. Light sources. There are several light sources available to the designer: incandescent, mercury vapor, fluorescent, metal halide, high- and low-pressure sodium.

i. Incandescent and mercury vapor should be avoided as light sources unless specifically required. Lamp efficacy is poorest with these sources, and lamp life is very short for incandescent.

ii. Fluorescent lamps are available in many sizes, wattages and color characteristics. Their efficacy and life are very good and they can be used in almost any indoor application. Energy-saving lamps are available as well as matching ballasts that can provide a highly efficient system.

iii. Metal halide lamps provide good color rendering and higher efficacy than mercury vapor lamps and about the same as fluorescents. A major drawback to metal halide is its short lamp life relative to the other sources.

iv. High-pressure sodium lamps are about the most efficient source available and typically have a longer life. Their efficacy is the highest available except low-pressure sodium but the color rendition is poor. This fact will limit its use indoors to nonexamination areas such as corridors and waiting rooms. High-pressure sodium lamps should be considered for exterior building and site lighting.

v. Low-pressure sodium lamps have the highest efficacy available but the poorest color rendition. As a source, low-pressure sodium should be limited to outdoor use.

c. Luminaires. Luminaire design can greatly affect the efficacy of a lighting system. The efficiency of the luminaire is a measure of how well the system delivers light to the space. Units should be chosen with the highest coefficient of utilization factor possible. Additionally, the following areas should be considered:

i. Ballasts should be chosen with high power factor, energy-efficient features, and core and coil protection against heating. Energy-saving ballasts should be matched with energy-saving lamps to maximize efficiency. Consideration should be given to use of electronic ballasts. The designer should include as part of the contract, document requirements for the installation of the special ballasts and lamps.

ii. Light loss factor takes into account temperature, voltage variations and dirt accumulation on luminaire and room surfaces, lamp depreciation, maintenance procedures, and atmospheric conditions. This factor is influenced by the level of maintenance performed to keep the space and luminaire surfaces clean and by replacement of lamps and ballasts when their output drops to poor levels. The specification of low-maintenance equipment will allow the designer to use a higher value in his calculations so fewer fixtures will be required.

iii. Heat can greatly affect lamp and ballast energy consumption, so the luminaire must be able to dissipate heat readily. The maximum efficiency for a fluorescent lamp occurs at a bulb wall temperature of 100°F (38°C). The luminaire should be able to pass air through it. This air should be at a relatively consistent temperature because shifts in bulk temperature will cause varying lamp color and brightness. To maximize air flow through the fixture, evenly spaced slots or vents near the lamp should be supplied rather than a single hole. Materials should also be considered because polished and diffuse anodized aluminum dissipates heat into the space better than white enamel, which absorbs and traps heat.

iv. Refraction and reflection produce the major amount of visible light or flux emitted from a luminaire. Therefore, the luminous efficiency of a light fixture can be directly measured against its effectiveness in this regard. Some of the refraction and reflection characteristics of luminaires are the angles of incidence and spectral characteristics of the incident flux as affected by moisture condensation or dust in the atmosphere, surface characteristic of the luminaire, and the source component characteristics.

d. Lighting controls. Lighting controls can be very simple or complex. A timeclock or individual photocell is about the simplest control scheme. Separate switching schemes should be used in areas with large amounts of daylight, such as on the perimeter. Lighting contactors can be added to control large groups of lights. Dimming of light sources should be considered. Motion detectors can be used for control of small-area lighting. A step-up in sophistication is a programmable controller that is hard-wired or that utilizes a carrier signal on the existing power system and receivers at the point of control.

B3.C2. Transportation Control

a. Solid-state drives. Solid-state drives can be used in lieu of the motor-generator (M-G) sets found in most elevator systems. Solid-state units rectify the incoming alternating current waveforms and directly control the output of the elevator drive motor. Use of these drives allows

Table B-2

Comparison Summary of Solid-State versus Motor Generators for Elevator Drives

	Solid-state	Motor generator (M-G) set
Efficiency	High	Moderate
Motor life	Good	Longer than solid-state
Line pollution	High	None
Maintenance	Low	Moderate
Overload capability	Poor	High
Reliability	High	Good
Space and weight	50% of M-G set	Relatively large
First cost	Approximately equal, maybe slightly less for solid-state	

instantaneous on-off control, whereas the M-G set would remain rotating as standby for elevator service. Table B-2 summarizes a comparison of solid-state versus motor generators for elevator drives. The major problem with solid-state is the creation of harmonic levels on the power lines that can affect sensitive equipment. Special filtering should be included.

b. Timed shutdown controls. If motor-generator set drives are chosen or required for elevators, timed shutdown after last call should be specified. The timer should be set such that the M-G set is shut off no more than 5 minutes after the last elevator call. It takes 10-20 seconds for M-G sets to resume operating speed.

B3.C3. Power Distribution Systems

a. General. The losses incurred in a distribution system are a function of the current flowing in it. Two methods to reduce the current are to use the highest distribution voltage feasible and to correct low power factor.

b. Distribution voltage. If a hospital complex is large and spread out, a higher voltage such as 4,160 volts should be considered. A total analysis will include higher equipment costs and transformation losses.

c. Power factor. Low lagging power factor is caused by inductive loads. A power meter only measures actual power and not apparent power, but a greater current is required to supply the apparent power load. This increase in current causes increased losses in the distribution conductors as well as the load conductors, i.e., motor

windings. The lagging power factor can be corrected by adding capacitance to the system or at the load, thus reducing the current. A better approach is to use power-factor-corrected ballasts and to match motors to their loads so that the power factor is as close to one as possible.

B3.C4. Transformers

a. General. Regardless of the type of core fill, there are basically two types of losses associated with transformers: core or no-load losses and load losses. The no-load losses occur when there is little or no load on the transformer, and the load losses are a result of the load current supplied. In general, the higher the temperature rise rating of the transformer, the lower the no-load losses and the higher the load losses incurred.

b. Transformer fill. Presently, there are four classic transformer fills available: oil, silicone, dry-type, and cast resin. There is diversity in initial cost and losses among the four types. All four types are available in building distribution systems.

i. Oil and silicone have very similar energy-loss characteristics for both 55°C and 65°C rise ratings. The no-load losses are the lowest available and their load losses are only greater than cast-resin type. Oil-fill transformers are the least expensive available except for dry type. The indoor installation costs for oil-filled transformers is higher than for other types.

ii. Dry-type transformers are widely used and are available in three temperature-rise ratings: 176°F (80°C), 239°F (115°C), and 302°F (150°C). Dry-type transformers have the lowest initial costs but the highest energy costs. The 302°F (150°C) rise unit will have the lowest no-load losses but the highest load losses, while 176°F (80°C) rise transformers have the highest no-load losses, the lowest load losses, and the higher cost. The break-even point for total losses is at about a 25 percent loading factor. The 302°F (150°C) rise rating allows no overload capability, whereas the 176°F (80°C) rise rating will theoretically allow a temporary overload of 25 percent.

iii. Cast resin-core transformers provide the lowest load losses but have no-load losses similar to dry-type transformers. Their price is considerably higher than the other types available.

c. Total analysis. When choosing a transformer, the most important energy consideration is the load profile. A comparison of complete costs of owning should be generated for all types of fill and temperature-rise ratings for the transformer load. A hospital runs 8,760 hours per year, so the loading will tend to be high. Additionally, all costs of installation, maintenance, and equipment should be included in the analysis.

B3.C5. Motors and Drives

a. General. Motors comprise a large portion of building load and are usually part of the mechanical systems of the building. Because of this, motors are generally specified in the mechanical documents, and consideration is not always given to the options available. High-efficiency motors generally have paybacks of 2 years or less and variable speed drives usually are the same, depending on the variability of the driven load.

b. High-efficiency motors. Standard-efficiency motors are available in T-frame and U-frame. The T-frame motor has the poorest efficiency, and the U-frame is usually 23 percent more efficient. High-efficiency motors are usually of T-frame construction and are about 6-7 percent more efficient than standard T-frame motors. To maximize the savings of a high-efficiency motor, the motor needs to be matched to the specific load. Motors reach their maximum efficiency at 80 percent loading, so they should be chosen to operate at that point for the bulk of their operating time. When evaluating high-efficiency motors, designers should be careful when reviewing manufacturers' efficiency claims. The nominal efficiency is developed from a bell-shape distribution curve of the testing of a large batch of motors. The motor received may be near the nominal efficiency or well above or below that rating. A minimum efficiency should be specified for best results.

c. Two-speed motors. Two-speed motors have applications in which a fan or pump has basically two levels of operation, such as day or night operating parameters. Two-speed motors come in two varieties: single winding and two winding. For most pump and fan applications, a variable torque, half-speed motor is used. The horsepower delivered at half speed is two-thirds of that delivered at full speed.

d. Variable-speed drives. Mechanical, fluid, and variable frequency/voltage units are available. The variable frequency/voltage drives vary the output for a standard A-C motor by varying the input frequency and/or voltage to the motor. Where required, special filtering should be included. These type of drives provide the highest energy savings. Applications are basically for fans or pumps with throttling devices that vary output according to need.

It is critical to develop a load profile to determine savings accurately. Technology has been changing rapidly and has caused prices to drop, making paybacks more attractive. Vendors should be contacted for assistance in estimating energy and cost savings.

B3.C6. Emergency Generators

a. General. Hospitals require emergency backup power, and this is usually provided by generator sets. This equipment constitutes a large capital investment that is utilized very infrequently. Planning during original design plus a small additional cost will allow these generators to provide a return on their investment by using them for peak shaving. Emergency generators used for peak shaving must comply with standards set forth in NFPA 70.

b. Peak shaving. Peak shaving differs from cogeneration in that its primary goal is the reduction of the electrical demand peak. The generators are operated only above a designated kilowatt level. The demand charge part of a utility bill is usually a large portion of the cost. The specific rate structure, the designated peak, and the building load profile will determine the number of annual operating hours. The additional costs to be incurred are for extra transfer switches or utility paralleling equipment. Increased maintenance costs and premium costs for a continuous duty generator set should be included in the economic analysis (see also Section B3.C9 of this Appendix).

B3.C7. Demand Controls (see also Section B3.D of this Appendix)

a. General. Controlling or shaving the level of the peak electrical demand will result in a savings on the demand charge. This technique does not reduce the building consumption but does reduce the utility costs. Demand control should be used for noncritical areas, allowing them to be shed off-line intermittently while not affecting the process. Control of the on and off times in sequence or by priority prevents simultaneous operation of these loads.

b. Packaged controllers. The controllers are microprocessor-based devices that continuously monitor the total demand and prevent a predetermined peak from being exceeded. One method of control is to shut down the designated loads that can be shed either on a priority or sequential basis. Another control method is time-of-day load cycling such as for water heaters and refrigeration equipment that can be shut down and allowed to coast during the peak cycle. Larger motors should be sequenced on and not allowed to start during the same demand interval.

B3.C8. Process/Appliance Efficiency

a. General. Efficiency of energy-consuming processes such as laundry or food preparation may be improved by altering the process or by the installation of high-efficiency equipment. Scheduling or sequencing of the process can affect the demand charge part of the utility costs.

b. High-efficiency appliances. Examples of high-efficiency appliances that should be specified are dishwashers that allow air drying rather than using the electric element; refrigeration equipment with additional condenser surfaces, thus reducing fan horsepower; and pilotless ignitors for boilers, water heaters, furnaces, and ranges.

B3.C9. Utility Rate Analysis

a. General. Usually, the rate schedule on which the building will be billed is dictated by the utility companies providing service. Rate schedules vary greatly from utility to utility, but most have options to save on costs. Riders have specific requirements to be adhered to, but if met they can mean a significant savings. Some utilities give customers a reduction in costs based on the voltage delivered to the site. If customer use is large enough, a rate can be negotiated.

b. Demand charges. The demand-charge part of a utility bill is based on the average peak kilowatt level interval supplied to the customer. This is not an *energy* charge but is the power company's method of charging customers for having generating capacity available. In some instances, the demand charge almost equals the energy of kilowatt hour charge. Different methods exist for basing this charge, but the trend is toward time-of-day and seasonal usage. It can be very beneficial to limit demand during the utilities' "on-peak" times when rates are highest. Some form of peak shaving or scheduling rearrangement can accomplish this.

B3.D. Energy Management, Monitoring, and Control Systems

One objective of an energy-management control system and/or equipment is to reduce energy consumption and demand cost effectively. Such systems can manage energy consumption or demand or both. Four options are generally available to hospitals for managing energy: manual controls; individual control devices, such as timeclocks or thermostats connected to equipment; stand-alone computer-based systems; and computer-integrated energy-management systems that also combine administrative capabilities with communication functions (see Table B-3 for a comparison of types of systems).

Generally, hospitals are using energy-management systems that use variations of basic energy-savings strategies: time-of-day shutdown, individual load (or duty cycling), and peak-load shedding. The first turns equipment on/off at a particular time of day and therefore limits energy use to where and when it is needed. The second controls loads by shutting down equipment intermittently during operation or according to a predetermined schedule. During periods of peak electric demand, noncritical loads such as water heaters or refrigeration can be shut down periodically, allowing their associated systems to "coast" until the peak load is reduced and the noncritical loads can be turned on again. Equipment normally unused during breaks or lunch hours can also be shut down. A staggered sequence for large induction motors can be incorporated as part of a time-of-day load-cycling strategy. Cycling may also include a shutdown schedule with optimal start/stop. In those cases where shutting down and starting up large horsepower supply fans is anticipated within an eight-hour cycle, necessary inspection and correction maintenance should be completed prior to implementation of such fan-cycling schedule. Starting and stopping large horsepower supply fans two or three times within an hour can lead to more frequent belt failure than is normally anticipated. Cycling of air handlers should only be considered when compliance with positive air flow and air change requirements can be assured.

The third strategy controls or shaves the level of peak demand. Demand control can be used for noncritical loads, allowing them to be shed off-line intermittently while not affecting the process. Control of the on and off times in sequence or by priority prevents simultaneous operation of these loads with the critical process loads. Examples of loads that can be shed during periods of peak demand are storeroom lighting, water heaters, space heating, and refrigeration equipment. Some systems employ additional strategies, such as enthalpy control (see Table B-4 for a description of strategies).

Determining which control strategy and type of equipment is cost effective for a particular facility requires an analysis of needs, capabilities, and resources available prior to the acquisition of any system. This front-end analysis should include initial energy audit, estimate of savings potential, and payback-analysis study of financing alternatives (i.e., summary of all benefits and costs arising from the project, and a reasonable time period over which those benefits and costs are expected to occur).

Selection of a system or subsystem should include qualitative as well as quantitative benefits of the investment. Some qualitative considerations are installation, expandability, ease of operation, system capabilities, understandability of displays, and service.

B3.E. Postdesign Activities

Energy conservation in hospitals is the responsibility of the administrative staff as well as the designer, architect, and engineer. A project manager or management team overseeing a construction or modernization/renovation project should perform specific activities in the interest of energy conservation. These activities include

B3.E1. In the bid and award phase:
Review and evaluate proposed alternatives and prior approvals where required for architectural, mechanical, and electrical/lighting systems to confirm compliance with energy-related design concepts.

B3.E2. In the construction phase:
Obtain operation and maintenance manuals, as-built drawings, and air-balance reports and participate in the start-up, check-out, and operating test of mechanical and electrical/lighting systems.

B3.E3. After initial occupancy:
Conduct postoccupancy survey to determine if mechanical and electrical/lighting systems function according to energy-conservation design objectives.

B3.F. Operating Management

Hospitals can substantially reduce their energy consumption and energy cost through an aggressive energy-management program which does not disrupt the environments required for health care delivery nor decrease comfort, security, or safety. An energy-management approach that has proven successful is *Total Energy Management* (TEM), developed by the Department of Health and Human Services (U.S. Department of Health, Education and Welfare, Public Health Service, Health Resources Administration, Bureau of Health Facilities, Division of Energy Policy and Program. DHEW Pub. No. (HRA)80-14516). Applications of TEM and other programs have demonstrated that certain components are essential for effective implementation. These include developing data on patterns of energy use; conducting an audit or facility survey to identify problems; and developing methods for energy conservation, maintaining records, obtaining cooperation of all hospital personnel, and good management, monitoring, and follow-up.

A key to managing energy and energy costs is the maintenance of meaningful and reliable data, i.e., energy accounting. The data must be systematically organized and easily accessible. Energy-accounting systems currently used by hospitals include those developed by the American Hospital Association, the Veterans Administration, and Blue Cross/Blue Shield of Greater New York.

There are numerous operation and maintenance methods for conserving energy in hospitals, some requiring minimal or no cost. The following guidelines represent the types of low-cost, short-payback conservation measures that can be applied to hospitals.

B3.F1. Heating, ventilation, and air conditioning provisions of Table 2 (Ventilation Requirements for Areas Affecting Patient Care in Hospital, Skilled Nursing, and Rehabilitation Areas) should be satisfied when implementing these measures.

a. In noncritical areas, stop air conditioning and fans before occupants leave.

b. Consider partial shutdown of air-circulating equipment during unoccupied periods.

c. Shut dampers when air-handling unit zone is unoccupied.

d. Turn fans off when area is unoccupied.

e. Reduce outside-air intake to minimum code requirements.

f. Repair air damper mechanism.

g. Shut exhaust when not required.

h. Repair air duct leakage and insulation.

i. Clean filters and coil units.

j. Install time clocks on air-handling units.

k. Shut off unneeded circulating pumps.

l. Cycle fans and pumps.

m. Reduce pumping flow.

n. Reset heating and chilled water temperatures.

o. Insulate heat pumping.

p. Reduce heat circulation by installing summer/winter controls.

q. Reduce room day temperature to minimum code requirements.

r. Set night thermostats back where possible (e.g., administration areas).

s. Shut off or reduce stairwell heating.

t. Reduce humidification to minimum requirements.

u. Reduce condenser water temperature.

v. Shed loads during peak electrical use periods.

w. Use outside air for free cooling whenever possible.

x. Reduce reheating of cooled air.

y. Recover heating or cooling with energy-recovery units.

z. Reduce chilled water circulated during light cooling loads.

aa. Install minimum-sized motor to meet loads.

bb. Replace hand valves with automatic controls.

cc. Utilize summer heaters for laundry and central sterile supply.

B3.F2. Lighting

a. Enforce turning off lights when not needed.

b. Revise cleaning schedules to minimize lighting other than during full-occupancy hours.

c. Install high-voltage transformers to receive power at a primary rate.

d. Reduce wattages where practical, e.g., parking areas, loading docks, storerooms, and exit stairways.

e. Investigate substitution of high-intensity mercury fixtures for high-wattage lamps.

f. Reduce wattage of bulbs in lamps.

g. Maintain a program of bulb replacement.

h. Reexamine the need for all outside signs and parking area lights to be on.

i. Use color-coded light switches to avoid nonessential lights being turned on during unoccupied hours. Designate those lights needed for cleaning and security.

B3.F3. Building Envelope

a. Redesign high heat-loss areas, including loading docks, vestibules, and entrances.

b. Add insulation to roofs and major wall areas.

c. Install dock enclosures and dock door seals at receiving and shipping points.

d. Reduce infiltration by caulking and weather-stripping.

e. Install storm windows or double-pane windows.

f. Repair doors and windows.

g. Keep windows and doors closed.

h. Use window shading.

i. Seal roof and wall openings.

j. Install vestibules at main entrances in cold climates.

B3.F4. Electrical Equipment

a. Initiate maintenance program to maintain electric equipment in the best running condition for minimum power needs.

b. Investigate relay or computer controls over power supply and schedule.

c. Combine electrical circuits of various buildings to affect metered billing rate.

d. Investigate the low power factor condition associated with new light sources.

e. Reduce the number and assortment of appliances running full time.

f. Shut off elevators whenever possible.

g. Shut off pneumatic tube system whenever possible.

h. Use emergency generator to reduce peak demand.

B3.F5. Boiler Plant

a. Reduce boiler pressure and hours of operation.

b. Clean or repair boiler annually.

c. Operate and maintain burners at most efficient levels. Clean heat exchangers regularly; inspect, maintain, and repair steam traps and steam lines.

d. Shut off steam to laundry when not in use.

e. Provide boiler water treatment.

B3.F6. Plumbing

a. Reduce domestic hot water temperature to minimum code requirements.

b. Repair and maintain hot water and steam piping insulation.

c. Install flow restrictors.

d. Install faucets which automatically shut off water flow.

Table B-3
Energy Management Control Systems

Type	Description	Advantages	Disadvantages
Thermostat	Random cycling based on setpoint temperature.	Controls energy consumption.	High level of inaccuracy. Does not control demand.
Time clock	Turn equipment on/off at predetermined times.		Limited number of controllable loads. Difficult to coordinate more than a few clocks. No planned cycling to reduce electrical demand.
Demand limiters	Turn electric equipment off when preset level of electrical usage is reached.		Does not consider environmental conditions.
Microprocessors	Utilize computerized memory to schedule and cycle electrical loads. Each load is entered individually. System usually connected to indoor and outdoor thermostat and programmed to modify its scheduling and cycling based on this feedback.	Flexibility of scheduling and cycling.	Keypad entry is time-consuming and complicated. Input subject to human error. Correction of mistakes is complicated. Computer codes used in programming must be memorized. Outdoor air thermostat feedback control proven to malfunction. Downtime memories affected by dust and static electricity. Errors or malfunctions may be undetected. Need trained operators.
Computer-integrated systems	Combines administrative capabilities with communication functions.	Able to perform sophisticated scheduling and cycling of electrical equipment.	Energy management only a small part of its function. Expensive. Need full-time operator. Keypad entry. Downtime.
Positive control solid-state system	Use solid-state logic devices for scheduling and cycling.	Easier to operate than microprocessors. Easier to program than microprocessors. Ideal for small builders.	Save approximately 80-85% of potential energy savings. Not as technologically advanced as microprocessors.
Direct digital control (DDC) systems	On/off control based on occupant input and/or time-of-day cycling.	Allows for both discrete and continuous feedback loop control. Allows proportional, integral, and derivative (PID) control. High reliability and accuracy. Flexibility in interfacing.	
Distributed processing control	Uses stand-alone intelligent Field Interface Devices (FIDs) as sensor inputs.	Equipment control is not interrupted when central station goes down. FIDs can be reset or reprogrammed by central station.	

Source: Time Energy Systems, Inc., Technical Manual, Houston, Texas, 1981.

Table B-4

Typical EMS Software Strategies

Type	Description	Results
Start/stop control (S/S)	Multiple S/S, 24-hour programs should be provided for digital points. This program will start and stop equipment at the designed times. Provisions for holiday scheduling should be provided.	Turns fans, air conditioners, boilers, lights, etc., on and off at the proper times.
Optimized start/stop	This S/S program will determine the proper time to start the environmental control system to provide comfort during occupancy hours. It will also determine the correct time to turn off equipment prior to the end of the occupancy period, allowing the building to "coast."	Energy savings result from starting the equipment on a variable requirement schedule as opposed to a fixed schedule. Additional savings result from letting the building coast at night.
Duty cycling	This program will turn off select loads for a percentage of time during a preset period. Both the on and off times must be adjustable. If indoor air temperature exceeds preset upper or lower limits, the software should be able to adjust the cycling times to compensate.	Since many systems are overdesigned, turning them off for a short period of time will not adversely affect comfort conditions. Certain loads, such as compressors, must have cycle time set carefully to avoid possible damage to the equipment. Duty cycling can also lower overall electric demand if the off times are staggered.
Demand limiting	A signal from the utility meter(s) is used to calculate KW demand. This number is used for usage reporting and is compared to a peak demand stored in memory. If actual demand will exceed peak demand, selected loads are turned off according to a priority schedule. Again, a provision should be made to compensate for when the program would cause indoor air to exceed preset temperature limitations.	Since demand charges can represent 40% or more of an electrical bill, demand limiting can result in substantial savings. Care must be exercised because very often maximum cooling can be required in a commercial building at the same time load shedding is most desirable. The more sophisticated programs use duty cycling.
Enthalpy control	Dry-bulb and dew-point temperatures are used to calculate the heat content of indoor and outside air (enthalpy). If the outside air enthalpy is less than the indoor air enthalpy, the outside air dampers are opened.	Enthalpy calculation allows the use of cool, dry outside air to replace a certain amount of mechanical air conditioning. It results in reduced energy consumption compared to use of outside air based only on dry-bulb temperatures.
Chilled water reset, hot water reset, hot or cold dec reset	These strategies are similar. The temperature is measured and adjusted based on a variable that reflects the load on the system. The variable may be outside air temperature, average space temperatures, or any other measure of load.	Varying heating and cooling equipment temperature setpoints reduce the energy used to meet given HVAC loads.
User-generated programs	This capability is necessary for the development of custom programs that the vendor cannot anticipate in standard software offerings. The following commands should be available to the user: • logic operators: and, or, not • analog operators: greater than, less than, equal, plus, times divided by, minus • controlled outputs: on, off, decrease, increase with or without time delay	User-generated programs are used for such purposes as: • boiler operation by outside temperature • night setback of temperature savings calculators • customizing standard vendor software offering "no energy zone" controls • precooling the building with outside air

continued next page

Table B-4 *(Continued)*
Typical EMS Software Strategies

Type	Description	Results
Utilities	• adjustable limit setpoints for analog points • user-generated print programs with selectable contents and initiators • error detection and printout routines for sensors, data-gathering panels, phone lines, and the computer itself • power outage and restart routines • operator check of status of equipment	
Chiller optimization	Program to operate the correct number of chillers in multiple chiller central plants based on the loads the right combination of equipment exhibited.	Energy consumption is reduced when operates for maximum efficiency.

Source: George R. Owens, "Specifying Your System, How to Get More than a Glorified Timeclock,"
Energy Management, March 1983, p. 31.
Note: Use of any of these strategies should comply with Table 2 of this document.

ENERGY GLOSSARY

Acceptable air quality: Air in which there are no known contaminants at harmful concentrations and with which a substantial majority (usually 80 percent) of the people exposed do not express dissatisfaction (ASHRAE 62).

Active system: A system that uses mechanical means to satisfy load demand as opposed to passive systems.

Air changes (AC or AC/HR): A way to express ventilation rates, which are the number of times the air volume of a given space will be replaced in a one-hour period, assuming the air distribution within the space is uniformly mixed.

Air conditioning: The process of treating air to meet the requirements of a conditioned space by controlling its temperature, humidity, cleanliness, and distribution (ASHRAE 62).

Air contaminant: An unwanted airborne constituent that may reduce acceptability of the air (ASHRAE 62).

Air pollutant: An airborne constituent that may adversely affect health.

Building envelope: The exterior enclosure of a building through which thermal energy may be transferred to or from the interior.

Constant volume system: A type of air handling system which provides precise air supply at a consistent volume.

Degree day, heating: A unit, based upon the difference between 65°F and the outdoor mean daily temperature. The mean daily temperature is the average of the maximum and minimum outdoor temperature during the 24 hours of a given day.

Degree day, cooling: When the mean daily temperature is greater than 65°F there are as many cooling degree days as degrees Fahrenheit difference between the mean and 65°F.

Demand: The amount of energy per unit of time required to satisfy the utility loads averaged over any given time.

Economizer cycle, air: A method of operating an air conditioning system to reduce conditioning load. Whenever the outdoor air conditions are more favorable (lower or higher heat content) than return air conditions, outdoor air quantity is increased.

Economizer cycle, water: A method of restricting the amount of domestic hot and cold water that flows from fixtures. This is accomplished with flow restrictors and pressure-reducing valves and spring-activated faucets.

Efficiency: The ratio of the useful energy (at the point of use) to the thermal energy input.

Energy management control system: Manual and/or automatic control and supervision of the operation of active and passive systems.

Heat gain: The amount of heat gained by a space from all sources, internal and external, including persons, lights, machines, sunshine, and so forth.

Heat loss: Heat flow from a building mass to the outside when the outdoor temperature is lower than desired indoor temperature.

Heat, latent: The quantity of heat required to effect a change in state, such as from water to steam.

Heat, sensible: Heat that results in a temperature change but no change in state.

Heat pump: A refrigeration machine possessing the capability of reversing the flow so that its output can be either heating or cooling. When used for heating, it extracts heat from a low temperature source and raises it to the point at which it can be used.

Infiltration: The uncontrolled inward air leakage through cracks and spaces and around windows and doors in any building element.

Insolation: The amount of solar energy that strikes a surface area. This is affected by orientation and configuration.

Life-cycle cost (LCC) analysis: A process of accounting for the total cost of the building or system over its useful life. It includes capital, operating, and maintenance costs.

Load: The demand for energy that is required at any given time to satisfy heating or cooling need(s).

Manual: Operated by personal intervention.

Nondepletable or renewable energy sources: Natural processes (e.g., solar radiation, wind, flowing water) which are organized in such a manner as to yield energy without depleting natural resources or disrupting natural processes.

Passive system: A system that uses nonmechanical means to provide cooling or heating, including energy stored in construction mass.

Power factor: The ratio between actual electric power consumption in watts and the theoretical power obtained by multiplying volts by amperes. The ideal situation is when the power factor is unity, KV x A = KW.

Recovered energy: Energy reclaimed and utilized that would otherwise be wasted, such as hot water drawn from laundry equipment.

Reheat: The application of sensible heat to supply air that has been previously cooled below the temperature of the conditioned space by either mechanical refrigeration or the introduction of outdoor air to provide cooling.

Reset: Adjustment, automatically or manually, of the set point of a control instrument to a higher or lower value to conserve energy.

R factor: Thermal resistance: A measure of ability to retard heat flow. R is the numerical reciprocal of U (see below), thus R = 1/U. R is used in combination with numerals to designate thermal resistance units: R = 11 equals 11 resistance units. The higher the R, the higher the insulating factor. All insulation products having the same R, regardless of material and thickness, are equal in insulating value.

Thermal transmittance (UI): Coefficient of heat transmission expressed in units of Btu per hour per square foot per degree F. It is the time rate of heat flow. The total U value results from combinations of different materials used in series along the heat flow path that compose a building section, including cavity air spaces. Overall (average) heat transmission (UO) of a gross area of the exterior building envelope is expressed in units of Btu per hour per square foot per degree F.

Unitary air conditioning equipment: A unitary air conditioner consists of one or more factory-made assemblies which normally include an evaporator or cooling coil, an air moving device, and a compressor and condenser combination, and which may include a heating function as well.

Variable air volume: Provides in varied volumes heated or cooled air at a constant temperature to all zones served. VAV boxes located in each zone adjust the volume of air reaching each zone depending on the requirements.

Ventilation: The process of supplying and removing air by natural or mechanical means to and from any space. Such air may or may not be conditioned (ASHRAE 62).

Waste heat: Heat that is too hot, too cool, or otherwise inappropriate for another purpose and is therefore discarded.

Zone: A space or group of spaces within a building with similar heating or cooling requirements that can be maintained throughout by a single controlling device system.